HOW INDIRECT TAX TECHNOLOGY WORKS

RAHUL SHARMA

DISCLAIMER

This book is intended solely for informational and educational purposes. The contents herein reflect the author's views based upon his learning, expertise, experiences, research, and interpretations at the time of writing.

Readers are advised to consult qualified professionals before acting on any information contained in this book. The author and publisher shall not be held liable for any loss, damage or inconvenience arising directly or indirectly from the use of, or reliance upon, the information provided. The views and opinions expressed in this book are those of the author and do not reflect the views of any institution, organization, or authority. References to laws, cases, policies, or practices are for general guidance only and may change over time. The content, figures and examples used in this book are used solely for educational purposes.

Product names, logos, brands, and other trademarks featured or referred to within this book are the property of their respective trademark holders. The mention of specific products or brand names in this book does not imply any association with, or endorsement by the respective trademark owners.

Some information provided in book chapters may not be permanent. It may change in accordance with the country's tax administration laws and policies regarding the adoption, editing, and decommissioning of new and existing indirect tax frameworks. Tax is always dynamic and is not permanent. The solutions proposed and described in this book are not intended to be copied and pasted for your firm's tax process without the involvement of proper stakeholders, the Tax Department, Taxologists, and Tax Technologists.

The objective of this book is to provide a global overview of indirect tax technology, covering the fundamentals across business, functional, and technical aspects.

By reading this book, the reader acknowledges and agrees to the terms of this disclaimer.

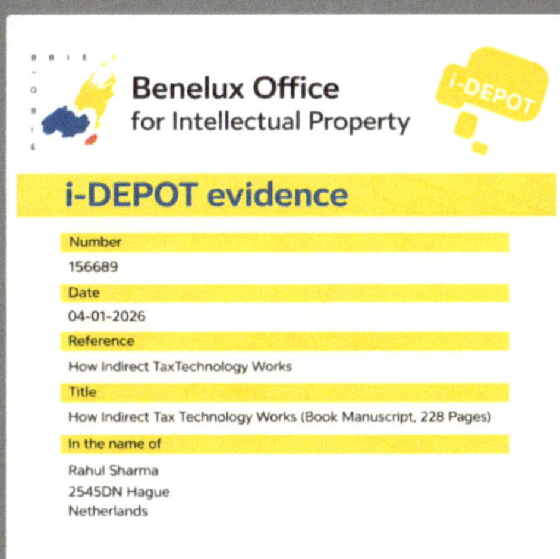

Benelux Office
for Intellectual Property

i-DEPOT

i-DEPOT evidence

Number
156689

Date
04-01-2026

Reference
How Indirect TaxTechnology Works

Title
How Indirect Tax Technology Works (Book Manuscript, 228 Pages)

In the name of
Rahul Sharma
2545DN Hague
Netherlands

Sincerely,
Rahul Sharma
Senior Solution Architect
Indirect Tax Technology
For rights inquires, e-mail: TaxTechnologists@gmail.com

DEDICATION

I dedicate this book to the firms and associates with whom I have had the pleasure of working over the past 15 years in the tax technology and consulting industries. It has been a wonderful experience for me to learn about tax processes involving determination, compliance, reporting, and other areas from the tax control framework, and to grow from a techno-functional background into an international tax technologist. Over the past 15 years, I have supported tax transformation, digitalization, and the automation of tax processes for prominent Fortune 500 firms, and I have interfaced with people from tax, finance, and IT backgrounds.

The tax and technology world is small, and information available online is limited. While collaborating with fellow tax function associates, and working on ERP Tax transformation, enhancements and support projects, I gained strong functional and practical tax technology knowledge. I later shared this knowledge and the skills I acquired with numerous individuals at both corporate and personal levels while working on tax technology projects. Both my mother and father were educators, and it gives me immense pleasure to carry forward their legacy by sharing the lessons and experiences I have gained with the global tax technology community.

Currently, much of the tax technology content published online is directed towards specific products or vendors. These sales-driven content often do not provide access to general knowledge about tax technology building blocks, resulting in a narrow and incomplete understanding of the subject. This knowledge gap in tax technology has motivated me to begin publishing articles and write-ups, leading to the creation of this comprehensive book.

This journey of learning, educating, and publishing articles has led to the creation of "How Indirect Tax Technology Works". This book aims to provide accurate, unbiased, contemporary, and practical information for tax professionals, finance and accounting specialists, IT audiences, and anyone interested in pursuing a career in tax technology. I have made every effort to ensure that this book remains product- and vendor-neutral for the benefit of all readers.

TABLE OF CONTENTS

FOREWORD

Indirect tax is an ever-evolving landscape, continually shaped by changes in legislation, the dynamics of global trade, and shifting economic priorities. In recent years, technological advancements have revolutionized how we manage, assess, and report indirect taxes to national tax authorities. As tax authorities increasingly embrace digital administration, real-time reporting, and advanced analytics, the need for transparency and compliance has never been more critical. This book is designed as an essential resource for tax professionals and anyone engaged in tax technology works, empowering readers to understand, adopt, and effectively leverage tax technology.

I have been acquainted with Rahul since 2010, when he joined Hewlett Packard's North Houston office as a contractor. He subsequently became a full-time employee and contributed to the firm's strategic tax technology initiative known as The Central Tax Engine (CTE). This project was architected, designed, and implemented to onboard over 50+ HP business applications, thereby facilitating the automation of transactional tax determination and supporting tax compliance and reporting across the organization's global entities. The CTE project incorporated custom-built tax software, middleware, interfaces, and external third-party tax software such as Sabrix and Taxware. In my capacity as the program solution architect, I oversaw the project, with Rahul serving as the SAP Finance lead and reporting directly to me.

Throughout the advancement of the project, I observed a significant growth in his skills and knowledge related to indirect tax and technological components - external tax engines, ERP tax software integrations, transaction tax data schema modeling, tax compliance reporting middleware, and an overall deepened understanding of tax-related matters. Rahul developed a profound affinity for indirect tax and technology, demonstrating a remarkable transformation over the three years I worked alongside him, evolving from an ERP finance professional into an indirect tax technologist. Notably, he exhibited a commendable commitment to professional development by training colleagues lacking expertise in tax technology in areas such as SAP Tax, tax engines, and the information technology aspects of the project. This initiative not only enhanced their ability to contribute effectively to the project but also ensured their ongoing relevance in the field. Furthermore, he authored numerous technical, user, and functional guides for internal use, which served to bolster educational efforts within the organization. I have observed Rahul's contributions to the tax technology sector for over 15 years and greatly admire his passion, commitment, and significant contributions to the industry.

When Rahul approached me to write a foreword for his book, I was genuinely pleased to accept the opportunity. After reviewing the text, I can confidently say that its main goal is to clarify the complexities of tax technology. Given the lack of formal, structured courses in academic institutions and the limited availability of vendor-specific online tutorials, many professionals face the challenge of a fragmented understanding in this field, often hindered by unfamiliar terminology and overlapping systems. Current educational resources tend to address topics like ERP tax, tax engines, and tax compliance reporting software, e-invoicing tax, and integrations in a disjointed manner, focusing more on specific products rather than offering a unified perspective. During my programming studies at university, I encountered a textbook that beautifully explained programming principles in clear language, covering foundational architecture, objects, functions, and models—rather than fixating on specific programming languages like C++, Java, or .NET. This book shares similar educational approach. It strives to illuminate the world of tax technology, detailing not only the essence of these tools but also how they work independently and collaboratively to enable modern indirect tax management. The structured approach of the book is truly inspiring, with each chapter acting as a "rung" that builds upon the last. This design empowers readers to evolve from fundamental concepts to advanced proficiency.

This book underscores the significance of essential skills in tax technology, highlighting that it involves not only tools but also the professionals who integrate tax, data, and technology. Modern tax professionals must understand process design, data flows, controls, and collaborate with IT and business stakeholders. By addressing these competencies, the book demonstrates how tax teams can shift from reactive compliance to proactive value creation. This publication functions as both a comprehensive guide and a valuable reference. It does not presume a high level of technical expertise, nor does it trivialize the complexities of the subject matter. Rather, it presents a structured and pragmatic perspective on indirect tax technology, integrating concepts, systems, and skills into a cohesive narrative. Whether the reader is embarking on an initial exploration of tax technology or seeking to enhance their understanding of an increasingly digitalized tax environment, this work will furnish the necessary knowledge to navigate current challenges and strategically prepare for the future of indirect tax.

Aimard Alexis
Tax Technology Product Leader,
Expedia Group

PREFACE

How Indirect Tax Technology Works will provide readers with information on the contemporary tax technology landscape, native and external tax software, and their integration with the ERP, fundamental concepts, solution architecture and best practices for their operation. The book's scope is indirect taxes and the associated technology. The book aims to enhance the knowledge base, fundamentals, skills, and insights of individuals and teams within the tax department and the enterprise's tax technology process. It will empower readers to look beyond conventional tax solution practices and move forward by understanding, adopting, installing, and operating modern tax technology landscapes comprising systems, integrations, tax drivers, and parameters.

The text provides an overview of the basics of tax technology, including tax software solutions and their functional architecture. It examines the interfaces with ERP systems and the integrated workflows and operations, making it a comprehensive guide suitable for any ERP and tax software within the tax technology landscape. This is because the tax technology software's application workflow and process blueprint is derived from tax laws, which are standard and product-agnostic (vendor/product/brand neutral). Tax software vendor's product names, brands internal modules, parameters, and nomenclature may differ, but the core working setup remains the same. It may fits well for any ERP - SAP, Oracle, MS Dynamics, Coupa, Sage, NetSuite, Epicor, Infor, Workday, Odoo, QuickBooks, custom, legacy ERP, as well as with any Tax software of firms like Thomson Reuters, Vertex, Avalara, SAP, Sovos, BizTax, Fonoa, Big4, or other tax technology firm.

Throughout the book, step-by-step explanations are supported by original, straightforward graphics that show how Tax determination, Tax Compliance Reporting, and e-Invoicing work independently and in harmony. It provides a comprehensive and practical overview of modern tax technology solutions deployed in thousands of multinational, Fortune 500 firms.

In a dynamic tax department of a globally operating organization, key functions are essential for effective tax management:

- Integrated Review and Assessment: Incorporating up-to-date tax laws, statutes, and cross-border treaties into advanced IT systems to ensure compliance with ever-changing regulations.

- Tailored Integration: Embedding company-specific financial and logistics models to accurately manage it's unique tax obligations and footprints.

- Accurate Tax Determination: Ensuring precise tax calculations during sales and procurement transactions to align with our financial goals.

- Proactive Compliance and Reporting: Committing to real-time compliance reporting to relevant tax jurisdictions, safeguarding it's reputation and minimizing risk.

- Forward-Thinking Tax Strategy: Developing innovative tax strategies and risk management plans that support sustainable growth in a complex global environment.

As tax laws, rules, and reporting obligations are becoming more complex and demanding, the tax department's work can no longer be sustained solely by tax accountants, tax SMEs, and tax advisors; the latest technological adoption is a must. As a result, these tax processes are now getting digitalized, streamlined and automated using tax technology, which combines a mix of tax technology tools, e.g. ERP native Tax solution, Tax engines (Tax determination software), Tax compliance and reporting software, and current upcoming e-Invoicing bolt-in software.

With the incorporation of tax technology solutions into the tax department, alongside the finance& tax accountants, Tax SMEs, Tax law specialists, and Tax advisors, one may now see Taxologists and Tax Technologists in the picture. Taxologists support the tax department in bridging the tax and IT gap, and tax technologists manage, operate, and maintain tax technology solutions. In short, contemporary tax systems, processes, and work landscape consist of Tax associates, Taxologists, and Tax Technologists, and it becomes essential for all three professional types to be in sync for a compliant, legal, and streamlined tax work spanning the entire enterprise.

The book provides an opportunity for Tax, IT, Finance, Accounting associates to transform themselves into effective Taxologists, giving them insights and foresight into tax technology software and its operations, thus enabling them to have a bigger and better role in this world of AI-driven automation and digitalization. It is a great reference guide for amateur and mid-level tax technologists to elevate themselves gradually to the level of tax solution architects and tax solution consultants.

This guide documents 15+ years of learning, training, work experience, and knowledge gained by the author while working across various industry domains. The content is practical and contemporary, drawn from real-world experience in tax technology and the knowledge will certainly empower tax technology teams. Each firm has unique business models, leading to specific tax determination and compliance reporting requirements. There is no one-size-fits-all solution; that is why this book lists many hybrid scenarios for optimal performance and minimum overwork.

The text will support your work across all tax technology work types, including ERP Tax transformation projects, Enhancement/Mini Projects, Process Improvements, Operations, Production support, Application Management Services (AMS), Product version upgrades, new integrations, product management, and any other generic tax department work. Also, whether you are in any tax technology software lifecycle phase –Exploration, Design, Build, Test, Deploy, Hyper care, the book content will support you professionally.

It's content will empower readers to understand the tax business, functional, and technical know-how, enabling you to contribute more with qualitative inputs, augmenting your value to the organization's finance and tax projects and teams, and making you fit and relevant for modern tax technology work. It offers a comparative analysis of tax processes and sub processes, highlighting solutions that utilize tax technology versus those that do not, empowering readers to develop both current (as-is) and future (to-be) solutions, weighing the pros and cons of each approach.

The author believes that once a reader gains a foundational understanding of how specific business tax software operates—not from a programming or application development perspective, but in terms of how the ERP tax software combination automates specific processes and sub-processes related to input-output transformations, data management, control flows, and the relationships between different parts of the system—they will be better equipped to effectively contribute to the design, implementation, operation, and management of such software. This knowledge empowers readers to add value in projects and operations as tax associates, taxologists, or tax technologists.

READERS OF THIS BOOK

How Indirect Tax Technology Works provides an overview of the workings of Indirect Tax Technology prevalent in the market. The author has written this book to help, mentor, and guide associates in a firm's tax technology set up, focusing on tax process streamlining, automation and digitalization.

Suitable readership includes the following job roles and profiles.

- **Tax Department:** Tax Managers, Tax Law Analysts, Tax Teams, Tax Advisors, Tax SME's, Tax VP, Tax Auditors, Tax Associate, Tax GPO's, Tax BPE's, Tax leads (Local & Global), Global Trade, Transfer Pricing etc.
- **Finance & Finance IT:** Finance Architects, Functional Finance & Controlling Consultants, ERP Finance Specialists.
- **Business (Tax) Users:** Global Service Centre associates – Super Users, Leads, Global Process Owners (GPO's) involved in sales, purchase business transactions involving ERP, Tax software's
- **Tax Technologists:** Tax Transformation Project Managers, Tax Technology Associates, Tax IT teams, Tax Product Specialists

- **Taxologists:** Tax Process Experts, Business Technology -Tax, Tax Business Analysts, Tax Solution Architects
- **Tax Authority:** Tax Assessor, Tax Auditor, Tax Administrator, etc.
- **IT Consultants:** IT consultants in sales, procurement, programming, human capital, warehouse, supply chain or any ERP module or industry who wish to move into tax technology
- **Professional Interest in Tax technology**: Those who wish to learn about tax and technology and would like to pursue a career at the intersection of tax, tech, and data
- **Graduate Students:** Graduate students from multi-disciplinary academic streams who plan to purse their career in Indirect Tax Technology

The book caters to individuals who have something to do or have a cross-functional interface with tax & technology in an organization, or who wish to learn more about this subject. It provides comprehensive guidance on the entire tax technology aspect associated with modern multinational enterprises.

FLOW OF THE BOOK

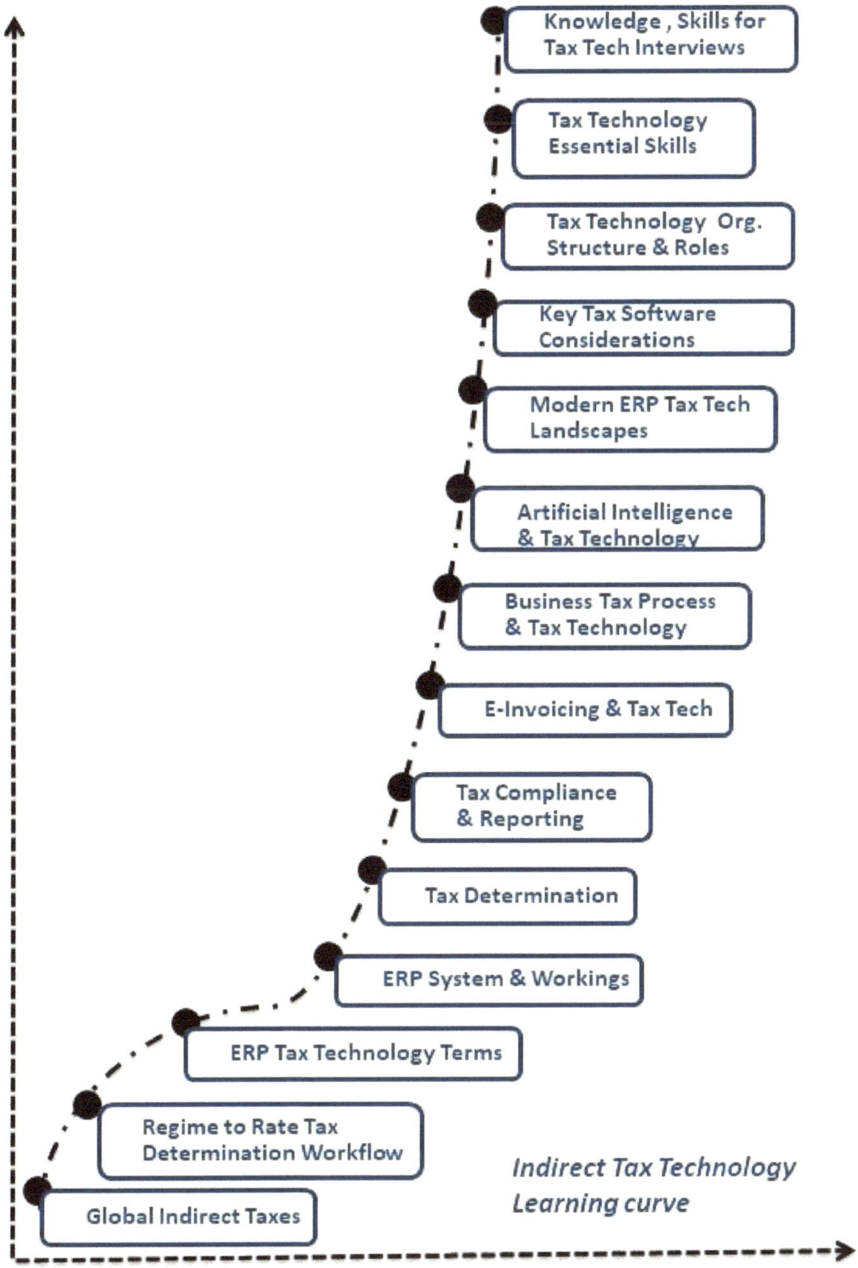

The book flow has been designed to educate the readers on tax technology in incremental steps. Like the way students in a college learn about a subject through sequentially interlinked courses. Tax and Tax Technology are complex subjects. Tax is dynamic, and the associated tax technology setup has its own moving parts. There is a sure way to understand this subject; otherwise, readers may become disillusioned and lost if there is not a proper learning structure and methodology.

It starts with basics on global indirect taxes, tax authorities, and tax levels, leading to the regime-to-rate tax determination workflow and associated tax objects, and later delves into ERP Tax technology terms to further develop understanding of the foundational pillars of tax technology. Having a clear understanding of the basics is paramount to moving ahead in tax technology and to understanding and grasping the book's contents. Post this; it educates readers on the core business process application, i.e., ERP systems, their components, technical tax, master data, and other associated tax aspects. Having ERP and its working knowledge, business processes, and Native EPP tax is a must to excel in tax technology, as ERP is the core of business operation, and transactions start and end with ERP.

In the next milestone, readers will know about the various facets of tax determination. Tax determination forms the backbone of any tax technology setup. The book mentions multiple techniques used for tax determination (tax computation process) – Native ERP, Tax Engine, Add-ons, Plug-ins and provides deep dives into their respective solution architectures and functional workings, alongside detailed comparative analysis.

Readers will learn about Taxonomy, ERP Tax Engine Integrations, Sales and Purchase Cycles, and Tax Footprints. Tax determination is an upstream process in any firm's tax technology setup and has a direct impact on downstream tax technology processes, such as tax compliance, reporting.

Readers will then be educated on the downstream processes of tax compliance and reporting tax technology softwares, including its design, landscape, architecture, and functionality, and how it works alongside ERP and the Tax engine. For tax functions, compliance and reporting are critical, as they are the end objective of any tax work and directly interface with tax authorities. After this, readers will learn about e-Invoicing models, the workings of e-Invoicing software, and the role of tax authorities. E-Invoicing in the current and near future will eventually play a significant role in real-time, near-real-time tax reporting.

Once readers have knowledge of ERP and Tax software, they will learn about various business tax processes and tax technologies to develop an integrated operational insight. Next, it educates readers on the AI (Artificial Intelligence) area related to tax, tax technology, and prospective AI footprints. It then delves into modern ERP Tax technology landscapes, educating readers on end-to-end tax process automation, digitalization for tax determination, compliance, reporting, and e-Invoicing.

The book guides readers through the factors firm's tax functions consider when selecting tax software solutions. In the latter part, the book educates readers on the overall enterprise-level tax technology organizational structure and the landscape, providing a holistic vision of practical work situations. The final parts shed light on the knowledge and skills required to further their tax technology professional journey through projects and interviews.

In short, the book guides readers through the knowledge and learning of upstream and downstream tax technology processes, with ERP at its core. The final objective of any tax work is to ensure accuracy and quality in tax data submissions to the tax authority on time. To achieve this, modern multi-national firms have deployed a myriad of tax technology tools at both upstream - ERP - Tax determination software, e-Invoicing and downstream tax compliance, audit, and reporting, with AI embedded in sub-processes of these tax software.

ABBREVIATIONS

AI = Artificial Intelligence

API = Application Programming Interface

ERP = Enterprise Resource Planning (Software)

GL = General Ledger

POV = Point of View

QA= Quality Assurance

SDLC = Software Development Lifecycle

SIT = System Integration Testing

Tax SME = Tax Subject Matter Expert

UAT = User Acceptance Testing

UNSPSC = United Nations Standard Products and Services Code

XML = Extensible Markup Language (XML)

*Rest majority of the abbreviations used are explained in the book content itself.

STRUCTURE OF THIS BOOK

This book is divided into the following fourteen chapters.

Chapter 1: Indirect Taxes

This chapter provides a solid foundation in indirect tax fundamentals for business transactions, including Value Added Tax, Goods and Services Tax, US Sales and Use Tax, Canadian GST, HST, PST, and Brazilian Tax, across world geographies and corresponding tax authorities, tax levels, tax types, and taxability determinants.

Chapter 2: Regime to Rate Tax Determination Workflow

The chapter introduces readers to the tax determination workflow and its associated components – Tax Authority, Tax Regime, Tax Type, Tax Jurisdiction, Tax Status, Tax Rate, Recoverability, and Tax GLs.

Chapter 3: ERP Tax Technology Terms & Meanings

The chapter introduces readers to widely used tax technology terms in the book and in real project work. It prepares readers for better reading and understanding of tax technology. These terms form the foundation bricks of tax technology applications and workflow.

Chapter 4: ERP Systems, Modules, Integrated Workings and Tax Technology Point of View

The chapter introduces ERP systems and provides readers with deeper insights. The chapter discusses ERP systems, their modules and submodules, business-function-integrated operations, vivid IT systems landscapes, ERP SDLC landscapes, associated tax technology POV, Master data, systems, and landscapes, deployment, and many additional aspects from real-life projects.

Chapter 5: Tax Determination

The chapter introduces the readers to the heart of tax technology, i.e. tax determination involving the use of native ERP tax solutions, a third party bolt-in tax engine and add-on's, plug in's tax software, later entering into tax engine and its workings, maintenance, taxonomy, detailed insights into vital sales and purchase cycle's workflow and associated tax footprints& drivers. Including comparison of ERP Native Tax solutions vs. Tax Engine vs. Tax Add-ons, EU ERP Tax scenarios.

Chapter 6: Tax Compliance & Reporting Solutions

This chapter introduces readers to the architecture, modules, and integrated workflow of modern tax compliance and reporting solutions. Readers will understand the tax technology involved in the end-to-end tax compliance and reporting process and its sub-processes – Data extraction, compliance checks, tax reports, tax return prep and filing.

Chapter 7: E-Invoicing &Tax Technology

The chapter introduces e-Invoicing, its workings, scope, e-invoicing models with and without tax authorities, e-invoicing functional architecture, and its integration with ERP, buyer/seller partner e-invoicing software, legal and functional requirements concerning e-Invoicing, ERP limits, and tax technology solutions.

Chapter 8: Business & Tax Processes - With & Without Tax Technology

This chapter introduces readers to business transactional lifecycle processes with and without tax technology. It will walk through the readers from upstream tax processes (sales and purchase transaction creation to tax determination) to e-Invoicing, and downstream processes involving tax data extraction, tax compliance, tax return preparation, and submissions to tax authorities, with tax technology viewpoints.

Chapter 9: AI & Indirect Tax Technology

This chapter introduces the influence and footprint of Artificial Intelligence (AI) within an enterprise tax governance framework, its sub-areas, processes, and parameters. Presenting a robust view on how AI will impact tax functions, tax process experts, and tax technologists' work, compares the delivery powers of AI vs. Tax engine, Tax compliance & reporting software: AI risks, benefits and AI v/s Tax functions.

Chapter 10: Modern ERP – Indirect Tax Technology Software Landscapes

The chapter provides readers with a modern landscape of Indirect tax technology, including ERP systems, Tax Engines, Tax Compliance reporting solutions, and E-invoicing software, along with possible IT architecture scenarios. Chapter references the modern ERP Tax technology landscape, which works similarly to our solar system: the Sun (ERP system) occupies a central place, and planets (tax software) are placed at specific locations and orbit it in particular ways for optimal joint working of systems and processes.

Chapter 11: Key Considerations for Right Tax Software

The chapter focuses on the factors a firm and its tax team should consider when selecting the right tax technology software. It revolves around key selection parameters for shortlisting and finalizing tax software: Tax authority coverage, ERP-friendliness, Tax content, and implementation and maintenance.

Chapter 12: Tax Technology Organizational Structure& Roles

The chapter introduces readers to the overall enterprise organizational structure involved in tax technology, covering business, tax functions, process experts, architects, and the placement of tax IT teams. For each work stream role, the associated work is detailed, and responsibilities are outlined for the overall tax technology work to better align, communicate, and deliver solutions.

Chapter 13: Essential Tax Technology Skills

The chapter introduces readers to the basic and advanced skills required for tax functions, tax process experts, and Tax IT associates required in tax technology work. The online knowledge base for tax technology is limited, and many associates struggle to identify the skills needed to work in this field. The chapter explores various knowledge areas and skills in tax technology that support impactful, value-driven delivery.

Chapter 14: Knowledge & Skills to Ace Tax Tech Interviews

The chapter prepares readers for tax technology interviews, where individuals from tax functions, tax process experts, and Tax IT associates form a panel to assess the interviewee's skills and knowledge in ERP Transactions, Tax determination, Tax Compliance Reporting, and e-Invoicing. These processes work in unison and are interdependent. The chapter will support readers in better preparing for gaining hindsight, insight, and foresight on the client's legacy, as-is, and to-be tax technology landscape, processes, and problem areas, leading to a successful, fruitful discussion and hiring.

CHAPTER 1

GLOBAL INDIRECT TAXES STRUCTURE

This chapter provides a basic overview and information on various indirect taxes applicable on business transactions like Value Added Tax (VAT), Goods Service Tax (GST), US Sales Use Tax (US SUT), Canadian GST, HST, PST, and QST in world geographies and corresponding tax authorities, tax levels, tax types and taxability determinants.

TAXABILITY DETERMINANTS
TAX TREATMENT
TAX TYPES
TAX LEVELS
TAX AUTHORITIES
GLOBAL INDIRECT TAXES
VALUE ADDED TAX (VAT)
GOODS & SERVICE TAX (GST)
SALES & USE TAX
CANADA PST,QST,HST
BRAZIL IPI, ICMS, PIS,ISS..
INDIA's CGST, SGST, IGST
CONSUMPTION TAX, GROSS RECEIPTS
VOLUME BASED TAX

Figure 1.0

1.1 INDIRECT TAX - TAX AUTHORITIES, TAX LEVELS, TAX TYPE, TAXABILITY

An indirect tax is levied by country tax administrations, which may have federal, state, provincial, city, and county-level presence. For example, the US has tax authorities at federal, state, city, county, and district levels, up to 7 levels (e.g., in California). In contrast, in India, it's at the central and state levels. In Europe, Asia Pacific, the Middle East, and a few Latin American countries, it's predominantly at the federal level. It's levied on business transactions involving the sale and purchase of items for consumption and expenditure. An intermediary collects it from the customer, who ultimately bears the tax burden, such as an individual or a business. The intermediary collects tax, prepares a tax return, and submits it to the tax authorities on a periodic basis. That's why it's called an Indirect tax: it differs from a direct tax, where the tax authority collects it directly from an individual or business on its income.

Country tax administrations have defined indirect tax laws that contain specific rules for indirect tax computations, and six major factors determine Indirect taxes. These are also called Tax drivers and play a vital role in the entire tax technology operations. What type of product or service is involved (product classification), From where the transfer of ownership has occurred (applicable tax jurisdiction /Nexus/Zone - the applicable jurisdiction where the tax collection and return liability has happened), To whom the product or service is sold to, The pricing of the product and service, How the product or service is used (e.g. resale, research, Exports, manufacturing etc.).

Indirect taxes are of two types.

a. Value based taxes, which is calculated as a percentage (%) of tax base i.e. the price, examples include Goods and Service Tax (GST), Value Added Tax (VAT), Sales & Use Tax, Harmonized Sales Tax (HST), Custom duty (Import duty/Tariff, Export Duty/Tariff), Consumption Tax (State, City, District sales and use tax, Canada Provincial Sales Tax (PST), Retail Sales Tax, Gross receipts (New Mexico and other US states Gross receipts/Excise taxes)

b. Volume based taxes – which are calculated as a fee per quantity e.g. cost per gallon /liter e.g. Excise Tax, Environmental fee.

Now we will read about the various value based Indirect tax types prevalent worldwide.

1.2 SALES & USE TAX (SUT)

- **United States (USA) & Puerto Rico**

The US has more than 15,000 tax jurisdictions with varying tax rates, which is why the majority of firms with US operations deploy a 3rd-party tax engine for tax computation. Sales and user tax is the primary indirect tax levied on business transactions at the state, country, city, and other local jurisdictions. A sales tax is imposed by the seller on the buyer for the sale of goods and services in the US at the state, county, city, and other local levels.

Use Tax is self-assessed tax which buyer incurs and collects the applicable taxes on behalf of the seller /vendor who has no local nexus (Nexus =Either a company is formed or registered or has employees and owns real estate in the taxing jurisdiction where title of ownership occurred (Ship To (Goods), Supply To (Service)) in the selling jurisdiction or in cases where the business has direct pay permits. It's essential to understand that use tax is not purchase tax. In the US, the invoice date is the legal fiscal date for determining sales and use tax. Unlike VAT, GST , there is no tax recoverability concept in the US Sales and use tax, and the tax is treated as an expense.

From a sales transaction workflow standpoint: The seller sells goods and services to the buyer and collects sales tax, later files the collected sales tax to applicable tax authorities (where point of title transfer occurs, i.e., tax jurisdiction or zone, comprising state, city, country, district, and other local level authorities), and makes payment. In a case where the goods or service are delivered, it's generally the Ship To address of the end customer to determine the jurisdiction of title ownership, whereas in a case where sales are picked up from a vendor or supplier, the plant /ship from address is the determinant for the jurisdiction of title ownership.

From a purchasing viewpoint, there may be two scenarios: (1) The buyer purchases goods or services from the seller and pays the sales tax to the vendor, and the vendor then files and makes payment of collected taxes to the state, city, country, district, and other local-level authorities. (2)In a case when the seller (vendor) has no local nexus (jurisdictional presence) in the area of supply, then the buyer self-accrues this sales tax, which is called use tax in this 'no nexus' case and later files tax returns and make payments to applicable the state, city, country, district and other local level authorities.

State, city, country, district, and other local-level jurisdictions in the US are empowered to make laws and rules defining the tax rates applicable. In addition to the five key transactional taxability drivers discussed there is a concept of customer tax exemption in the US. Under this, the customer or buyer may have a tax exemption certificate from the state, city, county, district, and other local authorities, and is exempt from paying tax for that specific jurisdiction. Such exemption certificates have start and end dates, along with notes indicating the use of products or services in some cases.

1.3 VALUE ADDED TAX (VAT)

- **Europe (EU)**

Europe follows the VAT (Value Added Tax) system, under which tax is imposed at each stage of the goods and services supply chain (Raw Material Supplier > Manufacturer > Wholesaler > Retailer > End customer). It's a recoverable tax (Output tax (VAT collected from the buyer on sales) is netted against Input Tax (VAT paid to the supplier/vendor for purchases), and the net VAT payable is remitted to the tax authorities by the business). However, VAT recoverability also depends on the taxing jurisdiction and the type of product or service involved. VAT rates in Europe are divided into primarily five categories: (1) Standard rate, (2) Reduced Rate, (3) Super Reduced Rate, (4) Zero rate, and (5) Exempt. Each country has its own tax rate for these tax categories (exempt and zero-rated have a 0% tax rate across all jurisdictions). Alongside Federal VAT and associated tax rates, in Europe, VAT registration of buyer and seller regarding goods ship-to location and place of supply (services) plays a significant role in determining applicable taxes with respect to Domestic VAT, Intra-community reverse charge, cross-border, Intra EU, Plants abroad, Triangulation treatments, etc. and making European VAT determination and compliance reporting complexity high. The applicable tax jurisdiction is determined by the destination country concept, i.e., the country to which the goods are shipped or the service is performed.

- **Asia Pacific (APAC) & Middle East**

The Asia Pacific region uses VAT (Value Added Tax) and GST (Goods and Services Tax). VAT rates in the Asia Pacific differ from those in Europe, and tax categories can have multiple rates ranging from 0% to 40%, i.e., it's not limited to the standard, reduced, exempt, or zero-rate brackets. Russia, China, Vietnam, Japan, Australia, and New Zealand have VAT; Singapore has a Goods and Services Tax (GST), which is a type of Value Added Tax (VAT). The VAT/GST framework in the APAC regions follows VAT practices prevalent in Europe. For example, VAT/GST is at the federal level; VAT/GST has tax slabs (instead of tax categories); the VAT treatment workflow (tax levied at each phase of the supply chain) is the same; and VAT recoverability exists, with few exceptions. In the case of Middle Eastern countries like the UAE, Saudi Arabia, Oman, Qatar, Egypt, and Turkey, the VAT framework is adopted. Taxability determinants follow the standard VAT framework as prevalent in Europe and the Asia Pacific, with few exceptions.

- **Latin America**

Mexico has a Value Added Tax (VAT) system. Central American countries like Argentina, Guatemala, El Salvador, Nicaragua, and

Panama have VAT. Honduras and Costa Rica impose sales and consumption taxes (indirect taxes) on certain services. Taxability determinants follow the standard VAT framework as prevalent in Europe and the Asia Pacific, with a few exceptions.

1.4 GOODS AND SERVICES TAX (GST)

- **India**

India follows GST – Goods and Services Tax; the GST authority determines the rules and rates. GST has a dual structure in India. Central Goods Service Tax (CGST), State Goods Service Tax (SGST), and Integrated Goods Service Tax (IGST).

It has replaced the complex tax system prevalent earlier, which involved multiple tax types in business transactions, such as Central Excise Duty, Service Tax, Surcharges and cesses, luxury Tax, state tax, entry tax, and entertainment tax.

CGST is the tax collected by the central government on an intra-state supply of goods and services (example, Jaipur to Jodhpur, within Rajasthan), SGST is the tax collected by the state government on an intra-state supply of goods and services (example, Mumbai to Pune), and IGST is applied on inter-state transactions and imports. The tax collected is shared between the central and state governments according to a predetermined formula. For example, if Goods are shipped from Gujarat (Ahmedabad) to Pune (Maharashtra), only IGST will apply, and the collected IGST will be shared in accordance with the understanding formula between the state and central governments. However, if it's within the state, for example, Pune to Mumbai, then both CSGT and SGST will be applicable, and CGST goes to the central government, and SGST goes to the state treasury.

Initially, GST was structured with multiple tax slabs—0%, 5%, 12%, 18%, 28%, and 40%—but after extensive reformation, it now has three tax rate slabs—5%, 18%, and 40%. Each product under GST has a GST code, which is assigned a specific rate under the new GST slabs.

1.5 GOODS AND SERVICES TAX (GST) + HARMONIZED SALES TAX (HST), PROVINCIAL SALES TAX (PST), QUEBEC SALES TAX (QST)

- **Canada (CA)**

In Canada, we have Goods and Services Tax (GST) – A form of Value Added Tax (VAT) applicable at the federal and provincial levels. Starting with Goods and Services Tax (GST) at the federal level, followed by Harmonized Sales Tax (HST), a Federal tax with provincial components, and, in addition, Quebec Sales Tax (QST), a value-added tax applicable in the province of Quebec. Also, as mentioned above under Indirect Tax types, in Canada, there is a consumption tax called Provincial Sales Tax (PST), levied on the end customer. In short, a business transaction in Canada may be subject to Federal GST, PST, HST, and QST depending on the province involved. For example, in British Columbia, one may have just HST %, whereas in Alberta, both GST and PST may be applicable, and in Quebec, both GST and QST are applicable.

The state governments have the authority to pass laws regarding the applicability of tax types, and what stands today may change tomorrow. While GST, PST, and QST – a form of GST (VAT) are recoverable (collected output taxes (tax collected from sales) are netted against the inputs (tax paid from purchases), PST (Provincial Sales Tax), which is a consumption tax, is not recoverable and is treated as an expense. Each tax type in Canada (GST, PST, HST, and QST) has special tax rates for goods and services, making Canada's indirect taxation computation moderately complex.

1.6 BRAZIL TAX

Brazil has many tax levels – Federal, State, and Municipal.

At the Federal level, there are II-Import Duty (levied on the import of goods), IPI (Federal VAT), and PIS/COFINS (Social Contributions), levied on gross revenues and on the import of goods and services. At the state level, it has ICMS, a state VAT imposed on the interstate and intramunicipal supply of goods and services. At the municipal level, there is an ISS (service tax). Each authority type has specific tax rates for the product (goods or services) involved in the transactions.

Alongside having three taxing authority levels, each with one or more tax types, and each tax type may have a different tax rate prescribed by the tax authority, Brazilian transactional taxability determinants under each taxing authority also involve many additional factors, like Vendor /Customer type, Establishment type (Commercial, Industrial), Product Type, usage, and origin. All these taxability drivers' combinations make tax determination in Brazil complex. IPI and ICMS are recoverable taxes.

1.7 SUMMARY

In this chapter, we've provided a basic overview of the Global Indirect Taxes structure prevalent across different geographies. In addition to this, we have also provided an overview of corresponding structure levels- tax authorities, tax levels, tax types, and taxability determinants. Readers are now aware of the topic 'Indirect Tax' and its vivid facets defined by various countries' tax administrations. We think it's essential to have at least a rough idea of the prevalent indirect tax requirements of regions and jurisdictions in the scope of your ERP Tax transformation project. In the next chapter, we will discuss the regime to rate workflow setup, which forms the fundamental equation in tax practices.

CHAPTER 2

TAX AUTHORITY TO RATE DETERMINATION

The chapter introduces readers to the tax determination workflow and associated components in this chain–Tax Authority, Tax Regime, Tax Type, Tax Jurisdiction, Tax Status, Tax Rate, recoverability, and Tax GL's. Tax terms are provided to users and will be used frequently throughout the book, helping readers better understand the subject. These terms are not only generic to tax functions but also to tax technology programs and they are used every day in discussions, meetings, and professional explanations.

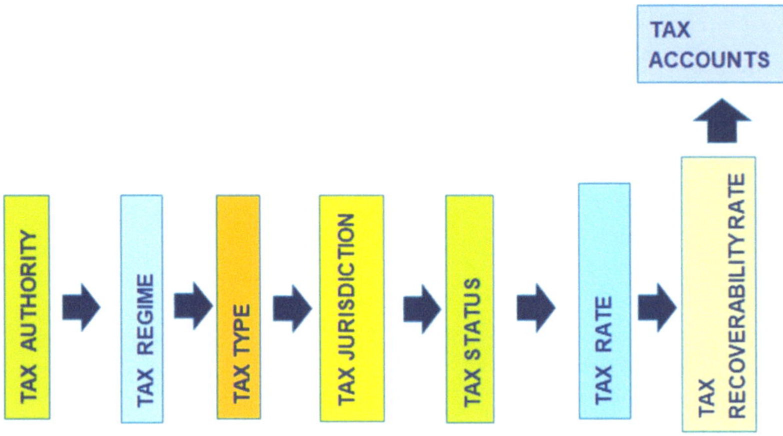

Belastingdienst	NL	VAT	NL	Standard	21%	0%
	NL	VAT	NL	Reduce Rate	9%	50%
IRS	US	State Sales Tax	Texas	Standard	6.25%	0%
		City Sales Tax	Houston	Standard	1%	0%
		County Sales Tax	Harris	Standard	1%	0%

Figure 2.0

2.1 REGIME TO RATE TAX WORKFLOW

For a tax technology consultant to succeed, they need to understand key tax terms used in Tax technology discussions, and to elicit and document tax requirements with Tax SMEs (Tax Dept.). Tax determination solution for business tax scenario follows 'Regime to Rate model' (Figure 2.0).

2.2 TAX AUTHORITY /COUNTRY TAX ADMINISTRATION

A tax authority is a government body that has the statutory power to collect and enforce tax liabilities. It is responsible for managing and administering tax laws within a particular jurisdiction. Its primary function is to ensure the accurate collection of taxes as mandated by legislative provisions—E.g., IRS for the US, CBIT for India, AEAT for Spain, etc.

2.3 TAX REGIME

A Tax regime or legislation is a set of tax rules and setup that determines the treatment of one or more taxes administered by a tax authority. E.g., VAT Tax Regime in the BE includes rules for VAT in the BE only. Firms' tax business flows must comply with the local country's tax law regime to be compliant.

2.4 TAX TYPE

A tax type is a distinct charge imposed by a fiscal or tax authority. E.g.: VAT for NL, Sales Use Tax in US states, and HST/GST/PST/QST in CA, CGST, SGST, and IGST in India.

2.5 TAX JURISDICTION

Also known as tax zone, its geographical area where a specific tax authority levies a tax or where a particular rate of tax applies. E.g.: Germany, San Francisco City, Saskatchewan, Ontario, or British Columbia, etc.

2.6 TAX STATUS

It is the taxable nature of a product/service in the context of a transaction for a tax type. E.g.: Taxable Standard rate, Zero rated, Exempt, Partial Exempt, Non-Taxable, Special rated, etc.

2.7 TAX RATE

It is the rate specified for a tax status in effect for a period; the tax rate can be expressed as a percentage or as a per-unit value. E.g. 0%, 15%, 5%.

2.8 TAX RECOVERABILITY

Rate of Input Tax that is allowed to be recovered or offset against Output Tax. E.g.: Businesses that only produce VATable goods and services can recover 100% of the VAT on most purchases. However, Businesses (e.g., Financial Institutions) that produce VAT-exempt goods and services may have 0% recoverability. Partial recoverability may also exist.

2.9 TAX ACCOUNTS

Specific GL Accounts to which the Tax Amount will be distributed. The tax amount will be distributed to particular account(s) based on the Tax Rate applied – strict requirements in some countries.

2.10 SUMMARY

In this chapter, you gained an overview of key tax parameters and the fundamental workflow hierarchy in descending order. Starting with the country tax administration, tax regime, tax type, tax jurisdiction, tax stats, tax rate-to-tax rate determination, and Tax GL. This equation forms the foundational architecture for Indirect tax determination, whether on paper, in an ERP, or in a Tax technology system. We also covered their definitions and roles, which are frequently used in tax technology. In the next chapter, we will dive deeper into key IT terms related to ERP and tax technology to help readers navigate subsequent chapters with ease.

CHAPTER 3

ERP TAX TECHNOLOGY TERMS & MEANINGS

The chapter introduces readers to various tax technology terms used in the book content and in real project work. It will prepare readers to read better and understand tax technology. These terms are often and widely used in tax technology projects and work. Especially when tax functions (tax department associates), tax process experts, and Tax IT associates are talking together, enabling all three parties to be on the same page. A basic understanding of these terms is vital for correctly understanding how tax technology software automates and digitalizes tax processes. They form the foundation for tax technology applications and workflows.

Figure 3.0

3.1 3RD PARTY BOLT-IN TAX SOFTWARE

As the name suggests, a third-party bolt-in tax software product is offered by an external firm and requires integration (standard or custom) with your firm's ERP to function. They may sit outside your ERP system and require an external integration to communicate and generate the desired output. Examples include tax engines, tax compliance& reporting software, e-Invoicing software's, Tax area look-up, tax exemptions, and other tax tech tools. Nowadays, these bolt-in tax software solutions offer standard integration packages for specific ERPs such as SAP, Oracle, Sage, and MS, and custom integrations are fast fading from the market. These third-party bolt-in tax systems are independent and can be connected to multiple ERPs, e-commerce platforms, and other non-ERP sales and procurement applications simultaneously, making them highly expandable and well-suited for firms with diverse vendor ERP/Business applications.

3.2 ADD-ONS /PLUG-IN TAX SOFTWARE'S

These tax software solutions, unlike third-party bolt-in tax software, are installed within the ERP system and do not require an external integration API. Once installed, this tax software will fetch transactional tax data during sales procurement and financial accounting transactions processing, and will populate the desired output. Their standard program is linked to ERP processes and includes internal tax touch points after installation, with a margin for further customization. The corresponding technical maintenance aligns with the ERP release cycles and follows the firm's standard SDLC (Software Development Life Cycle) QA (Quality assurance) framework. Examples of ERP Add-ons tax software include Meridian, TaxMarc, Ryan, and Deloitte ITL.

3.3 TAX REPORTING DATABASE

A tax reporting database contains transactional tax data used for compliance and tax return reporting. The database contains only those parameters applicable to tax compliance work and tax returns, and is intended for tax functions. Modern tax engines and tax compliance reporting tools include a feature that allows document line-item information captured in a specific pattern. Documents include legal sales, purchase invoices, as well as financial accounting postings applicable to tax submissions. The final objective of this database is to enable tax functions to prepare and submit tax returns to the respective authorities. Within such tax software, there are application menus for extracting, processing, and preparing the data in the prescribed format structure and with the required parameters (fields–values) as specified by the tax authorities. A firm may have a custom tax reporting database within its ERP or an external data lake for compliance and reporting. A well-organized, qualitative tax database is perhaps the most essential tool for tax functions, as without data, they lack insight and foresight into what they are submitting and whether it is accurate.

3.4 TAX AUDIT DATABASE

A Tax audit database precedes a tax reporting database; it is a term generally used in tax engine systems. When a sales, purchase or accounting transaction occurs, and its end-to-end journey is successful, i.e., posting has happened in the ERP production system, that transaction gets audited in a database within the tax engine application. The term 'audit' implies that the transaction is successful and has been recorded/posted in the ERP, because those transactions (documents) only matter in legality. Later, the Tax reporting database extracts this data and places it separately for tax reporting purposes, as explained in the above section.

3.5 TAXONOMY

Tax taxonomy is the process by which a firm maintains the listing (classification) of its entire product range, alongside the applicable tax rates prevailing in the world jurisdictions where it sells and buy those products. The Taxonomy data provides a real-time insight into the prevailing rate and tax treatment of a specific ERP product in a particular jurisdiction. This supports users, super users, and tax functions in tax rate validations and verifications for sales and purchase transactions. Tax Taxonomy files are generally maintained in MS Excel formats by tax functions and shared across the organization. In a scenario where a tax engine is present and has tax rates available for commodity codes, not all business users can log in to the tax engine and identify the tax rate applicable in specific jurisdictions, as this process involves multiple steps and screen navigation and is often time-consuming. Whether a firm has a Tax engine or not, the tax taxonomy file is a quick, user-friendly, and compliance-supporting tool.

3.6 TAXABILITY MATRIX

A taxability matrix is a Tax Taxonomy file published by external tax engine firms that lists all possible products (goods and services) alongside the applicable tax rates and tax treatments (Standard rate, exempt, zero rate, etc.) for global jurisdictions. Such files are generic and not client-specific and can be extracted from the Tax engine, for mapping firms' ERP product codes with tax engine commodity codes (UNSPSC, Harmonized, Independent, and Custom).

3.7 TAXING NEXUS

Taxability nexus defines the applicable tax jurisdiction, tax treatment, and tax liability generated for a business transaction. For example, in the US, if a seller is not registered to conduct business in a specific state, there is no nexus, and the buyer will self-assess and remit to the tax authority. Similarly, in Europe, if a seller does not have a VAT registration in the place of supply, they lack the legal power to charge and collect domestic VAT, which affects the tax treatment. In short, the taxing nexus determines the presence of a seller (either registered or having a Tax ID) and the corresponding tax charging and collection authority they have. Different country tax administrations have specific rules on this.

3.8 TRANSACTIONAL TAX DATA

Transactional tax data comprises transactional and tax data. Transactional data includes finance, logistics, and master data parameters (e.g., company code, location parameters, value, vendor/supplier data), and tax data includes tax parameters (tax rate, tax amount, recoverability, tax GL, tax code).

3.9 TRANSACTIONAL TAX LIFECYCLE

The transactional tax lifecycle involves an end-to-end journey of a sales, purchase, and finance accounting transaction. From the business user running the transaction on ERP, followed by tax determination, Tax postings, conducting compliance & internal audits, finally leading to preparation, review, and submissions of the tax returns with the tax authority, and archiving of data as per the country tax administration laws.

3.10 TRANSACTIONAL TAX XML

Modern tax APIs use XML. Data between the ERP and external tax software is exchanged in XML format. A transactional tax XML contains data relevant to the tax software application, including transactional and Tax data. The term is widely used in the context of external tax engine installation, where the request call (ERP to Tax Engine) includes transactional data, and the response call (Tax Engine to ERP) includes both transactional data and tax data (processed and published by the tax engine). Such XML files provide deep insights for tax technologists when conducting troubleshooting and root cause analysis. XML data also includes the applicable rules and the tax engine application module touch points, providing all the information for the tax treatment journey.

3.11 BROWNFIELD ERP TAX TRANSFORMATION

A brownfield ERP Tax transformation involves leveraging most, or a significant portion, of the existing business tax flows, with the opportunity to further enhance the overall tax control framework. Examples include firms migrating part of their business units to an external tax engine from Native ERP, or strengthening the Native ERP tax computational setup itself. In this approach, selectively identified existing business tax flows of the financial supply chain, which are 'problem areas' or 'complex', are reviewed, and necessary process improvements and flow edits are incorporated. The concept 'Brownfield' is the same, whether it is for ERP or Tax.

3.12 GREENFIELD ERP TAX TRANSFORMATION

A Greenfield ERP Tax transformation program involves the deployment of tax technology set up from scratch. That is, discovery, design, build, test, and deployment of the entire business tax flows occur across all entities, i.e., an overall revamp of the tax setup. It provides an excellent opportunity for tax functions to establish a world-class tax control framework involving determination, compliance reporting, and e-Invoicing. Examples include a spin-off company case from a parent entity implementing acquired units' and associated businesses on a new ERP and using a new tax engine or add-ons/plug-ins for tax determination. The fundamental concept of 'Greenfield' is the same, whether it is for ERP or Tax.

3.13 E-INVOICING SOFTWARE

An e-Invoicing software supports a firm's sales and purchase transactions by transmitting electronic invoices to buyers, suppliers, and tax authorities in a specific format, data model, and set of parameters. It is not tax-determination or compliance-reporting software. It is just a tool that enables the transmission and receipt of ERP's sales, purchase invoices from customer, supplier and tax authority systems. An e-Invoice software bolt-on integrates with the ERP system, internally or externally, supports the generation and receipt of outgoing and incoming e-Invoices, and later transforms them into the ERP document format and postings and vice versa. Examples of e-Invoicing software are Avalara, Edicom, Vertex Ecosio, Thomson Reuters Pagero, Basware, SNI, Tradeshift, RTC, and Taxually etc.

3.14 ERP

An ERP is enterprise resource planning software. Some firms have custom ERP systems, meaning they have developed the application in-house and operate and maintain it. ERP facilitates the flow of information across the organization for all business functions; it is an integrated system that operates in real time and serves as a central repository shared by all business functions. Examples of major ERP software include SAP, Oracle, Microsoft, Infor, Acumatica, Workday and Sage etc.

3.15 ERP-TAX SOFTWARE INTEGRATION

It is the integration between the ERP system and the tax software. An API that enables communication and handshake. This can be custom (developed by the firm's DevOps team) or standard. Integration involves data schema mappings between the ERP, source system data fields (table-field level), and tax software target fields to enable data transfer and further processing. Nowadays, standard integrations also offer additional functionalities like tax code generation and the choice of select logistic data parameters, and audit log functionalities etc. Integration software has evolved with time and is no longer just source target system data parsing applications.

3.16 INDIRECT TAX AI

Indirect Tax Artificial Intelligence (AI) sits within the tax software. A classic case is when a tax engine application contains codified translations of worldwide tax authorities' laws, rules, rates, and content; in short, the entire tax legislation is digitized within the application. Moreover, when an incoming transaction calls the tax engine, the application accurately identifies the tax jurisdiction, tax rate, and tax amount. Tax engines are artificial tax intelligence computational software themselves. Another case is where the tax compliance and reporting software inbuilt AI (pre-defined + having custom flexible mechanism) supports the tax function to run tens of vivid sorts of compliance-related checks on tax data - anomalies, overcharge, undercharge, exemptions, legality, facilitate internal audits towards tax return data preparations and submissions.

3.17 NATIVE ERP TAX

Native ERP Tax refers to a setup in which the ERP system's tax determination and reporting module is used for tax computation and reporting. In this case, no third-party tax software is involved, and the firm is using the ERP standard tax functionality to manage tax operations. With the advent of complex regulator frameworks, real-time reporting, thousands of tax rules and rates, firms are gradually moving away from Native ERP Tax towards leveraging external tax software for compliance.

3.18 TAX API'S

A Tax API, or Tax application programming interface, is the communication mechanism via which the ERP and Tax software communicate. API is a standard term and not specific to Tax. It connects two systems to handshake and exchange data elements. The Tax API can be custom, standard, or a mix, depending on the ERP Tax IT landscape.

3.19 TAX AUTHORITY / COUNTRY TAX ADMINISTRATIONS

Every country has its own tax department, called the tax authority or tax administration; for example, the FTA (Federal Tax Authority) in the UAE, the IRS in the US, the GST Council in India, the BZSt in Germany, and HMRC in the UK. These tax authorities make rules and regulations for the computation, collection, and remittance of indirect taxes on business transactions within their jurisdictions.

3.20 TAX CLASSIFICATION

Tax classification is the technique that involves tagging the products – goods and services with an indicator that defines taxability – standard rate, reduced rate, exempt, zero rate. In the case of native ERP solutioning, this is very helpful and a standard practice. When a transaction is run, this indicator, which is generally an alphanumeric code, also serves as a tax driver in the computational program and supports applicable tax treatment.

3.21 TAX COMMODITY CODE

Tax commodity codes are the standard nomenclature for products and services. In the current world setup, each product and service has codes defined for all possible goods and services, which customers and country tax administrations use to identify the nature of the transaction. Country-specific nomenclatures may also vary; for example, in the US, it is UNSPSC, in India, GST and SAC codes for goods and services, and in Brazil, its own nomenclature.

3.22 TAX COMPLIANCE REPORTING SOFTWARE

Tax reporting and compliance software is third-party software that helps a firm's tax functions run compliance checks, prepare, assess, approve, and submit tax returns to tax authorities. This software first extracts transactional tax data from the ERP system and organizes it at the filing entity (under country) level, creating a data lake. On this data, a set of tools helps the tax department perform validation/ verification checks, ensuring compliance. Finally, this software supports the standard tax return preparation and submission process, including e-filing at tax authority portals. Examples of Tax Compliance Reporting software include Avalara, Sovos, Vertex, Thomson Reuters, Taxually, VAT IT, Taxera, Ryan, Deloitte ITC, EY GVRT, Simply VAT, Tax Systems AlphaVAT, etc.

3.23 TAX CONTROL FRAMEWORK

A firm tax control framework involves a comprehensive blueprint, or tax IT architecture, that effectively complies with all applicable tax authorities rules and regulations. The framework is designed to ensure high compliance and legality across all tax-related work and processes. It encompass set up of business tax models for optimum profits, supply chain optimization, mandated SOP's for direct& indirect tax practices involving tax computation, tax compliance, reporting, audit defense, archiving. Including other business, functional and technical aspects having tax footprints with one singular objective – to attain maximum compliance with worldwide legal and statutory tax authorities in its business scope.

3.24 TAX DATA MODELING

Tax data modeling is the process of retrieving applicable financial and operational tax parameters from the finance and operational processes for use in tax software solutions. It includes the fields and value mappings of the source field & values (ERP finance, sales, and procurement) process and the target field-value (tax solutions program) process. The same technique is also applied to tax compliance reporting software and e-invoicing programs to effectively transmit transactional tax data for upstream and downstream tax processes. In modern tax tech setups, this data modeling is done at the integration level (front-end data mapping). For non-standard API setups, Excel is used for discovery, design, and Dev. Ops team leverages that for the data model program.

3.25 TAX DRIVERS

Tax drivers are elements that drive tax determination and also support the movement of transactions (documents) to tax compliance and reporting software. They are elements from master and transactional data. The artificial intelligence of modern tax software works based on tax drivers, which are custom nomenclature elements of a firm and not generic (e.g., material code, plant ID, entity code, VAT ID).

3.26 TAX ENGINES

A tax engine is a third-party bolt-in tax solution that fully automates the sales, purchase, and finance accounting tax determination process. The tax determination process involves the identification of accurate tax rates, tax amounts for applicable tax levels (Federal, state/province, (City, county, district, etc. for the US), and also now it can populate tax codes specific to the business scenario. The tax engine is an artificial intelligence system that incorporates all applicable country tax administration rules and rates into its application. Examples of Tax Engine include Vertex, Thomson Reuters, Avalara, Sovos etc.

3.27 TAX EXEMPTION CERTIFICATE

A tax exemption certificate is issued by the tax authority to a firm (business) to exempt it from tax on the seller's side. The concept is widely used in the US, and tax authorities (at state, city, county, and local levels) issue a document listing the firm's name, the product/service involved, and the exemption start and end dates. In other regions of the world, such as Canada, Europe, and the Asia Pacific, these concepts are evident in specific jurisdictions. Modern tax technology software has functionality to incorporate such requirements and provide the desired tax treatment. Examples of Tax Exempt Certificate software's include CERTify Tax, Avalara, Vertex, Thomson Reuters, SOVOS, DMA etc.

3.28 TAX TOUCH POINTS/FOOTPRINTS

In a sales and purchase process, specific documents are created for sales, e.g., quotations, sales orders, delivery, and billing. Similarly, for the procurement process, we have purchase requisitions, purchase orders, incoming deliveries, invoices, and payments. Not all sub-processes within the sales and procurement require tax determination internally within the ERP or via the tax engine. Tax touch points or integration points are the points at which tax calls for tax determination trigger in a business process.

3.29 TAX IT

Tax IT refers to the integration of tax and IT, i.e., the use of tax technology. Tax IT symbolizes the automation, digitalization, and streamlining of tax laws, rules, processes and workflow using IT (Software).

3.30 TAX JURISDICTION

Tax jurisdiction is the location where transactional tax liability arises for a business transaction involving goods or services. Tax liability is the obligation of a business to report and remit the taxes charged and collected to the applicable tax authority. It may be at a country level (e.g., UK, France, UAE) or country–state level (India, dual GST setup), or in combination with state, city, county, district, and other local authority levels (USA).

3.31 TAX JURISDICTION CODE (TJC)/TAX AREA ID

This term in the ERP refers to a specific zone in the United States, which comprises a state, city, county, district, and other local levels. Modern tax engines use their own tax jurisdiction code or Tax Area ID formats, which may include a State code, Zip code, Geo code, and an In-city/Outside city indicator. They may be alphanumeric, with a limit of 8 to 10 characters. For example, TX770704410 may indicate that the zone (area) falls in Texas State 'TX', Houston city, Harris County (Zip code 77070), and Geo code 4410. This technique is used to tag address master data (customers, plants, warehouses, vendors). During master data creation, the ERP system makes a call to the tax engine or another address verification tool to capture the information. Later, when sales and purchase transactions are run, this value flows alongside standard address data elements to enable the tax engine to identify addresses (taxing zones) with precision. It is important to note that the Tax Area ID or the Tax jurisdictional code alphanumeric structure is a custom element of specific ERP or 3rd party vendor tax software and may not be generic.

3.32 TAX LOCALIZATION

Tax localization involves a custom setup of tax processes in the native ERP system or external tax software. Native ERP or external tax software may provide a solution for tax determination; however, there is a series of configurations that need to be done in such systems to enable the tax determination or tax compliance reporting processes to work—for example, setting up taxpayers' data in tax software or tax codes in the ERP. No tax solution offers 100% automation out of the box.

3.33 TAX SYSTEM IMPLEMENTOR

A Tax Implementor or Tax System Integrator (SI) is a firm that helps a firm design, build, and deploy a tax technology solution. These firms have established tax technology practices and have a legacy in setting up indirect tax technology solutions for clients. These firms have tax

SME's, Taxologists, Tax Technologists, and ERP Finance Accounting & Tax professionals, Business Analysts, Tax project managers on board, and they bring years of learning, expertise, experience, and skills to the tax transformation program. The majority of large tax software vendors also have their own professional services divisions that can support the implementation of tax technology solutions. Examples of Tax System Integrator firms include Deloitte, Accenture, IBM, EY, KPMG, PwC, WTS, ATC, BDO, Innovate Tax, Ryan, and Grant Thornton.

3.34 TAX WORKFLOW SYSTEMS

Tax workflow systems help firms collect and manage client data through portals, harmonize it into a format and structure that enables seamless integration with integrated tax & accounting software. In this process, such systems support collaborative tax operations, with task accountability and tracking mechanisms, and include built-in checks to detect anomalies and errors, ensuring high-quality data for tax compliance and reporting. Tax workflow systems offer many other additional functionalities. Examples of Tax workflow systems include Alteryx, Orbitax, Loctax, Blue dot, Tax Canary etc.

3.35 TAX CODE

A tax code is generally a two-digit alphanumeric code that is configured in the ERP system as per the unique business tax treatments prevalent in specific jurisdictions, generally derived from country tax administration-prescribed tax return boxes. That way, business transactions are classified 'tagged,' and for tax functions, it's easier to segregate and compute values for tax return boxes. From a point of determination also, tax code has high significance as in cases where native ERP tax is used for tax calculation, a tax code contains tax rate and tax GL value, when business transactions are punched in with tax code (manual or automated), the tax rate embedded inside the tax code leads to tax value computation (tax value = tax rate % * tax base) and later that value is published in the tax GL having additional finance data, finally in a posted document one can see credit, debit and tax line items. In cases where 3rd party tax engine or tax Add-on software is used for tax rate calculation, the tax rate and even tax codes can be populated from such external systems, and tax GL is determined by the tax code already present in the ERP. It's important to note that any tax code used in the external tax engine or add-on's solution should already have a presence in the ERP system; otherwise, the transaction will fail. Other than the tax rate, the tax GL, and the tax code also contain additional parameters like tax types, account keys, condition information, and tax category, which help drive the basic tax determination process in the ERP. In modern tax compliance reporting, a tax code is a vital mapping link between document line item tax values to tax return boxes, in e-invoicing software, tax administration-mandated tax codes can come into play, which helps tax authorities to identify transactional scenarios and check compliance. A Tax code is a permanent, irreplaceable tax object in tax technology.

3.36 TAX FUNCTION

A tax function consists of tax associates (tax department), taxologists (process experts), and tax technical (tax IT) i.e. individuals from tax dept. and tax IT. They work in cohesion to enable tax requirements incorporation in IT systems. In this book, wherever tax function is listed, it implies joint involvement of tax associates, Taxologist and Tax Technologist.

3.37 SUMMARY

After reading this chapter, you should be able to understand the various ERP, Tax, and Tax Technology terms while reading articles, books, listening to webinars, podcasts, reports etc. The list is quite comprehensive, enabling a holistic view. Without a good understanding of the basic building blocks, understanding tax technology becomes difficult; therefore, it is highly relevant to understand these terms and develop a clear, crystal-clear vision of their definitions to understand ERP and Tax Technology. Also, the application of these terms in tax technology project works and discussions displays maturity and experience. In the next chapter, we will look into the ERP (Enterprise Resource Planning) system, its architecture, and its technical aspects.

CHAPTER 4

ERP SYSTEMS, MODULES, INTEGRATED WORKINGS, AND TAX TECHNOLOGY POINT OF VIEW

The chapter introduces ERP systems and helps readers gain deeper insights into their workings and features. Having a strong understanding of ERP is the first step in the tax technology journey, because it is the core of the entire tax framework. The chapter discusses the ERP system, its modules and sub modules, business function integration (with a simple case study), vivid IT systems landscapes, the ERP landscape, associated tax technology POV, Master data, System & landscape, deployment, and many additional aspects from real-life projects. Followed by the capabilities of the ERP system in managing the modern tax determination and tax compliance reporting requirements, shortlisting the shortcomings and limitations of the ERP system with specific examples, use cases, and real-time situations. The chapter educates readers on the challenges tax teams face in the absence of tax technology software and how modern tax technology can streamline, digitize, and automate tax processes.

An ERP system is a core business process automation system, and it is vital to have a good understanding of its architecture, modules, sub modules, processes, and integrated operations. Understanding ERP is the first step towards Indirect tax technology.

4.1 ERP SYSTEM

An ERP is an Enterprise Resource Planning Software, a business process automation software, which first automates organizational business processes and later enables users to access, run, and operate those processes digitally, with the data associated with such processes stored (logged) in its database.

An ERP -

- Facilitates the flow of information across the organization for all business functions
- Integrates cross functional system that operates in real time
- Provides a central repository (database) that is shared by all of an organization's business functions

Figure 4.1

As seen in Figure 4.1, an organization has different departments (*business functions*) – Manufacturing involving plants, inventories, factories, and warehouses; Finance involving payables, receivables, down payments, assets; HR involving hiring, separation, payroll, employee benefits, etc. An ERP system has corresponding modules to automate and streamline such business function processes, which are called modules (Finance, Sales, Procurement, Human Capital, Customer Relationship Management etc.). In short, the business term '*Business functions*' is called '*modules*' or 'building blocks' in functional language and each business function has its own unique process; different business function processes can have integrations at various process steps. The combination of modules in an ERP is often called a *suite*.

4.2 ERP SYSTEM MODULES

An organization (a firm) may have one or multiple business operations. For example, manufacturing, suppliers, procurement, human capital, sales, finance, etc. All these processes are automated using different ERP modules (business-process-specific components within the ERP that communicate with each other). As markets and businesses expand, more modules are being added to the ERP, alongside industry-specific modules (Oil & Gas, Environmental), which offer tailored features. Many ERP systems include standard modules and allow firms to license additional modules based on their business requirements. Firms may also not use some modules that come with the standard package if the business requirement is not present.

Some prominent modules are:

- **Finance and Accounting:** Invoice & Billing tasks, account reconciliation, vendor payments (AP), customer payments (AR), profit and loss reporting, balance sheet, tax reporting, etc. Financial accounting is at the heart of an ERP, as nearly all business functions and processes involve it.
- **Human Capital Management**: Specific to organization employees: Hiring, training, payroll, separation, employee data mgmt., tax withholding, time off, etc.
- **Customer Relationship Management:** Focused on customers: Initial contract, sales, purchase history, post-sale maintenance and support, service and warranty agreements, etc.
- **Supply Chain Management:** Focused on supplier and vendor-related processes to ensure that a shortage of raw

materials or assembled goods does not occur to balance demand and supply, e.g., inventory availability at the right place at the right time.

- **Inventory and Warehouse Management**: Real-time inventory levels (outbound and inbound), inventory location, locate and ship the product process, etc.
- **Order Management:** Quotations, sales orders, outbound delivery, customer billing, etc.
- **Procurement:** Purchase requisitions, purchase orders, goods receipts, inbound deliveries, etc.
- **Manufacturing:** Involves processes such as material requirements planning, planning and scheduling, manufacturing execution, and product lifecycle management.

4.3 ERP SYSTEMS IN THE MARKET

SAP, Oracle, Microsoft Dynamics, Sage, Salesforce, Workday, Zoho, etc. There are tens of ERP systems available in the market. While some ERPs may have comprehensive module coverage, some may have limited module availability. A firm needs to check that out before making a purchase.

Tax Technology POV: Tax software has distinct modules, unlike ERP systems. More detailed information on the tax software architecture, modules, and operations is explained in the later chapters. By tax technology, we mean tax software, which may be external (e.g., Vertex, Avalara, Fonoa, and Meridian) or an ERP firm's separately licensed product (e.g., SAP ERP has DRC for compliance, reporting, and e-invoicing).

POV = Point of View

4.4 INTEGRATED OPERATION OF ERP MODULES

In the distant past, firms had multiple IT systems (Mainframe Systems, MS Excel, Custom ERPs, Legacy ERPs) for their business functions, e.g., Finance and accounting, sales, human capital, and material planning. These systems focused on one or more business functions and were independent of each other. As a result, extensive custom integration was required for process and data flows, and there was no centralized view for organizations. Whereas in the modern ERP's, these modules catering to the unique business function needs are now internally integrated with each other, share a common database, use a standard programming language, and have a common nomenclature for processes and data (master and transactional). In the ERP system, business transactions occur uniquely in each module and flow through the other modules via an integrated process, enabling end-to-end completion.

To better understand the workings of an ERP, its modules (business functions, software units), their integrations, and the processes and data flows, we will use a simple business flow. In the Figure 4.4, we have a firm, MED Pharma Company, a dummy pharmaceutical firm based in the Netherlands that makes medicines for its customers in Europe.

It's involved in the manufacturing and sale of drugs and purchases raw materials (chemicals) from its supplier in the Netherlands.

We are limiting the entire supply chain to the Netherlands to explain the ERP workings and avoid complicating the tax piece. Also, we have included the main modules relevant to this case study to avoid overcomplicating the objective.

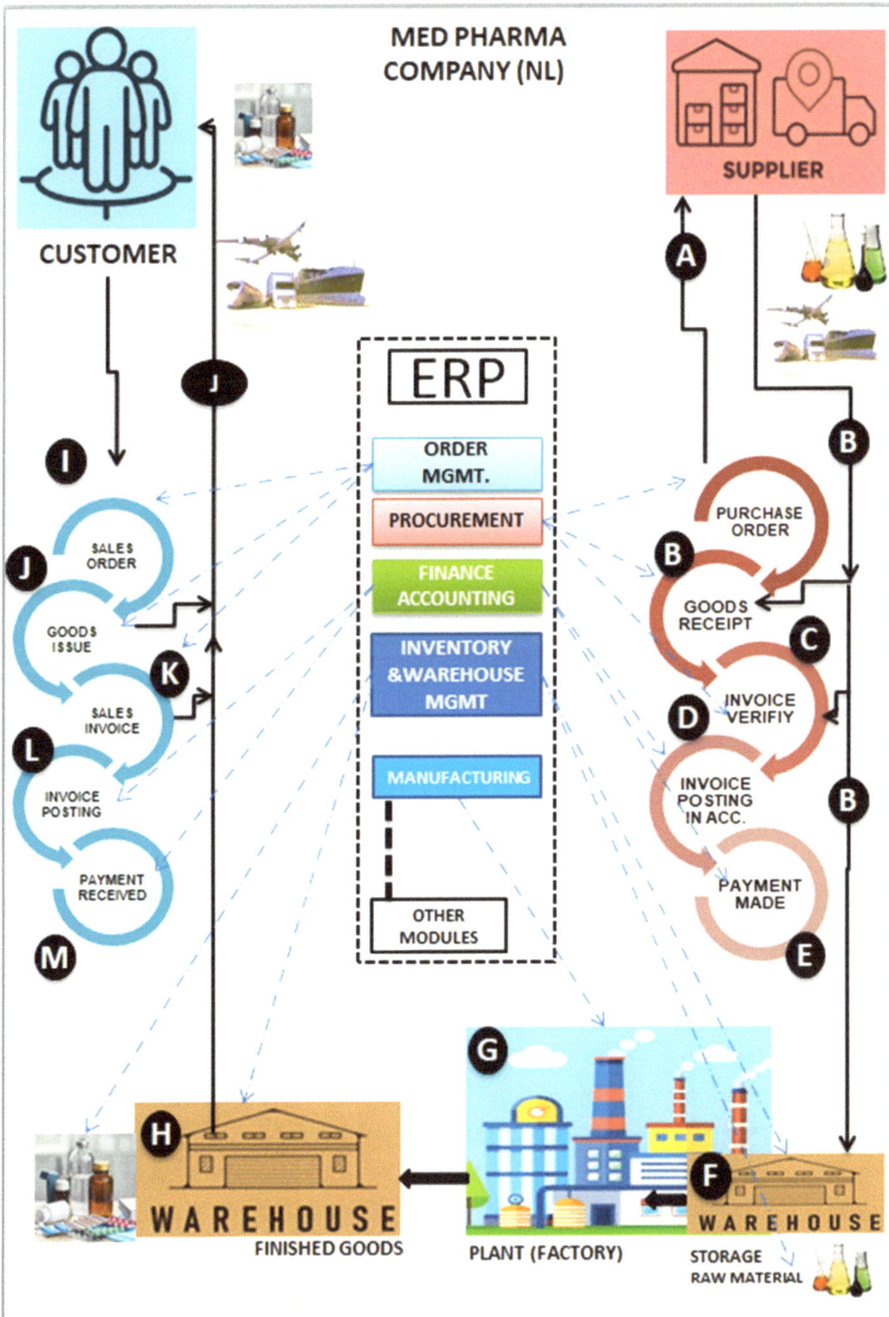
MED PHARMA
COMPANY (NL)
CUSTOMER
SUPPLIER
ERP
ORDER
MGMT.
PROCUREMENT
FINANCE
ACCOUNTING
INVENTORY
&WAREHOUSE
MGMT
MANUFACTURING
OTHER
MODULES
A
B
C
D
E
F
G
H
I
J
K
L
M
SALES
ORDER
GOODS
ISSUE
SALES
INVOICE
INVOICE
POSTING
PAYMENT
RECEIVED
PURCHASE
ORDER
GOODS
RECEIPT
INVOICE
VERIFIY
INVOICE
POSTING
IN ACC.
PAYMENT
MADE
WAREHOUSE
FINISHED GOODS
PLANT (FACTORY)
WAREHOUSE
STORAGE
RAW MATERIAL

Figure 4.4

The process starts with step A. Based on the production requirement (derived from actual sales under the lean manufacturing model), a Purchase Order is created in the *ERP's Procurement module* for the Supplier. Post which, the supplier ships the raw materials (chemicals) to MED Pharma Company and also sends an invoice. The raw material is sent to the Plant warehouse (B), and the *Inventory & Warehouse management* module is involved, triggering a raw material stock receipt and an inventory update (F). The module provides updated information on inventory levels (specs, type, and quantity) and the location within the warehouse, which is attached to the plant. In parallel to this process, the ERP Procurement module receives an invoice from the supplier (C) and, post which, verification is conducted physically in the Plant warehouse (Goods type – quantity and other specs) to ensure that the actual product and units delivered are as expected. After verification, the supplier's invoice is posted in the *Financial Accounting* module (D), and the payment is later made to the supplier by the *Financial Accounting* module.

The plant or factory is now involved, and manufacturing begins (G). In the ERP, the manufacturing process stages are managed by the *Manufacturing module,* which has its own set of processes. Post manufacturing, the final product, i.e., consumable medicines, is moved to a finished goods warehouse, where the *Inventory and Warehouse module* again comes into play, providing accurate insights into the medicine type, units, and storage location.

Now, when a customer places a sales order containing medicine type and units, which happens in the Order management module (I), firm Med Pharma Co. NL moves the goods (medicines) from its finished goods warehouse (J) involving *Inventory and Warehouse management* module and ships the goods (medicines) (J) to the customer site (Goods issue) using applicable transport means. Post which, a sales invoice (billing) is issued to the customer (K) in the *Order management module*, and also the invoice is posted in the accounting (L) via the Finance Accounting module. The customer receives the invoice and makes payment for the same, and it's posted in the *Financial Accounting* module. In a real-life scenario, there will undoubtedly be more modules, depending on the firm's business function requirements.

Thus, in the above case study, we can see how different ERP modules work in unison and have footprints on the entire value stream of the supply chain. They work in an integrated manner, automating and streamlining the workflow. That's one reason ERP is called an integrated system: its functional modules process data together and enable data flow.

Tax Technology POV: The tax software's function is to compute tax, run compliance checks, prepare tax returns, and support tax filing with the tax authority. For that, it needs finance logistics and organizational data, plus additional tax driver information from the ERP's. They are artificial tax intelligence machines**.** Its architecture is different.

4.5 ERP COMPONENTS

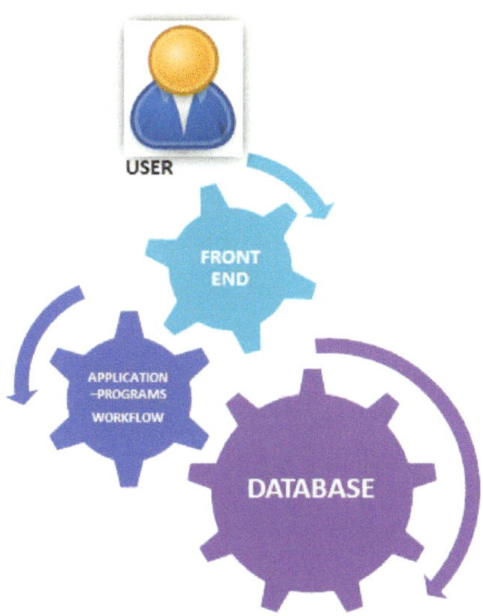

Figure 4.5

An ERP has three components –

- *Front End:* A front-end user-friendly interface, which enables users to create and manage operations, e.g., payroll runs, sales ordering, and payments. This layer is for humans to see functions, processes, and data.
- *Application:* An application (program code) that runs such operations in the background. The application program is included in the standard package and offers customization flexibility.
- *Database:* A database (tables) and interlinks contain data.

All three components work in cohesion to deliver the expected output for that specific module (business process)

Tax Technology POV: Tax software also has three components – front end, application, and database.

4.6 ERP MODULES WORKFLOW & TAX FOOTPRINTS

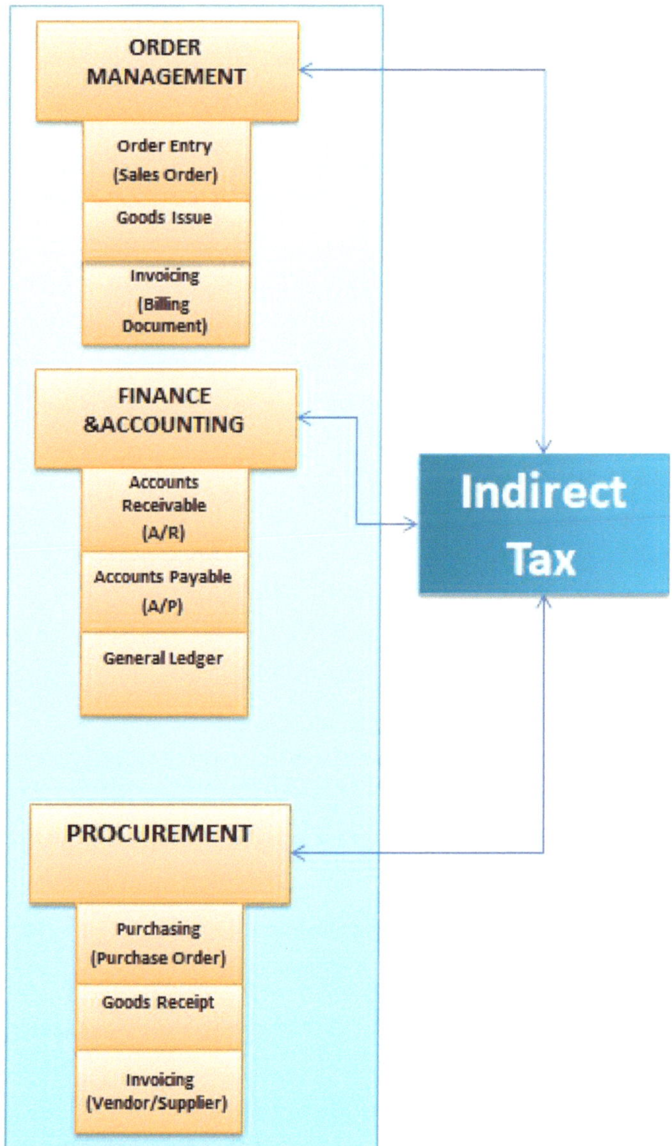

Figure 4.6

An ERP module has submodules (integrated sub-processes (alongside integrated module-level processes)), for example, in the above figure 4.6, we can see Order Management has Order Entry, Goods issue, and Invoicing, which are stacked together in a specific flow direction: Order Entry >Goods issue >Invoicing.

For Finance Accounting, we have Accounts Payable (Paying vendors/suppliers), Accounts Receivable (Posting incoming monies from customers), and General Leader. In this case, these submodules don't have a flow; AP and AR are independent, thus within a module, its submodules can have a definite process flow or may operate independently. Similarly, for Procurement, which includes Purchase Order, Goods Receipt, and Invoicing. These sub-module processes operate in a specific flow: Purchase Order > Goods receipt > Invoicing, etc.

Similarly, we can have sub-processes within the Supply Chain Management, Human Capital, Customer Relationship Management, Inventory Management, and Manufacturing modules.

Tax POV: Generally, the Order Management, Procurement, Finance, and Accounting modules and sub-modules trigger tax calculation, as shown in the figure. Tax, from a business, functional, and technical viewpoint, sits under the finance accounting module umbrella, but does get involved in other modules' operations and processes that have tax footprints.

4.7 ERP CONFIGURATION & CUSTOMIZATION

An ERP needs to be configured for operations. It doesn't come with out-of-the-box, ready-to-use functionality; it needs to be personalized to the business's needs and requirements, and modules need to be functionally integrated (company-specific objects, parameters, functionality activation) with respect to data and process flows. Technical integration (front-end interface, process workflow, application program, and database) is already there. Functional and technical associates handle such aspects in accordance with designs developed by solution consultants based on business requirements.

Tax Technology POV: Tax engine also requires configuration– Master data set ups (taxpayer, tax ID, jurisdictional registrations, customers, vendors for exemptions) and company-specific tax policy /tax treatment rules leveraging tax drivers.

4.8 ERP DEPLOYMENT TYPES: ON PREMISE, CLOUD AND HYBRID ERP

An ERP system software can be installed on site (on company hardware (servers) and internal intranet networks) or on cloud (3rd party servers) like Amazon, Microsoft or private cloud (remote servers) interconnected by internet. This cloud model is also called Software -as-a-service (SaaS). There is a third model, called hybrid, under which an ERP is installed both on-premise (generally at firms headquarters) and on cloud for subsidiaries. Country laws also play a factor in such models. For example, few Middle Eastern nations don't permit cloud deployment of their businesses for data security reasons. Certain government departments ERP's are often deployed on premise.

Cloud deployment is the future offering plethora of technological benefits –reduced hardware, less technical support costs (technical patches, upgrades are applied automatically) to business. Leverage internet of things (IoT), Blockchain, AI – Machine learning's, Robotic process automation (RPA), Generative AI, greater security and integration with other cloud based IT solutions and scalability are other advantages of cloud.

Tax Technology POV: A tax engine can also be deployed onsite, hybrid or cloud. It follows the way the ERP is installed generally.

4.9 MODERN ERP'S SETUPS SCENARIOS IN GLOBAL FIRMS

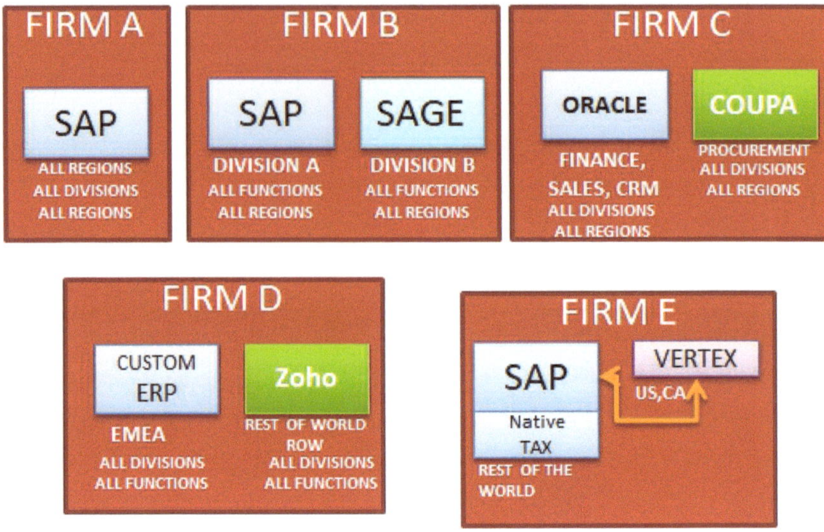

Figure 4.9

An ERP landscape may differ from firm to firm. An organization may have multiple ERP systems (including custom ERP systems) from separate ERP software vendors on its IT landscape. Custom ERP systems are developed by the organization's development team and aren't third-party ERPs (external vendors). A firm can also have multiple divisions (product portfolios), e.g., home appliances, chemicals, commercial hardware, and services, as well as a geographical presence in various countries.

For example, in Figure 4.9, we see vivid ERP landscape scenarios.

Firm A runs its business using only the SAP ERP system across all divisions and their associated business functions globally (ideal landscape). With many ERP transformations underway, firms are targeting this positioning for centralized operations. Firm B has SAP ERP for division A and Sage ERP for division B for all functions and regions. In Firm C, we see that SAP ERP is used for Finance, Sales, and CRM, and that Coupa ERP is used for procurement across all regions. Firm D, which uses a custom ERP for EMEA operations and ZOHO ERP for the rest of the world entities. In short, an ERP landscape for modern multinational Fortune 500 firms can include multiple ERP systems, positioned in combinations based on their geographical presence, business divisions, and business functions. Firm E may uses Vertex (a tax software) for US and Canada and Native SAP Tax for rest of the world.

Understanding the ERP landscape, ERP systems, business functions, and the countries in scope for a firm is the very first step towards understanding its operational blueprint for successful delivery of Tax & tax technology solutions.

Tax Technology POV: In the context of tax software, a firm may have one tax software integrated with various ERPs, non-ERPs, Excel, custom applications, and e-commerce apps, i.e., a many-to-one relationship. That is the benefit of having tax software. A firm does not need multiple tax software for a multi-system landscape. For example, one tax engine can integrate with various ERPs, e-commerce portals, and even Excel databases via APIs or connectors.

4.10 ERP AND REPORTING

Figure 4.10

Alongside business process automation and operations (managing day to day business as usual works), an ERP system also supports various types reporting – Internal (management reporting) and external (to statutory and legal bodies), this is because ERP database contains data from all modules and any specific data for a particular period can be extracted to populate reports using standard (ERP specific transaction codes) or custom programs.

Tax Technology POV: Tax software offers better reporting and a database containing transactional data relevant to reporting. The ERP sales purchase, and finance data is fed into the tax software via API/Connectors, stored in the tax software database, and the tax software application extracts and transforms it into a format and structure with the required data elements for tax reporting to tax authorities. For example, tax compliance and reporting software's can populate tax returns, supplementary reports for tax authorities. Tax engines also has reporting database offering transactional reporting functionality for the entities in scope.

4.11 ERP MASTER DATA & TAXABILITY IMPACT

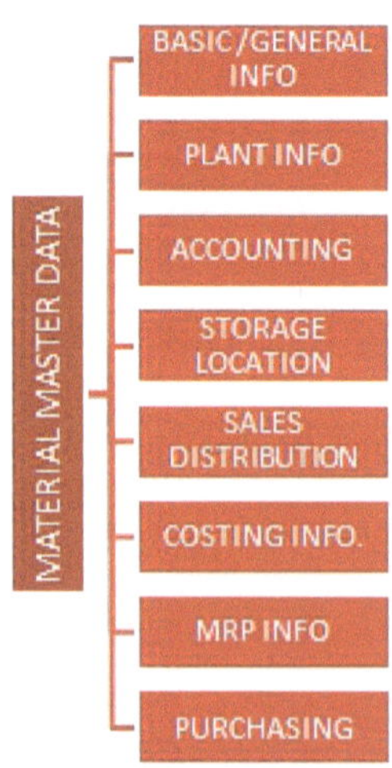

Figure 4.11

An ERP system integrates people, processes, and technologies in an organization. The data in the ERP is consistent across all modules.

For example, consider a firm involved in making medicines – and in that case, 'Contraceptive pills' –a product, will have a common name and material code (e.g., CONPIL23) across all functions – Sales, CRM, Finance, etc. This 'contraceptive pill' material is now a *master data* record, with additional information such as part name, units, expiry date, lot no., serial number, plant/warehouse no., and other specifications. Master data is like an individual's driving license, listing their name, date of birth, valid-to/from dates, jurisdictional authority, a bar code, DL number, class of vehicle to drive, etc., and providing a unique nationwide identification of an individual across all authorities.

This common sharing of master data across organizational business functions results in the creation of centralized databases (e.g., storing all medicines in a single database table), rather than each business function having its own unique databases (Excel, multiple standalone ERPs, custom databases), which creates ambiguity.

This feature of ERP to have a centralized repository of common master data facilitates an organization and its employees to have real-time insight into the inventory, do business with confidence, and propel upstream manufacturing in a lean manner, avoiding both overproduction (leading to wastage) and underproduction (leading to a shortage of supply).

The same holds well with finance processes, which include finance master data objects that incorporate financial information like general ledger accounts - payable, receivable, expense, tax (direct, indirect), collections, assets, revenue, etc., and are shared generically within an entity's (legal operating unit) business functions. This leads to an accurate estimate of working capital, and the organization can provide financial reporting to legal and statutory bodies with accuracy. ERP replaces spreadsheet-based financial accounting, which is highly error-prone, bulky, slow, and requires custom macros to connect to and extract the desired data. There are numerous strategic and tactical benefits to using an ERP for business.

Like material, we have other master data elements in an ERP, such as Plants, Warehouses, General Ledgers, Cost Centers, Company Codes, Projects, Customers, and Vendors.

To do business, a firm needs to execute a transaction, i.e., a business transaction, in which such master data element are punched in alongside transactional data; these master data elements also enable data visibility in other modules. For example, while creating a purchase order, the receiving plant information is entered in the transaction line item. This entry enables an update (inventory update) in the plant maintenance module. Similarly, during billing and invoicing transactions during sales or procurement, credit and debit events happen involving the customer/vendor and the firm's general ledger accounts, which leads to the update of ledger data, which resides in the financial accounting module, i.e., the data flows from one module to another with the use of master data elements in the ERP.

Tax Technology POV: A master dataset is required in tax software as well to enable operations, e.g., taxpayer name (legal entity), company code, tax ID, jurisdictional registrations, customers, vendors, tax drivers, etc., and similar to the ERP, these master data elements enable data flow between tax software modules.

4.12 ERP SYSTEM VIEWS

An ERP system has three views to cater to its three user types- Business, Functional, and Technical.

- *Business user view*: This view has menu options for the business user to run business transactions

- *Functional view:* This view contains menus that a functional consultant uses to configure the ERP.
- *Technical view:* This view provides menu options for developers (programmers) to make changes or enhancements to the ERP program code.

There may be tens of roles defined in an ERP, which limit a user (business, functional, or technical) to one or multiple roles, enabling access to specific view areas, business functions and processes, sub-processes, company codes, divisions, and combinations. This is to ensure compliance and prevent unauthorized transactions.

Tax Technology POV: Tax software generally has two views – the Business user view and the functional view. Client developers are not authorized to modify the programming code of the Tax software applications, as that's the IP (intellectual property) of the tax software firm, and tax vendors don't want it exposed or leaked. The tax software vendor sends regular legal and technical patches to maintain the software system and keep it up to date with tax law changes. If a custom development requirement is a must, the tax software vendor will involve their own consultants to facilitate it.

4.13 ERP LANDSCAPE SYSTEMS

Figure 4.13

A firm's ERP landscape has primarily three sub-systems:

4.13.1 Development

In this system, the functional and technical associates conduct development work, i.e., either front-end configuration or customizations (application level technical works involving programming). After solution discovery and design phase for a project, enhancement, or bug fix, the build happens in this system. After some testing (Functional unit testing) by functional and technical associates, the build (configuration or customization objects) is moved to the next system, i.e., Test.

4.13.2 Testing

In this system, business users test it with relevant business scenarios to validate and verify the development. They check input parameters and if the actual output is as expected. In modern enterprises, this system is often subdivided into two systems. This is because, in the development system, master and transactional data quality is generally poor, and concurrent cross-functional (multi-module) developments create a shaky dynamic, leading to doubts about testing quality.

Figure 4.13.2

4.13.2.1 Testing (SIT)

Test system – also nicknamed SIT (System Integration Testing)- to differentiate it from the UAT system. Here, functional and technical associates test the business scenario and further validate the quality of the development. The system has better data availability, fuelled by production system refresh (a process that periodically replicates production data into the test and UAT systems to enable real production testing simulation).

4.13.2.2 Testing (UAT)

User Acceptance testing (UAT), in which business users test the system with relevant business scenarios to validate and verify the development. They check input and output parameters and if the actual output is as expected. The business users pass/fail the results. If the result is a as expected i.e. pass, the built components are moved into the production system, and functionality is achieved. If the UAT result is failed, the incident/change request/service request is returned to the functional or technical consultant for rechecking the build and performing necessary rectifications. The process repeats, restarting the development system.

It's worth noting that a firm may have just one ERP system for both Test and UAT, or separate ERP systems.

4.13.3 Production

It's the system in which real-world business transactions occur. It's a highly sensitive system, and no functional or technical associate has access to do developments here. Only authorized business users can access this system with defined roles and access points. This is the final system in an ERP system's landscape. Even if someone has accidental access or if any built-type work is done in a production system, it should never be done, as it will cause operational disruption and lead to profound business impact.

In addition, a firm may have systems such as a Sandbox (which isn't connected to any other system and is mainly used for training and prototype development), a staging system during project work, a cutover system, etc. A project may involve a multitude of dynamic systems depending upon deployment strategy – Big bang, phased go-live, etc. However, as a standard, Development, Testing, and Production systems form the backbone of the ERP systems landscape.

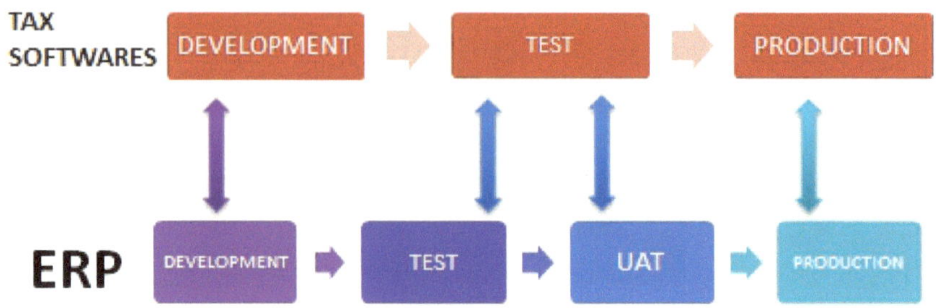

Figure 4.13.3

Tax Technology POV: In terms of tax technology, where we may have third party tax software's deployed on firms IT landscape for tax determination, compliance reporting and e-invoicing, the ERP Dev-Test-Production systems are connected (integrated) with corresponding tax software's Development, Test& Production systems (Figure 4.13.C) to enable configuration consistence related testing quality and built movement –either done solely in the ERP, or tax software or done in both ERP and Tax software.

4.14 DEVELOPMENT TO DEPLOYMENT METHODOLOGY

The ERP built (configurations and customizations) in the development environment is loaded onto an object, and the object makes its way to production. For example, in SAP, the object is called transport, and SAP Basis teams support its movement. A built move in the ERP Development to Test to Production follows the standard SDLC (Software development lifecycle) process, incorporating Quality Control (QC), Change Management (Change Mgmt.), and Release management (RLS. Mgmt.) Processes. These areas include incident, service request, and change request creation (i.e., an ID for the business requirement, which enables tracking); business requirement document (BRD) creation, often including technical design system configuration documents; test documentation; and syncing with the weekly/monthly release cycles. An emergency requirement-related build can be moved urgently after special approvals, skipping the standard release cycle. There are specific software solutions on the market to manage SLDC, QA, and CHG. Mgmt., RLS. Mgmt. process, e.g., Azure, `JIRA, Service Now, Freshworks, HP ALM, Ninjaone.

Tax Technology POV: The tax technology components built within the third-party systems integrated with the ERP also follow a similar SDLC, QA, and RLS. Mgmt., Change Mgmt. process of a firm. They do have separate BRD, TDD (Technical design document), though. However, testing is done in the ERP system to verify the end-to-end functionality. A limited unit testing can be done within tax software's also. They are also managed and tracked through the same project and incident management software the firm uses for the ERP.

4.15 TAX CHALLENGES IN AN ERP SYSTEM

The chapter guides readers through the ERP system's capabilities for managing modern tax determination and tax compliance reporting requirements. It shortlists the ERP system's shortcomings and limitations with specific examples, use cases, and real-time scenarios. The chapter educates readers on the challenges the tax team faces in the absence of tax technology software and on how modern tax technology can streamline, digitalize, and automate tax processes.

As tax technology is evolving, tax authorities are getting smarter every day. There is a positive push for enterprise Tax software. Tax software is like 'Tax ERP,' which integrates with your business application ERP and automatically computes Tax for every purchase and sales transaction. It also populates your Tax returns using Tax data from your ERP database.

Figure 4.15

Accurate Tax returns are the final objective of the entire tax exercise, i.e., to make sure that the tax value in every Tax return form box is 100% accurate - That's what accurate and efficient tax compliance is with respect to Tax legislation. That level of accuracy comes when you have accurately determined Tax in your ERP, coupled with precise Tax classification (tagging transactions with Tax codes, which define transaction tax types, e.g., standard rate, cross-border, etc.). Tax codes in ERP tax software set up have two critical roles. To help transactions locate GL accounts for posting & enable Tax returns form development. Tax codes tag a transaction and route it to eligible Tax boxes in the Tax form.

ERP systems are not designed to manage the tax determination and tax compliance reporting requirement. An ERP system is a 'brainless tax box' with no built-in tax logic to apply to business transactions; it has zero tax intelligence. It cannot drive Tax rate determination or tag transactions with relevant Tax classification tax codes as standard functionality. While many ERP specialists may argue this, it's a fact. No ERP system comes with any tax authority logic (Tax laws, tax legislation); it's customized & hard-coded with tax data and anything dynamic (like tax) must not be hard-coded.

In an ERP, custom tax codes are created; these codes include custom embedded tax rates. When business user makes a transaction, tax codes are manually or automatically selected based upon the transaction scenario i.e. tax code is picked up set up from 'Tax code selection table' (this table has multiple columns, the end column has tax code, based upon the transaction data e.g. Column 1{Country}, Column 2 {Transaction Type (Output /Input)}, Column 3 {Tax Type}, Column 4 Tax classification} ...Column N { } the tax code is picked, and the tax rate embedded within the tax code is applied. An illustrative example is below.

Country	**Process**	**Tax Type**	**Tax classification**	**Valid from**	**Valid To**	**Tax code**
UK	O	VAT	1 (Std. rate)	1.1.2000	31.12.9999	U1
UK	O	VAT	2(Reduced rate)	1.1.2000	31.12.9999	U2
UK	O	VAT	0(Zero rate)	1.1.2000	31.12.9999	U3

Later, the returns reporting period transaction dump is exported into spreadsheets and tax managers populate Tax forms.

By doing this, the Finance, Tax & IT department completes its business-as-usual tasks. But this is a non-compliant situation. If your Tax data (Tax Code, Tax Rate for the business scenario) is inaccurate, no matter how savvy your tax return spreadsheets are, noncompliance is evident: 'Garbage in - Garbage out'.

Tax legislation is dynamic. For example, barcode scanners today may be subject to 12% VAT; a month later, they may be subject to 5%; or they may be taxable for customers, nontaxable for NGOs, or the government entities, etc. Tax rates are defined by tax authorities, who issue a circular on their website; they don't personally call all businesses tax managers.

In ERP-led tax automation, a cumbersome, manual, and painful process kicks off to update tax code and tax rates for applicable transactions. The tax manager must regularly review the tax laws of their country to identify all applicable tax scenarios across all relevant jurisdictions. If such a change is not detected on time, it's a serious compliance problem; it means the business is overcharging or undercharging, which can lead to class lawsuits, assured audits, followed by penalties by tax authorities and loss of goodwill, brand loss, and layoffs of accountable persons.

A single tax authority-led tax update miss is enough to cost a firm hundreds of thousands of pounds (e.g., if a UK firm pays 15% input VAT instead of 5% on a £10m purchase, the loss is £100K). This is because you may never get back the incorrectly incurred input VAT from the tax authority. This is a classic example of when firms blindly rely on vendors and suppliers who charge tax, and their end users manually enter 'vendor tax rate fit' payable tax codes to book the payable invoice.

In the GCC region, tax authorities have refused to grant refunds for requests for inaccurate or overpaid input VAT. Overcharging tax is illegal, but paying overcharged tax and later claiming a refund from the government is also unlawful. Recently, in the UK, the Government busted a financial syndicate that stole millions in VAT refunds from the UK tax authority by issuing fake invoices in the names of bogus suppliers and vendors. Though this is an intentional financial crime, intentional non-compliance, and being apologetic later, is not accepted by tax authorities.

In a standard ERP native tax set up, if tax manager observes a tax rate change, he logs a ticket and asks IT for help to accommodate this change, IT has its own turnaround time, they develop BRD (Business Requirement Document), Technical specs, do build in Development, conduct IT testing, support UAT, get approvals, alongside managing change management, release management and quality assurance SDLC (Software Development Life Cycle) process before moving the tax logic into production. For risky objects, companywide regression testing must be completed (to avoid misfit components going into production & disrupting it), and finally, the new tax code (a single-row edit in that massive tax code selection table) goes into production.

The tax department is happy because now they are compliant, business is working as usual, and IT gets appreciation and funds (as per industry estimates, the minimum dollar value of such enhancements is $2000, based upon 40-hour work (BRD, Specs, Build, Test, Go-live) and $50/Hr. resource cost). As compared to the annual license cost of Tax software, which can run from $50K - $500K (depending upon corporate size, transactional volume, geographical scope, legal entities), internal IT cost to manage Tax IT work tickets, enhancements, and projects can efficiently run from $500K - $2M annually, i.e., four to five times. In the author's own experience, the cost to make a small change in tax type for India's 2019's 'Swachh Bharath Tax' requirement delivery costed around $35K for a major firm.

For a firm that sells only few products in a limited jurisdiction, it looks like an acceptable deal to use ERP native tax. However, for firms with business in many countries and tens of products and services with different taxability, it's a nightmare to ensure your Tax rates and Tax codes are always accurate. Moreover, due to ERP standard operating procedures, tax updates are often not included promptly; as a result, the business has to perform extensive manual workarounds to rectify the resulting inaccurate invoices.

While Tax receivables can be semi-automated, the ERP has limited ability to help firms manage Tax accuracy in their payables. ERP has to be hard-coded for every tax logic, which is neither easy, feasible, nor reliable. Otherwise, why do hundreds of Fortune 500 firms use tax automation software for billions of transactions. By using ERP for tax automation, firms are on a path of noncompliance. It puts tax managers, IT heads, and Finance managers at grave risk, as someone has to take accountability for tax noncompliance with this 'hard-coded' & 'designer' Tax logic in the ERP, which, with tens of tax codes for each tax scenario and situation, only worsens the problem.

As ERP cannot auto-update tax rates and tax codes, firms have to undergo the 'Detect-Analyze-Ticket-Build-Test' process again and again, a never-ending process. It causes unnecessary strain on finance, tax, and IT functions. It's an expensive, risky, and old school type approach to doing tax things and asking ERP to do things it's not designed for or supposed to do. ERP software is for business process automation, not for tax automation.

Tax Engine – an artificial 'tax intelligence supercomputer' has Tax law led Tax logic programs pre-configured and gets auto updated with any Tax changes. In any major Tax software seller firm, every day, hundreds of legal and tax professionals' scan-receive-analyses and document tax rate updates for each tax authority and their DevOps team develop technical program applications for those requirements, later pushing legal updates into the client tax software's, leading to computing accuracy in tax determination. Nowadays, tax software returns tax codes to the to the ERP at the line-item & invoice level, which drive appropriate Tax GL A/C entries, enriching transaction data to the highest levels of compliance and removing the need for tens of tax codes for tax rates in the ERP system.

Moreover, if firms use Tax compliance software (alongside Tax Engine), with a pre-qualified tax codes tagged transactions, the Tax compliance and returns process becomes seamless, this is because Tax compliance software's use Tax codes to route transactions to Tax form boxes, there may be one to one or many to one relationship logic between Tax Compliance software tax codes and Tax returns boxes. Since the Tax engine has already determined appropriate tax codes, transactions are enriched, the compliance and returns filing process is seamless, giving tax managers precise 'six sigma' level reverse traceability (defense against Tax authority-led audits and top-notch ERP GL – Tax engine extract reconciliation at the line item level.

That means the tax function can extract all transactions at the line item level for a particular Tax box of a specific Tax period and justify its tax veracity – Tax rate & amount is accurate & Tax box relevancy (invoice is fit for a particular Tax box through Tax code tagging).

That way, end-to-end real tax automation is achieved. Tax digitization is of no use if it lacks automated tax logic. Tax software is for Tax process automation, ERPs are for business process automation. Both compliment each other. Business drives innovation and process improvements in the ERP and Tax department should have a top-notch say in the organization on the best software tools for tax automation, because tax managers and tax associates are guardians of the firm's tax legal and statutory compliance policy with respect to domestic and international tax authorities.

4.16 SUMMARY

In this chapter, we have shown you thc ERP system's modules, integrated cross-functional processes, tax footprints, configuration and customization aspects, master data, system and landscape, and associated tax challenges when using Native ERP tax functionality. Readers are now aware of ERP operations and how specific process interfaces have tax touchpoints. ERP is the core of any tax operation; business transactions are created in the ERP and then imported into tax technology software. An ERP is like a Sun in our solar system, occupying the central position, around which everything else revolves; its understanding is the very first ladder in tax technology. In the next chapter, we'll discuss the upstream tax process, i.e., tax determination, and the various tools and methodologies adopted globally.

CHAPTER 5

TAX DETERMINATION

The chapter introduces readers to the heart of tax technology: tax determination using native ERP tax solutions, an external 3rd-party bolt-in tax engine, and add-ons and plug-ins. Accurate and qualitative tax determination is the key to good, effective tax compliance and reporting. The chapter starts with the tax determination process involving the native ERP, then moves to the tax engine, its workings, maintenance, and taxonomy. The chapter educates readers on the vital sales and purchase cycle workflow and the associated tax drivers; i.e., it introduces the concept of tax drivers, which run the show both upstream and downstream in tax technology solutions.

The tax determination chapter covers the fundamentals of tax determination extensively and in a defined knowledge & learning structure. Later sections compare the pros and cons of ERP Native Tax solutions, Tax Engines, and Tax Add-ons, concluding with the overall value proposition. The tax determination process is here to stay despite modern Artificial intelligence software, because tax engines are themselves artificial intelligence software. Once readers understand the working dynamics of tax determination, they can more quickly grasp downstream tax technology processes, enabling them to contribute to overall tax technology more efficiently.

Later, it delves into a specific viewpoint on the European ERP Tax transformation scenario, under a Greenfield project approach (start from scratch), comparing the adoption of native ERP tax functionality, a tax engine, and tax add-ons.

5.1 NATIVE ERP TAX DETERMINATION

Long before the advent of 3rd-party external tax engines and Add-on, Plug-In tax determination technologies, native ERP Tax functionality supported tax determination for the ERP sales, procurement, and finance business processes.

'Native' ERP Tax functionality is inherent. It is a standard module within the ERP. It doesn't require separate licensing or installation, just like finance & accounting, manufacturing, supply chain management, project management, sales, purchase, human capital, controlling, etc.

No matter how far the tax computation process has digitalized and automated, native ERP tax will always play a role in the overall tax determination process, and it's irreplaceable in its entirety. This is because the Native ERP Tax programs are the first technical touchpoints with the ERP sales, procurement, and finance accounting processes and enables further processing of tax data.

Native ERP tax functionality not only supports tax determination but also assists the tax functions in tax reporting. In the contemporary world, the tax authority's complex regulatory landscape demands periodic , near real time or real-time tax reporting and submissions, along with ever-changing tax rules and rates, to ensure accurate determinations. Native ERP tax delivery performance is fast-fading and unable to keep up, leading to the deployment of external tax software.

The core tax determination process architecture in any ERP is the same, whether it's SAP, Oracle, MS Dynamics, Sage, SalesForce, Infor, etc. This is because the fundamental tax determination process is prescribed by the tax authorities, not ERP firms; its standard, ERP-product-agnostic, and generic for all firms. It's the same process adopted by tax advisors and tax law experts for determining tax. The nomenclature of tax suites, modules, methods, names, and elements may differ from one ERP to another.

The process involves tax setup – standard configurations (which one may find in product implementation guides) and custom maintenance of tax content. Native ERP provides empty containers (tables) for organizations to develop their own tax determination setups.

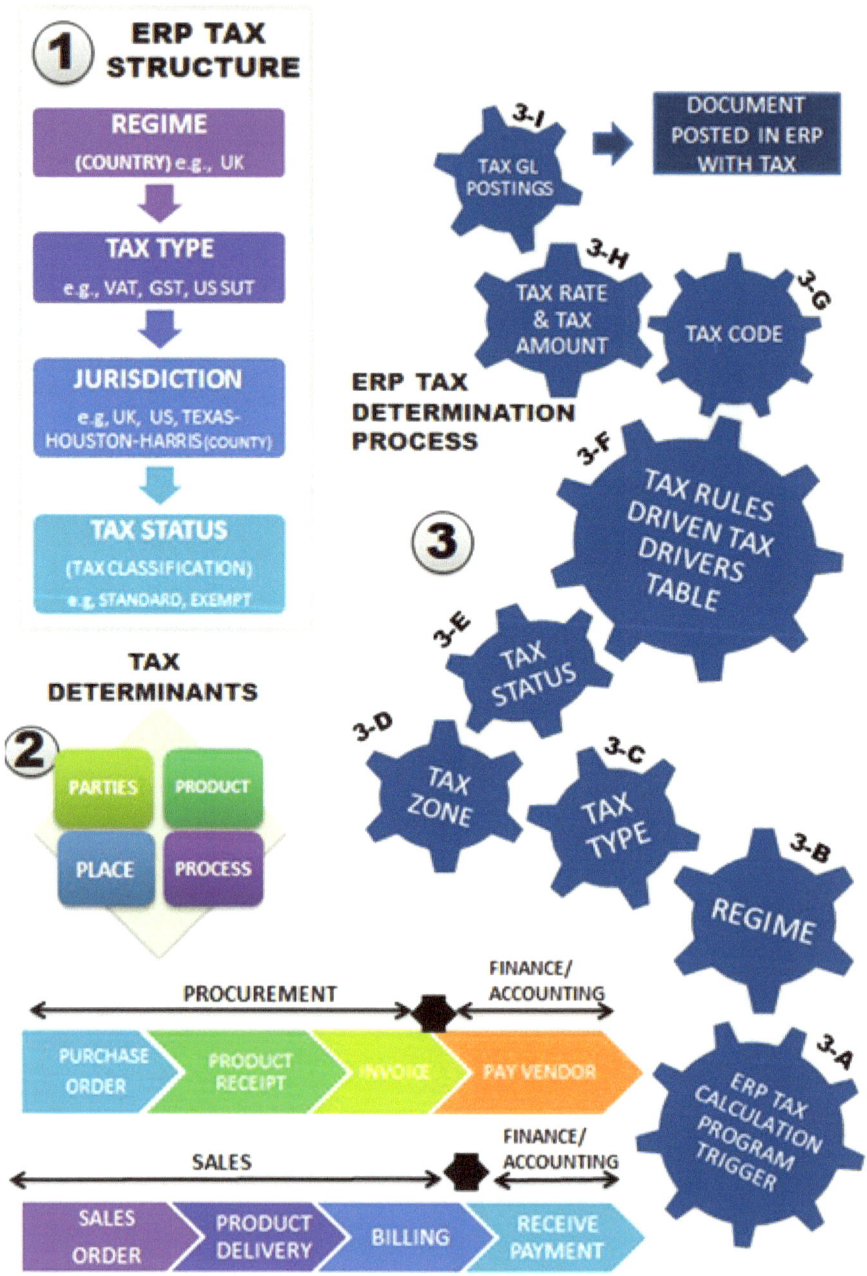
1
ERP TAX STRUCTURE
REGIME
(COUNTRY) e.g., UK
TAX TYPE
e.g., VAT, GST, US SUT
JURISDICTION
e.g, UK, US, TEXAS-HOUSTON-HARRIS(COUNTY)
TAX STATUS
(TAX CLASSIFICATION)
e.g, STANDARD, EXEMPT
TAX DETERMINANTS
2
PARTIES
PRODUCT
PLACE
PROCESS
ERP TAX DETERMINATION PROCESS
3
3-I
TAX GL POSTINGS
DOCUMENT POSTED IN ERP WITH TAX
3-H
TAX RATE & TAX AMOUNT
3-G
TAX CODE
3-F
TAX RULES DRIVEN TAX DRIVERS TABLE
3-E
TAX STATUS
3-D
TAX ZONE
3-C
TAX TYPE
3-B
REGIME
3-A
ERP TAX CALCULATION PROGRAM TRIGGER
PROCUREMENT
FINANCE/ ACCOUNTING
PURCHASE ORDER
PRODUCT RECEIPT
INVOICE
PAY VENDOR
SALES
FINANCE/ ACCOUNTING
SALES ORDER
PRODUCT DELIVERY
BILLING
RECEIVE PAYMENT

Figure 5.1.0

Let's dive in further to understand the native ERP Tax system architecture. In Figure 5.1.0, we can see the ERP Tax structure (1), the Tax Determinants (2), and the Tax computational process (3).

5.1.1 ERP Tax Structure

A standard ERP tax structure consists of four blocks in a downward hierarchy, as shown in Figure 5.1.1. This tax structure is delivered as standard by the ERP vendor and seldom requires any customizations. The information present in these structure modules is generic and not client-specific. The ERP Tax structure provides a foundation for firms to configure their tax setup on top of it.

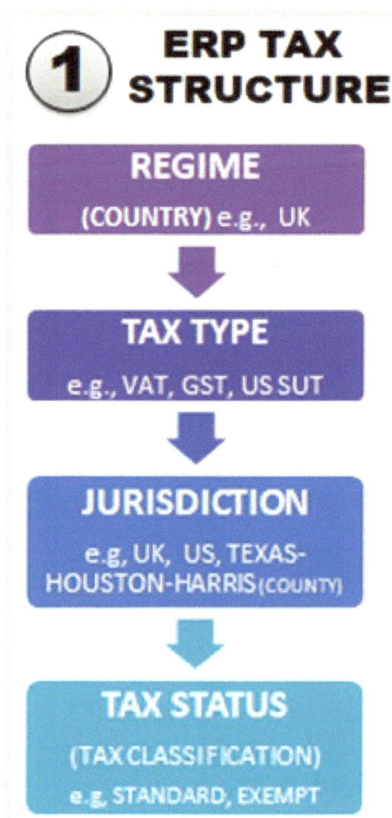

Figure 5.1.1

5.1.1.1 Regime

The top module is the 'Regime' or 'Country'. Each country has its unique place in the ERP Tax structure; the 'COUNTRY' has the highest hierarchy, and all tax structures set up fall under it.

5.1.1.2 Tax Type

The second module in the hierarchy is 'TAX TYPE'. Every country (tax administration) has a Tax type, e.g., VAT, GST, and Sales Use Tax. This is also generic data, and each country is tied to a unique Tax Type. E.g, UK = VAT, Singapore = GST, US = Sales Use Tax. This data is generic and client-independent, i.e., the country's tax authority has already prescribed the tax type in its law.

5.1.1.3 Jurisdiction

The third module, i.e., jurisdiction data sub classifies the applicable lower-level jurisdictions in a country. A country may have Tax authorities at the federal level (e.g., VAT in the UK, France, Singapore, the EU, Middle East, and APAC nations have, or at a dual level (CGST, IGST, SGST in India at Country & State levels) or at multiple levels (US Sales Use Tax at State + City +County +District + Additional levels). This tax framework enables the ERP Tax system to compute and post the taxes at various levels applicable to the business scenario document line item in scope. This data is generic and client-independent; i.e., the country's tax authority has already prescribed the jurisdictional levels in its law.

5.1.1.4 Tax Status

The fourth module, i.e., Tax status, is basically tax slabs (in tax terms) or tax sub classification, e.g., standard rate, reduced rate, zero rate, exempt, super reduced rate, outside of scope. Countries' tax slabs are divided into these tax statuses. This framework helps the ERP Tax system to tag the applicable tax status to corresponding product tax classification indicators – a custom configuration involving tagging an alphanumeric code to tax classification indicator in product master data (e.g., 1 for standard rate, 2 for exempt, zero as zero rate), later to be used as a tax driver in the ERP Tax computation process.

In short, tax statuses (tax slabs) are standard parameters that let the firm leverage them as a nomenclature 'tags' to classify product taxability status. This data is generic and client-independent, i.e., the country's tax authority has prescribed the prevailing tax slabs in its law. The tax status module doesn't contain the tax rate because tax rates are dynamic. Although the quantum of tax status may also change for a country, e.g., in July 2023, Vietnam introduced 'Luxury tax slab' (Special Consumption Tax (SCT)) in addition to existing slabs. GCC nations didn't have VAT before 2018; now VAT (Tax type) is there, so things are dynamic in the tax world.

5.1.2 Tax Determinants /Tax Drivers

Figure 5.1.2

When we talk about tax determination, whether using ERP Native Tax, offline using spreadsheets, or using an external tax engine, there are primarily four tax determinants. The fundamental logic of tax determination remains the same, and the majority of tax authorities worldwide follow this computational foundation, along with additional rules and exceptions. These tax determinants are present in ERP master data elements and are fetched during the transaction tax determination process, as explained in detail in Section 5.1.3 (ERP Tax Determination process).

5.1.2.1 Parties, i.e., **'Who'** is involved in the business transaction, this determinant helps the system identify the parties (buyer and seller) involved in the transaction. The legal party, i.e. the operating firm, the buyer (sales), the vendor/supplier (purchase), the fiscal classification of the legal entity, its registration, and other factors. In the ERP system, the process uses custom alphanumeric codes assigned to parties (e.g., the operating entity ABC Corporation B.V. may have a company code of '5004', and supplier Maxim Chemicals B.V. may have a vendor/supplier code of 33221100, etc.). This data helps the ERP system to identify the buyer and seller.

5.1.2.2 Places, i.e., **'Where'** – The geographical location of the buyer and seller. A supplier may have three location types – Bill from (Invoice from), Ship from, Supplier registered site (point of order acceptance), and similarly a buyer may have three location types –Ship To, Bill To, and Buyer registered address (Point of order origin). This determinant helps the system to identify the supply chain geographic parameters, which leads to the identification of regime (country) and Jurisdictions (Taxing Zone) as seen in Process 3-B and 3-D (Figure 5.1.0).

The 3-B process depicts the country, and the 3-C process involves the country codes and, if applicable, lower-level jurisdictions. For example, in Europe, VAT is set at the federal level, so the value defaults to the country (e.g., the UK). In India, GST is at a dual level, with value containing country and state data (e.g., IN-MH, IN-GJ). In the US, it's at state-city-county-district –additional lower levels (e.g., US-TX-HOUSTON-HARRIS...). This determinant is selected from the business transaction parties' master data and logistics (plant and warehouse). E.g., some jurisdictions in Europe may consider the bill from location as supplier's site, rather than ship from location (plant, warehouse) for service related transactions, in India it's the Ship from (rather than bill from, Seller reg. site) location type when it comes to supplier, in the US, it's Ship To location type (point of title ownership transfer) for buyer (rather than Bill To, Buyers reg. address). In short, the Places determinant provides country-, sub-authority-level-, and location-type-applicable data to the ERP tax computation process.

5.1.2.3 Products 'What': Product is the goods or service in scope, i.e., the nature of the transaction, for example, a laptop, a chemical agent, IT services, etc. Also, this determinant may contain one or more additional tax drivers, e.g., the intended usage of the product - resale, research, and manufacturing.

A tax regime, or a country's tax authority, has specific rates for products and services under its tax law and rules (product taxability).

5.1.2.4 Process: ERP processes and sub-processes, e.g., Sales process with sales order, approval/release of SO, delivery note creation, goods/service issue, sales invoice, with adjoined finance processes involving invoice postings and customer payment received as sub-processes. Similarly, we have a procurement process with purchase order, goods receipt, invoice verification, an adjoined finance process for invoice posting into accounting, and payment made to the vendor. There may be many additional processes and sub-processes requiring tax computation. In the ERP sales, procurement, and finance transactional business processes, there are unique technical processes in the ERP Tax structure, and it is often tagged internally with a unique alphanumeric code, e.g., AP – Payable, AR- Receivable, FI for Finance, SO as sales order etc. The process identifier triggers tax touch points for the ERP Tax determination program and workflow to work.

5.1.3 End-to-End ERP Tax Determination Workflow

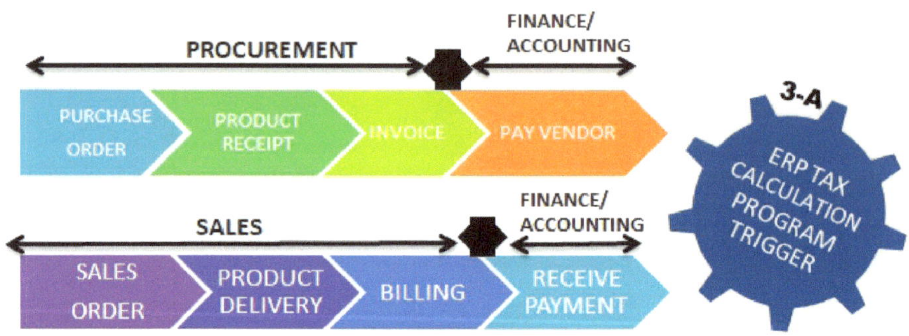

Figure 5.1.3

- **3-A: ERP Tax Determination Program Trigger**

As shown in Figure 5.1.3, the ERP Tax determination process is triggered by the creation of sales and purchase documents and their associated sub-processes.

How ERP Tax determination program is triggered: Once the sales or purchase procedure (process involving series of steps (conditions we call them in the ERP, they refer to specific criteria and values used to determine prices, discounts, freight, surcharges, and other business-transaction details), the process then stops at Tax condition type (tax determination step), and this step leads to the triggering of ERP Tax determination program, an application containing programming code leveraging tax drivers, tax data tables, custom rules sequencing.

Figure 5.1.4

- **3-B: Regime**

The program then picks up the tax regime (country) by fetching the data from parties involved in the business transaction -operating unit /buyer (purchase), seller /vendor (purchase). This data is available on the party's address master data (country). The program cross-checks the country code against the Tax regime module (5.1.1), and determine the tax jurisdiction (country). For example, a US-based firm 'ABC Inc.' is selling spices to a US-based customer 'XYZ', then the firm's master data has 'US' as the country code. The program cross-checks this country code 'US' in the regime module to derive the United States as the country, and tags the regime as the United States in the program.

- **3-C: Tax Type**

The program then retrieves the applicable tax type from the Tax Type module, as explained in section 5.1.1.2. For example, continuing with the US firm to a US customer sale, once the regime (United States) is determined; the program identifies and tags the tax type as Sales Tax (assuming the US firm ABC Inc. has nexus in the US customer 'XYZ' location).

- **3-D: Tax Zone**

In this stage, the program fetches additional address data elements (state, city, county, zip, and geo code) from the US Firm 'ABC Inc.', like state, city, county, zip, and geo code, and also from the customer 'XYZ' address parameters, and identifies the tax zone applicable. Since US follows Ship To location based taxability, considering the customer is based in the state of Texas, Houston city, Harris county (assuming with no further lower level tax jurisdictions), the Tax zone will be identified as Texas-Houston-Harris i.e. now there will be three tax levels for the tax type 'Sales tax' (State tax %, City tax %, Country tax %).

- **3-E: Tax Status**

In this step, the program will check the tax status or tax slabs in all applicable tax zones, as explained in section 5.1.1.4. In the US, there are no such tax slabs, so we will use the UK as an example, where we have three tax slabs – standard rate, reduced rate, and zero rate. In short, the tax zone determines the tax status (tax slabs), and if there are no tax slabs in a specific tax zone, then the program has null values for this parameter.

Figure 5.1.5

- **3-F: Tax rules-driven tax drivers tables**

Now the ERP Tax calculation program has all the tax drives captured and is ready to hit the tax rules-driven tax driver tables. These tables are empty containers where firm tax and Tax IT associates can enter data in accordance with the expected output. These containers (tables) are arranged in a sequential pattern, one after another, and the sequence order is defined by a set of rules (subprograms).

The main tax calculation program leverages these sequencing rules and scans the tables table by table to find the best-fit entry. These tables may have vivid format (no of columns) field containing tax drivers data, the program scans the tables and try figure out the right match containing combinations of tax drivers data, for example, a UK firm, which is selling ('O' as output for sales) hard drives (material having tax classification as '1' standard rate) and has tax status as 'standard' can be seen highlighted below will hit the first entry in this tax driver Table 3-F and will stop there, fetching U1 tax code.

Country	**Process**	**Tax Type**	**Tax classification**	**Valid from**	**Valid To**	**Tax code**
UK	O	VAT	1 (Std. rate)	1.1.2000	31.12.9999	U1
UK	O	VAT	2(Reduced rate)	1.1.2000	31.12.9999	U2
UK	O	VAT	0(Zero rate)	1.1.2000	31.12.9999	U3

Table 3-F (Tax driver table) (Illustrative)

In the above case, one may see the use of tax regime (UK taxing authority level, which is at federal level), tax type, and process and product details. It's important to note that different ERP's may have vivid name of the programs, rule, sequences and tables, field nomenclatures, however, the core fundamental functioning process is the same - extraction of tax drivers from sales, purchase process, referring them to core tax structure modules for regime, tax type, tax status, tax classification data generation, and later using these tax drivers and data to extract the tax code. Some ERPs may have an additional tax driver to fetch the tax code listed in the table.

- **3-G: Tax Code**

That's the core objective of the entire ERP Tax calculation program, i.e., fetching the tax code, since the tax code is the key for tax rate and tax GL determination. The whole exercise, involving 3A>B>C>D>E>F steps, is to determine the correct tax code for the business scenario. The program captures the tax code, in this example 'U1', from the tax driver table 3-F and starts fetching the tax code's properties from the tax code master data.

- **3-H: Tax Rate and Tax Amount**

A tax code contains a tax rate, e.g., 20% for the UK standard, and the program picks up the tax rate from the tax code properties and applies it to the new tax base value, generating the tax amount. The program captures such financial information (net tax base, currency, etc.) during the initial integration period and reserves it for later stages, like stage 3-H.

- **3-I: Tax GL posting**

Now that the tax rate and tax amount are computed, the program fetches the tax GL (general ledger) from the tax code based upon the tax type and posts the tax GL with this amount and rate. Once the Tax GL posting occurs, the document is created in the ERP system. The document posted will have a tax line item containing information about the tax GL, tax rate, tax amount and this completes the entire lifecycle of the ERP tax determination process.

5.2 TAX ENGINE

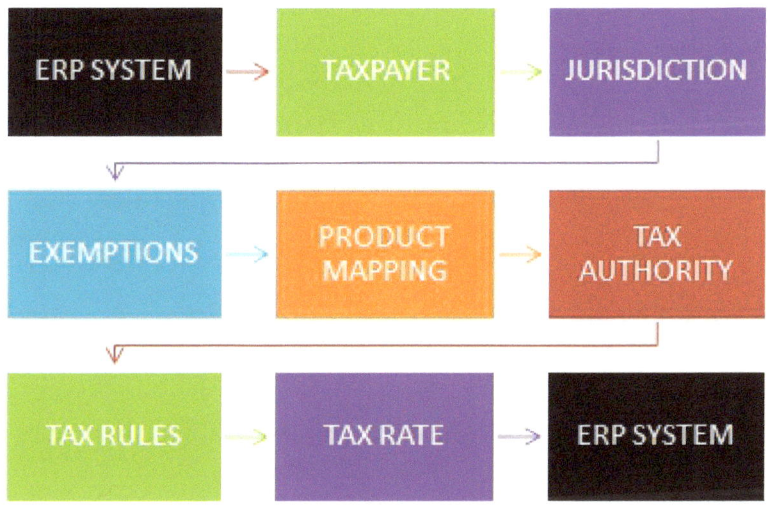

Figure 5.2

A tax engine is a software application that processes transaction data (business data) and computes tax rates and amounts using artificial intelligence. The Tax rate and tax amount are sent back to the ERP system, where they are published in the line item data for that specific transaction. The Tax engine has many modules (programs) built into the application through which transactional data flows and is assessed for tax. Thomson Reuters ONESOURCE, Vertex, Avalara, Taxware, and Sovos tax engines are mostly used in today's multinational firms for automating indirect tax computation at a global scale. There are additional tax software programs, but they may be limited to country-specific tax computation. In this section, we will discuss the operation of global tax engines that enable tax departments to automate tax computations for operations in the US, LATAM, EMEA, and APAC regions.

When the business or tax department integrates the tax engine with the ERP using a web service API, custom connectors, or standard connectors, the tax computation operation is updated.

Now, instead of ERP processing and computing tax, the tax engine processes the transaction data (Company code, posting/invoice/ document date, ship-to/bill-to/sold-to parties, material used, product code, invoice amount, and many additional fields). The ERP – tax engine API captures all such values and creates an XML structure.

The majority of Tax engines use XML structure for transmission. This XML has fields that are specific for integration, for example, in ERP; the company code field may be DCOCD, whereas in the tax engine, the same field may be called LINE.HEADER.COMPANYCODE. So data modeling would be like DCOCD<>LINE.HEADER.COMPANY CODE.. In the majority of cases, the XML has a schema that is near the Tax engine. The purpose of this XML transmission is to capture transaction data from the ERP, pass it to the tax engine, and return the transaction and tax data (tax amount, tax rate, tax jurisdiction) to the ERP, where it is absorbed at the line item level. Here, we will refer to the business and transaction data as 'XML data' for ease of technical and functional use.

Once the XML is inside the tax engine, it journeys through a sequential set of modules (programs) (Figure 5.2). The majority of tax engine architectures are similar because the process of computing tax on a business transaction is the same as done offline by a Tax professional.

5.2.1 Tax Engine Architecture & Workings

- **Taxpayer**

The taxpayer is the firm that records sales and purchase transactions, also called the entity or company code. The module contains the legal entity information – Name, Company code, Tax registration, etc. The first module is the Taxpayer. The incoming XML containing transactional data is routed to this module, and the legal entity is identified. Firm's tax/Tax IT needs to configure the legal entities master data in this module and their organizational and tax registration data.

- **Jurisdictions**

The module contains the legal entity's registration information for proper taxability, as well as the jurisdictional data (geographical IDs – Country, Province, County, City, District etc.) to identify the point of title transfer and the ship-to and ship-from locations, i.e., the financial supply chain's geographical footprints. The XML captures the location parameters through this module, which will help the tax engine's tax rules logic for accurate tax computation, after understanding the business scenario. This data is part of standard tax engine content, and Tax/Tax IT doesn't need to create this geographical data in the tax engine, they only need to tag the jurisdictions where the taxpayer is registered.

- **Exemptions**

This module of the tax engine contains exemptions, customers, vendors, and the exemption certificates issued by the tax authority. In case the customer or vendor has a tax exemption status, the XML customer/vendor field matches up with such records, and the corresponding tax treatment is applied (Taxable, partially taxable, zero-rated, etc.). An exemption is a tax certificate issued to a firm that is not liable to pay or collect tax for various reasons – for example, based on use (resale, scientific research) or material (medical supplies). When XML reaches this module, the tax engine program checks it to determine whether the transaction is exempt, partially exempt, reduced-rate, or zero-rated. The firm's Tax/Tax IT team needs to maintain the exemption and certificate data in the tax engine.

- **Product Mapping**

The product mapping module contains tax engine commodity code data, and here the ERP product and service codes are mapped to those codes. The XML contains the ERP product and service codes (Material No. and Material Group). Once mapped, the tax engine can identify the corresponding commodity, as the commodity plays a vital role in tax rate determination. Material type is a significant tax parameter in tax computation, e.g., air conditioning units in India are taxed at 18%, whereas food and beverages are taxed at 5%. The material is identified, and a corresponding tax engine commodity code is assigned; i.e., the commodity code field is populated in the XML. There are two options (1) Map the ERP Product/Service codes in the tax engine with tax engine commodity code, (2) The tax engine commodity code value can also be passed directly from the ERP, under this scenario, firms Tax/Tax IT team needs to map ERP products/services codes to the tax engine commodity codes in the ERP product/service master data and enable its passage during to the tax engine during the tax call.

- **Tax Authority**

The module contains the applicable global tax authority's data, based on the location parameters. The tax engine identifies the nexus (the relevant tax jurisdiction and authority), whose rules and rates will govern the tax treatment. For example, if it's a US transaction, the state, city, country, district, secondary district, etc.; if it's an EU transaction, the VAT authority; if it's an Indian transaction, the GST authority (CGST, SGST, and IGST). This tax authority level identification and its capture at the line-item data in the ERP enables tax managers to accurately file tax returns with the relevant authorities, as required by country tax laws. This data is part of standard content from the tax engine; in rare cases (e.g., when the tax vendor delays the tax engine content, but the tax authority is already active), one may create a custom tax authority as a workaround solution.

- **Tax Rules**

Every tax authority (tax administration) has tax laws, which contain comprehensive lists of tax rules. In the tax engine, the entire tax legislation is codified. A tax engine contains standard rules (as specified by the tax authority) and custom rules (written to accommodate specific company tax requirements). In this module, the corresponding tax rules are identified based on key tax driver data – Taxpayer, registrations, location data, commodity codes, exemptions, and value, etc. These tax rules are dynamic and are automatically updated (via tax legal content updates released by tax engine vendor) when there is a change in the tax legislation of any country. However, any custom rules in scope needs to be updated and maintained by firms Tax functions. Custom rules are created for cases where the standard functionality isn't able to support the desired tax treatments.

- **Tax Rate**

The final module is where the tax computation takes place; it's the tax rate module. In all the preceding modules, the tax engine reads the XML data and identifies the key tax values (Location, material, tax authority, date, etc.). Now, the tax engine has all the required elements, and the Tax rate module computes the tax rate based on tax rules (tax laws automated as a program). The applicable tax rate is determined, and the tax engine populates the corresponding tax amount. The tax rate and tax amount are passed on to the ERP system. This data is part of the standard tax engine content; however, firms Tax functions may create additional tax rates in exceptional cases, using tax drivers as conditions.

- **Tax Code**

Nowadays, Modern tax engines can also populate the ERP Tax code during the return tax call to the ERP. These tax engines have custom tables containing rows of key tax drivers like Input (Purchase)/Output (Sales), Goods/Service, Rate classifications (SR, ZR, EM etc.) and scenario indicators (Intra EU, Import, Export, Domestic) having unique ERP Tax code targets, and at the end of transaction tax cycle (inside the tax engine), the tax engine analyses above listed parameters and ERP Tax code is popped out from the tax engine, alongside tax rate, tax amount and recoverability data. This feature enables automatic detection and outward passage of ERP tax codes within the tax engine; i.e., custom tax code determination logic isn't required in the ERP, making tax determination and Tax GL postings super automated.

- **Recoverability**

The recoverability parameter is another output from the tax engine that helps the ERP identify recoverability: full recoverability (deductible), partial recoverability, and zero recoverability (nondeductible). The recoverability aspect can be standard and customized, too.

The tax rate, tax amount, for the applicable jurisdiction (tax levels) is populated in the XML tax fields, which are pushed into ERP, where ERP absorbs the values. The tax data is then populated in the business transaction, the transaction is posted, and a document number is generated. This entire cycle occurs in a few milliseconds. Please note that there may be additional tax modules in different tax software; however, the above six are core tax modules.

- **Tax Content Updates**

Tax software firms have teams of tax experts who monitor such changes globally. They send updates in the form of software files, which are automatically absorbed by the tax engine, and the tax rules are updated (in both cloud and on-premises deployments, if the automatic update checkbox is activated). This data comes from the tax vendor and is automatically or manually imported into the tax engine.

5.2.2 How to Maintain a Tax Engine

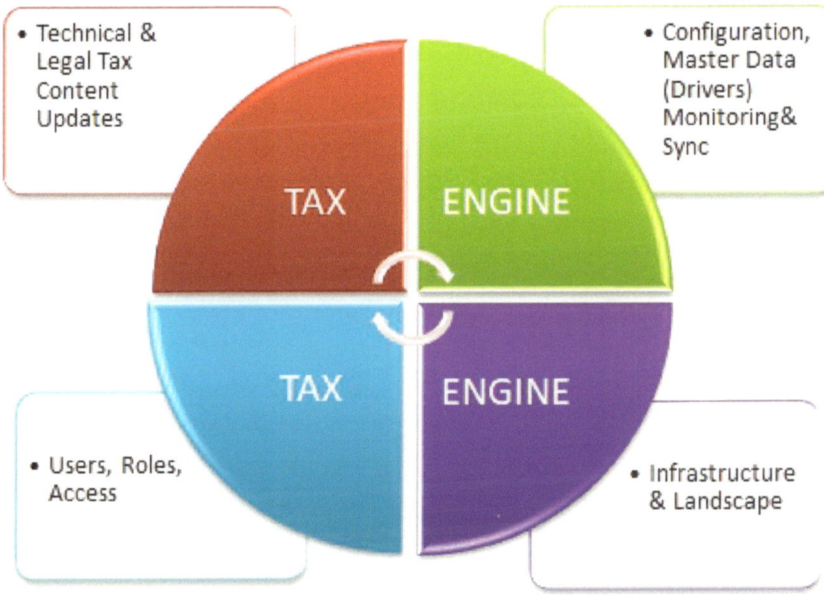

Figure 5.2.2

A Tax engine is an application that computes tax for a business transaction. It's a software product that has its own significance in a firm's tax function. Like an ERP application, it has many sub-modules, e.g., a tax API for handling incoming tax calls, hundreds of tax rules designed and built for worldwide tax authorities and tax rate combinations. These tax rules apply appropriate tax treatment based on key tax drivers (tax determinants).

A Tax Engine includes tables, large geographic databases, subprograms, and multiple tax tools that help Tax SMEs and tax technologists check expected tax output for any scenario. A Tax Engine also includes tax reporting and audit databases, where transaction and tax data are written at the line-item level. In short, a Tax Engine is a tax business application software and does need a structured maintenance standard operating procedure.

Here, we will assess key system maintenance points (non-functional)

5.2.2.1 Legal and Technical updates

Tax laws are dynamic; a case of Beer today in California may be subject to 12% Sales and use tax, but after a month, it may be 9% based on changes in state, county, city, and other tax authorities' tax laws. Similarly, a notebook in the UK (domestic) may be subject to 20% VAT today, but after a week, it may be subject to 23% VAT. The World has 15000+ tax authorities led tax treatment combinations (approx.14,000+ in the US alone and 1000+ in the rest of the world) and tax rates are constantly changing for products and services.

To ensure timely updates to your Tax engine regarding tax rates, tax rules, and tax jurisdictions, the Tax engine vendor releases monthly updates in a file containing all relevant tax data (tax rate changes) for products and services across all tax jurisdictions. The Tax Data update also has any new jurisdictions added (e.g., new city boundaries, new territories), new tax rules for specific tax authorities, tax law changes, etc. To ensure compliance, these tax data updates should be applied in tax engine development, testing and production systems.

Many clients enable automatic absorption of these updates for their cloud-based tax engine; In a manual scenario, the Tax engine administrator should import it on a timely basis and diligently, else, a firm risks incorrect tax set up in the Tax engine, and tax determination accuracy will be negatively impacted, which will lead to tax compliance issues –overcharging, undercharging tax, transaction tax errors leading to lots of workaround work, incorrect tax filling, etc.

Such tax content updates may be legal and technical in nature, Legal updates accommodate tax authority related notifications – tax rules, tax rates, tax jurisdictions, recoverability aspects, whereas technical updates are meant to support and sustain the tax software product technical health – database, tables, data modeling, programs.

Enabling it – The firm's tax function must develop a workflow using an existing incident resolution system or another software tool to ensure timely, sure-shot delivery on this subject, if it's a manual operation.

5.2.2.2 Post Tax Data Import Impact Assessment

As a precautionary step, the Tax function should pre-assess the impact of the tax content file after import. This is to ensure whether any custom configuration (tax rules, tax rates, etc.) got impacted, as it may be possible that now the standard update has covered up for the custom rule e.g., assume from April'2026 onwards intra GCC country transactions are zero-rated, however, Tax engine didn't release an update, to mitigate risk, firm created an XYZ123 rule with a specific rate.

However, in June'2026, the Tax engine standard content now has that rule. The custom rule is not desired, so now the XYZ123 rule can be deleted, as it will conflict with the Tax engine standard rule (custom rules or user-defined rules have more precedence than Tax engine standard rules, and they override their rule conditions and impact), which will lead to errors and tax compliance issues. Though it may sound undesirable, it often reveals a potential problem that could become a future blocker.

Enabling it – Once the tax department receives a communication from the tax administrator confirming that an import was successful, the tax functional associate may be assigned a ticket for this work and prepare a summary. This will significantly help end-dating (deleting) custom logic blocks that are no longer required.

5.2.2.3 Configurations & Master Data Monitoring

Firms have their own customization in Tax engines (Entities, Customers – Certificates, Taxability Mapping, Tax rules, etc.). If there is a project, enhancement or operations related requirement for change, the below process is recommended. There may be scenarios in which multiple teams are involved in tax work. In that scenario, what one team is doing is not known to another team. Unlike in an ERP system, where there is a single window of configurable objects, the tax engine has no such visibility (unless one runs a daily activity log). Also, in a tax engine, two or three associates can work on the same item, without each other's knowledge. This creates issues because the cross-team joint review is absent; for example, team A may be trying to add new entries to a specific table to enable tax logic, whereas team B may be end-dating entries in another table for some other reason. Often, tax engine changes in production are implemented without updating/informing cross-functional teams.

Enabling it – There should be a common communication platform, which tax engine associates can share the updates on the work they are doing. That way, there is no dark area and surprises when work is done in a mutually exclusive way.

5.2.2.4 Users & Access

A Tax engine requires proper controls regarding users and roles, and the access levels they are granted. Why? Because, unlike modern ERP's, where there is a highly structured chain of transport (Development>Testing>Production) to move configuration items to production, tax engines don't have such a mechanism, which Tax engine firms must develop and understand. In Tax engines, the configurations are first exported from Test/Quality systems. Standard Tax data export function (full or partial tax objects): a file is downloaded to the local computer and imported into the production system. By mistake, if any Tax engine associates exports and imports with an irrelevant object in production, it will disrupt production and severely impact production invoices (sales and purchases).

Also, as in ERP systems, where users can't make configuration changes in the production system, in a Tax engine, any user with functional access can make changes directly. An undesired change will disrupt the Tax engine, negatively impacting business tax continuity. Moreover, unlike in ERP, where object-specific revert can occur in the prod system, in a tax engine, one must perform a database restore to a prior version. In short, the engine is a very vulnerable system. While there is a provision to check who did what. However, there is no provision to stop an undesired and unauthorized change.

Enabling it – Tax engines are well-organized software, i.e., they have defined user roles. By user roles, we mean restricted access - e.g., View only access, administrator access, super user access, etc. Also, in tax engines, users' access can be limited to a few regions, entities, sub-modules (Admin, Entities, Tax Set-Up, Tester, Reporting, System, etc.), or restricted vertically and horizontally. The tax engine administrator needs to review each user, their role, and responsibility, and edit/assign only relevant access in the tax engines. They must do a cross-check of roles - responsibilities from a tax business point of view, and then see required software access (By Partition, By Sub Module, By Entity, and the access necessary -View, ability to edit, run reports, etc.).

This must be done diligently, and every user must be scrutinized, and their job role activities must accurately match with the access level, neither less nor more. Also, if access is provided, a basic peer review must be conducted to ensure the user has basic tax-engine experience, especially regarding dos and don'ts.

5.2.2.5 Infrastructure & Landscape

A Tax engine is an application, it has to deliver fast to ERP / Business application transaction calls, tax engine application should guarantee 24*7*365 availability, with significantly less maintenance. The load balancer should be able to flip tax engine instances based on transaction tax requests, ensuring an overall turnaround time of only a few milliseconds. If the tax engine is on-site, the databases should be configured to create a version copy every 15 days, up to a maximum of 1 month. Additionally, a few settings must be configured manually in the tax engine whenever a new partition or client is created. These are mostly IT infrastructure team works, which they also do for other business applications. Also, during downtime maintenance windows provided by the tax engine vendor, Tax IT needs to inform business, so that they are aware and any real time or background jobs impacted can be re-processed.

5.3 TAXONOMY

The Art of Mapping Products with Tax Engine Commodity Codes

Figure 5.3

In a landscape where a 3rd-party bolt-in tax engine is integrated with business ERP software, accurate product mapping becomes an essential activity. Product mapping is an art to map business products, which can be goods and services with appropriate tax engine commodity codes as defined by tax authorities. In Tax Technology, multiple tax drivers help the tax engine accurately identify the tax rate, tax amount, and tax jurisdiction. These are -

- Where are you selling to or buying from (Customer/Vendor location)
- What are you selling or buying (Product/Services)
- To whom are you selling to or buying from (Customer/Suppliers)
- How much are you selling or buying (Quantity)
- Where are you shipping from or getting shipped to (Plant/Warehouse)
- Additional tax drivers

5.3.1 ERP Goods & Service Material code

In this chapter, we will focus on 'what are you selling or buying' aspect. For example, a mining firm may have detonators, imaging systems, valves, and ammonium nitrate as physical goods, whereas in services, it may have rock blasting and exploration engineering services. Now, in the ERP, these products are named according to the company's custom nomenclature, and each client may have a different nomenclature for goods and services in their respective ERPs.

For example, firm ABCD GmbH in Germany may be using SAP, and in SAP, detonators are named as DETO777 (Material), etc. While a similar mining firm in Australia may be using Oracle ERP, detonators are named as TRIG98. In short, every firm has its own nomenclature policy for materials (goods and services). The question is how a tax engine will identify the type of product for tax computing. The tax engine is a black box - a tax program application which leverages artificial intelligence derived from tens of big, small programs which scan the incoming transaction data (Tax drivers) and tries to assess the applicable tax scenario - cross border or domestic, goods or service, tax type – Standard rate, reduce rate, exempt, zero rate etc., tax jurisdiction – where tax is to be reported and remitted.

When a client purchases (licenses) a tax engine from tax software vendors, the company has to do customizations in both ERP (Tax localization) and Tax Engine (client-specific master data, rules, etc.) to enable accurate tax computation for all applicable use cases, i.e., indirect tax scenarios for all global entities in the scope of the tax engine.

One such customization is product mapping, which is required in all tax engines. Here, the firm's tax function or the implementer identifies the appropriate tax engine commodity code for applicable company products. A firm may have thousands of products (Goods and services); however, it may have a few hundred or dozens of material groups, each grouping products (material or service) with similar attributes. Now, since the material& material group is also a part of transaction tax data that goes into the tax engine (from ERP during the tax call), firms can map the material or material group to the associated tax engine commodity codes in the tax engine.

Ideally, whenever a new material master is created, the relevant tax engine commodity code should be entered in the Material master field. In the ERP-Tax Engine integration mapping (Custom or standard), such a field must flow through. That way, less customization is required in the Tax Engine (mapping hundreds of material groups or thousands of products) with tax engine commodity codes. The tax engine must be customized at a minimum level.

5.3.2 Tax Engine Commodity Codes

Let's try to understand what a tax engine commodity code is. A commodity code in Tax Technology is the product tax code defined by the tax authority, enabling it to identify the goods or services involved in the transaction. Because, ultimately, it's the tax authority to which a firm files its tax returns,, and in a case where a tax authority gets interested in knowing material information about an invoice, having such tax commodity codes embedded in the tax line item data greatly helps in Tax audit defense preparedness and in many tax jurisdictions, this field is mandatory by tax law. While that may be one advantage with respect to tax audits, in a tax engine landscape, such mapping is required; otherwise, the tax engine will probably mark all products as fully taxable. It's important to note that each tax engine software has its own generic front-end product tax codes (visible to tax engine users), which are mapped in the background to product codes listed by tax authorities. That way, customers don't have to map each product to the custom codes for every nation; the tax engine handles that. In cases, where the firm has licensed the country tax content from the tax software vendor, the tax engine commodity code may also contain tax authority defined codes like NCM& NBS for Brazil, GST& SAC codes for India. In such cases, the tax functions can map ERP Product and service codes directly to the legal product service codes inside the tax engine.

5.3.3 ERP Product - Tax Engine Commodity Mapping

Not to get confused, a company's ERP has its own nomenclature of products (Material), a tax engine has its own nomenclature of products (tax engine commodity code). Each nation or group of nations (like the European Union) may have its own nomenclature of products (Customs Tariff codes). Here, in a tax engine landscape, the customer doesn't have to bother with Custom Tariff codes for each nation where it does business. The company has to map its ERP products (material) with the tax engine commodity codes only; the remaining piece of correlating commodity codes with country tax administration prescribed product codes works automatically by the tax engine in the background application program, which has tax logic, tax content, and artificial intelligence for every indirect tax authority supported by the tax engine.

There are four predominantly product-tax commodity groupings globally.

1. HARMONIZED
2. BRAZIL
3. INDIA
4. USA

The majority of VAT nations (EU, UK, Africa, LATAM, APAC, Canada, Middle East) follow harmonized commodity behavior, i.e., a specific product or service in these nations can be mapped to a particular commodity code in the tax engine. The Harmonized System is the most widely used trade classification system in the world. One hundred seventy-seven countries use it to classify over 5,000+ commodity groups. India, the USA, and Brazil have Independent product tax codes.

For Example, A software firm has Anti-Virus software nomenclature as VIRUSSOFT in its ERP material master and in the harmonized network the Anti-Virus software is addressed as 88764.5687 commodity code, that means for all entities, firm has in these nations, the mapping is to be done between VIRUSSOFT & 88764.5687 either in the ERP (entry in the Foreign Exchange Tab – Custom Tarrif field) or in Tax Engine (Product Mapping).

Now, whenever the tax engine receives this value, VIRUSSOFT, due to the mapping, it can identify it as 88764.5687, which, according to the tax authorities of harmonized nations, is Anti-Virus software. In Brazil, products are defined by NCM codes and services by NBS codes. In India, goods are determined by GST codes, whereas SAC codes identify services. In the US, though, there are no separate definitions for goods and services; they are called US commodity codes, and most Tax engines have a separate internal application partition for the US, as these tax engines evolved from the US.

This mapping exercise is part of every tax technology project, and accurate mapping helps the tax engine identify the product and its applicable tax type in that business jurisdiction (Standard rate, reduced rate, Zero rate, Exempt). If done unprofessionally, there can be thousands of invoices with incorrect tax treatment.

Along with systems mapping, a proper change management system using online web sheets placed at an accessible share point site with proper access, controls must be deployed for edits, updates for different regions tax rate, tax types, tax status of products, which eventually (post implementation) is managed by tax managers or tax SME's. This data file is also called Taxonomy file.

This Taxonomy file will serve as a single point of reference for Tax functions, supply and procurement teams whenever a new product is introduced, a legacy product is phased out, or when investigating a tax issue with IT. It's important to note that, though such mapping is ideally done by Tax SMEs, in Tax Technology Implementation, tax managers are often very busy with monthly and quarterly return reporting. Firms usually ask experienced tax technologists to do this. However, they may have mapped products with commodity codes precisely; without the tax manager's review and approval of the mapping, absorption (implementation) into the ERP or tax engine is not advisable, as this work affects tax legality. Tax SME's are the final and supreme guardians of tax authorities. Their involvement, review, and approval are required for tax compliance.

5.4 THE ERP – TAX ENGINE INTEGRATION

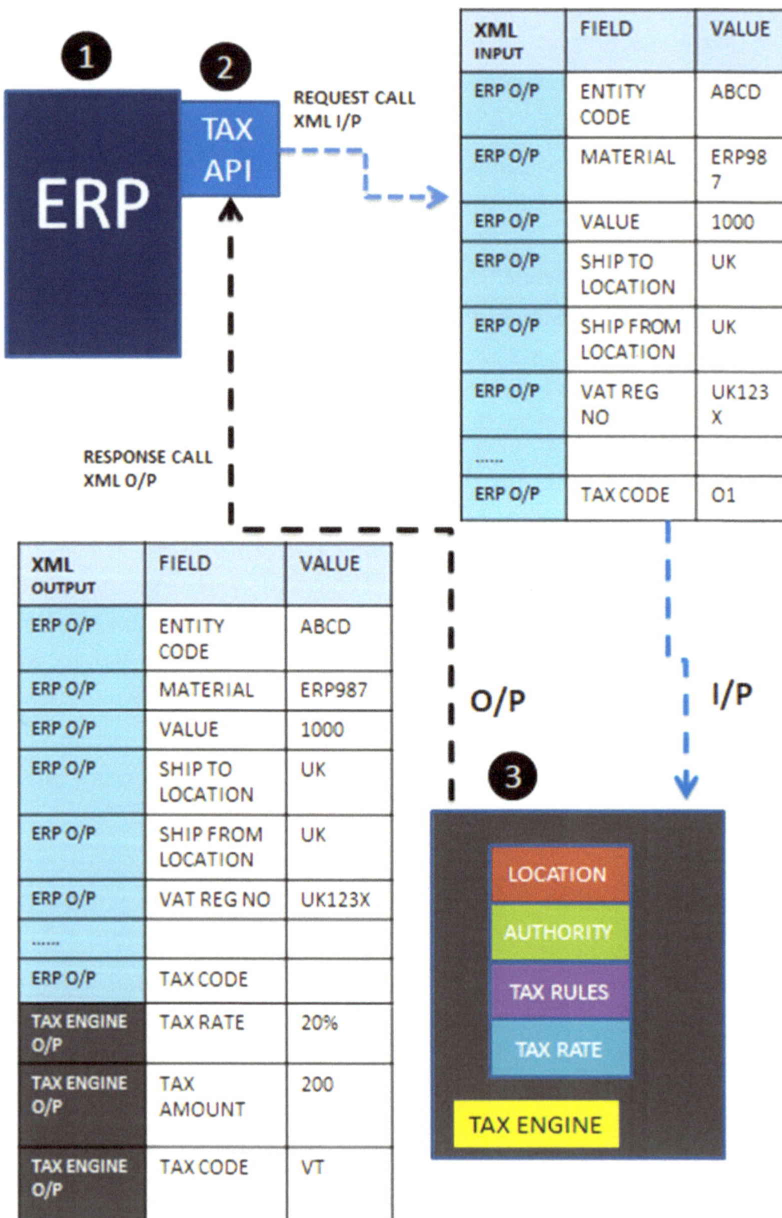

XML INPUT	FIELD	VALUE
ERP O/P	ENTITY CODE	ABCD
ERP O/P	MATERIAL	ERP987
ERP O/P	VALUE	1000
ERP O/P	SHIP TO LOCATION	UK
ERP O/P	SHIP FROM LOCATION	UK
ERP O/P	VAT REG NO	UK123X
......		
ERP O/P	TAX CODE	01

XML OUTPUT	FIELD	VALUE
ERP O/P	ENTITY CODE	ABCD
ERP O/P	MATERIAL	ERP987
ERP O/P	VALUE	1000
ERP O/P	SHIP TO LOCATION	UK
ERP O/P	SHIP FROM LOCATION	UK
ERP O/P	VAT REG NO	UK123X
......		
ERP O/P	TAX CODE	
TAX ENGINE O/P	TAX RATE	20%
TAX ENGINE O/P	TAX AMOUNT	200
TAX ENGINE O/P	TAX CODE	VT

Figure 5.4

Indirect tax technology is a specialized area that automates tax computation, compliance, and returns reporting. It involves a successful integration of ERP and Tax Engine. As part of this integration, it's understood that the ERP will provide all essential key tax drivers to the tax engine, and in return, the tax engine will populate accurate tax rates, tax amounts and send them back to the ERP. In Figure 5.4, for ease of understanding, the ERP O/P and Tax Engine O/P structures are shown with a few fields; in reality, they can range from 50+ to 100+ fields, depending on the worldwide scope of the firm's operations.

5.4.1 ERP

The first step in tax technology is tax computation; for that, a firm's ERP system/'s must have the correct tax drivers (tax determinants) maintained in the customer, vendor, GL, and material master data. This is an essential requirement, without which the entire tax automation machine will undoubtedly fail. Tax drivers are like essential 'Minerals & Vitamins' for the Tax engine software. Tax engine is not a standalone black box that can predict tax rates; it needs inputs from the ERP system to identify, analyze, and compute tax rates and tax amounts, and in some cases to determine the appropriate ERP tax codes. Once ERP master data is enriched with essential tax drivers (generally referred to as master data sanitization projects, in sync with tax transformation projects, these projects are managed by MDG (Master Data Governance) teams in large corporations) the ERP system is 'eligible' to integrate well with its counterpart - the tax software.

5.4.2 TAX Integration

Nowadays, ERP and Tax Engines integration can be real-time (synchronous tax calculation) or offline (asynchronous tax computation), depending on the business setup. Businesses that have custom tax set up in an ERP use a tax engine to validate ERP-computed tax rates in batch mode, whereas companies that have no custom tax set up in the ERP use real-time tax rate calculation. Ideally, the best practice is to use a tax engine for real-time tax computation. The integration is an API – Application programming interface (Tax API), where there is a mapping between ERP's Table -fields and Tax Engine's Table-Fields (data modeling/schema mapping). Alongside data mapping, it contains a program which drives the capture of ERP accounting and logistics data values during the transaction (sales/purchase), creates a structure (Figure 5.4, ERP Request call XML I/P) pushes it through the Tax API onto Tax engine. Post internal computation, the Tax Engine O/P structure (Figure 5.4, Tax Engine O/P Response call XML O/P) is pushed out of tax engine towards the ERP, the ERP system absorbs the tax rates, tax amounts and Tax code into the sales and purchase transactions line item data and the document is posted in the ERP. All of this happens in real time, within few mill seconds (i.e. when the front end user has created the purchase or sales transaction and hit's the save/simulate or park tab).

5.4.3 Tax Engine

The tax engine is like an artificial intelligence machine; it has tax rules, tax rates, tax logic, and company-specific business tax policy set up modules. The entire tax authority's tax legislation and tax laws are fully automated in the tax engine, which automatically keeps itself up to date with any changes to the tax laws. Many newcomers in the tax technology field view the tax engine as a mere tax table that returns the tax rate to the ERP; that's an incorrect assumption. A tax engine is like a 'Tax ERP'; it has many submodules tightly integrated, as per the tax authority's published tax determination workflow. The tax engine is a virtual tax manager (Tax supercomputer). It first identifies the transaction scenario – Origin, destination, goods or service, invoice amount, product or services, units, tax registrations of buyer or seller, Nexus, cross border or domestic etc. and tax amount is computed.

The ERP transaction data flows through a dozen or more submodules of the tax engine, and each submodule has a significant impact on the values that form the structure of the Tax engine transaction tax data (Transaction = ERP-generated accounting values, Tax = Tax engine-generated tax values, together it's called Transaction tax data in tax technology). As shown in Figure 5.4, the tax engine has completed the ERP O/P transaction with Tax Engine O/P Response call XML O/P.

Post this, the enhanced structure hits the ERP via. the tax API and the tax values are absorbed into the ERP's sales and purchase transactions, and the transactions are posted. These tax values are returned by the tax engine at the line-item level of the ERP transaction; i.e., even if there are hundreds of line items in an ERP sales or purchase transaction with different taxability, the tax engine will yield different rates and amounts for each line item. That's the beauty and power of the tax engine. New versions of tax software also generate tax codes, which help drive correct GL account entries (e.g., as seen in Figure 5.4, Tax engine O/P structure, Tax engine has generated a Tax code 'VT'. Here the default tax code sent by ERP is 'O1' (for sales transaction); however, the tax engine has populated 'VT' tax code, which is the true tax code representing the business scenario. Such tagging of transactions helps finance and tax teams of firms with accurate tax compliance and returns reporting to statutory bodies or tax authorities. Contemporary tax engines also include tax data warehouses, where all transactions are logged and stored, and reports can be generated in PDF, Excel, or Web forms for validations, reconciliations, and variance analysis. While for UK to UK, it may look like a simple tax determination, within such countries (limited tax rate brackets/slabs), multinational firms may have hundreds of vivid tax scenarios applicable, especially for countries like the United States, where there are multi-level tax jurisdictions, and thousands of tax rate scenarios, a tax engine is vital.

5.5 ERP SALES PROCESS- TAX ENGINE INTEGRATION SOLUTION ARCHITECTURE

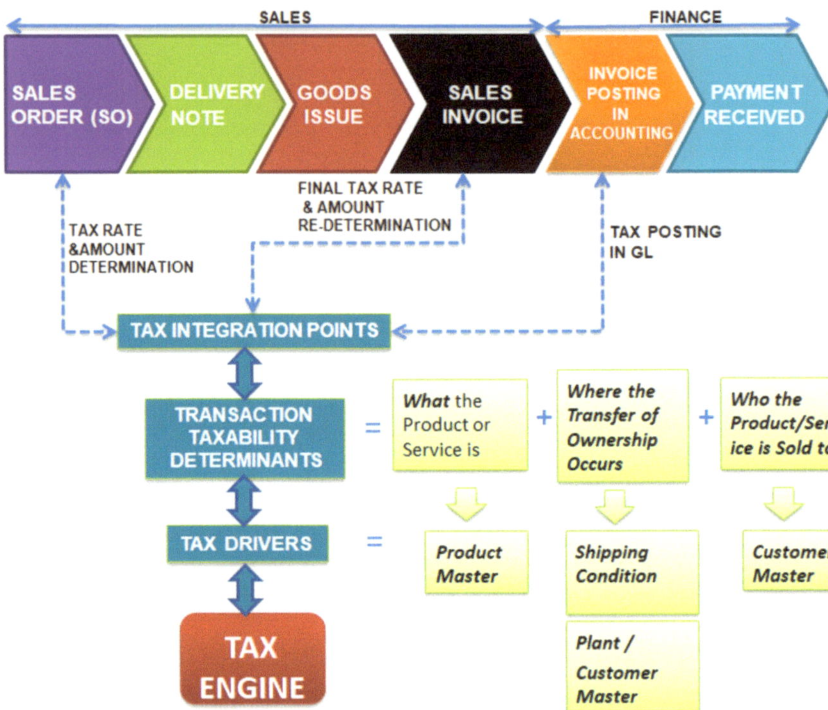

Figure 5.5

ERP's sales process incorporates all the steps associated with receiving and processing sales/revenue. We will try to understand sales process areas, sub-processes, tax integration points, transaction taxability factors, and detailed key tax drivers within the transactional taxability factors master data.

Figure 5.5.1

5.5.1 ERP Sales Process

As shown in Figure 5.5.1, a sales process comprises the following main process areas.

- Sales Order
- Delivery Note
- Goods Issue
- Sales Invoice
- Invoice Posting in Accounting
- Payment received

The Sales and Finance modules in ERP are where all the steps associated with a sale are recorded.

5.5.2 Tax Engine Integration Points

In this section, we will try to understand the sales sub-process that calls the tax engine, i.e., the Tax integration points.

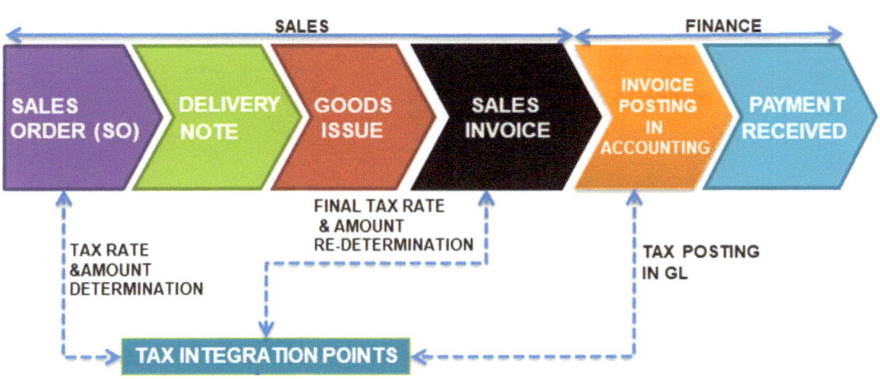

Figure 5.5.2

As shown in Fig 5.5.2, not all steps in the sales process require tax determination.

- **Sales Order:** A call is made to the tax engine for tax determination only. Tax Rate and amount are returned but not posted to the General Ledger.
- **Delivery Document:** No tax call, recalculation, or posting is made.
- **Goods Issue:** No tax call, recalculation, or posting is made
- **Sales Invoice:** Final call is made to the tax engine for tax recalculation and posting of the liability
- **Invoice Posting in Accounting:** Call is made to the tax engine to enable tax posting in the GL and creation of an accounting document in the ERP finance module for the sales invoice.
- **Payment received:** Once customer makes the payment for the invoice, the entry is updated in the ERP.

5.5.3 Transaction Taxability Determinants & Key Tax Drivers

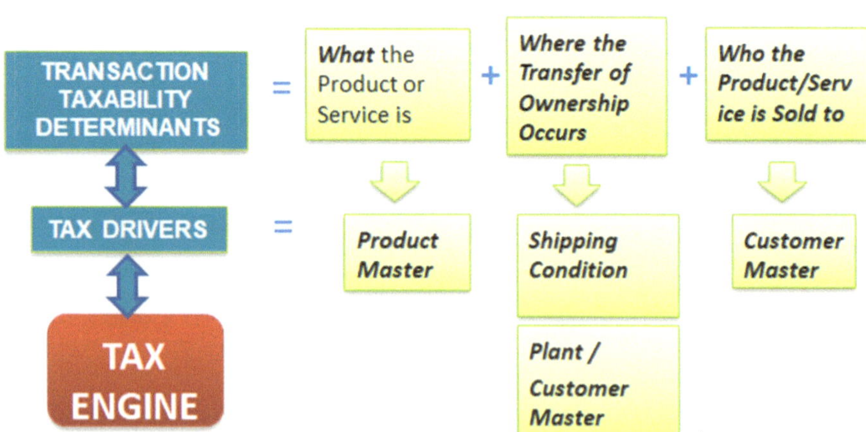

Figure 5.5.3

As shown in Fig. 5.5.3, we will examine the taxability factors that determine the tax engine's behavior.

- ***What*** the Product or Service is: The product (Goods/Service) master provides this information and is a key taxability factor in tax determination. E.g., Material No or material group mapped to the tax engine commodity codes. In some projects, the ERP product master also includes the tax-engine commodity code, directly generated by the ERP. This allows the tax engine to determine the type of product or service used in the transaction. In a tax authority regime, tax laws have specific tax rates for different products and services.

- ***Where*** the Transfer of Ownership Occurs: This is identified by Shipping Condition / Point of Title Transfer and by Plant and Customer master data. It's essential for a tax engine to know end-to-end business flow for tax scenario determination accurately and apply tax rates pertinent to applicable tax jurisdiction, e.g., Ship To, Bill To, Sold To, Ship From, Bill From, Order origin, and Order acceptance parameters.

- ***Who*** the Product/Service is Sold to: This tax determinant helps the tax engine determine the customer and whether any special tax treatment is required. The customer ID is determined from the customer master. For example, in the US, Canada, and certain EU countries, customers may have a tax-exemption certificate, a resale certificate, or another document that exempts them from tax or subjects them to special tax treatment. Also, the customer's tax registration status in the sales jurisdiction affects tax.

It's important to note that for a given project, there may be many additional tax drivers. The type and quantum of tax drivers leveraged for integration and implementation are directly dependent on the firm's unique business tax flows requirements and its solution design. Though a few tax drivers are mandatory, a few may be optional for some projects.

5.6 ERP PROCUREMENT - TAX ENGINE INTEGRATION SOLUTION ARCHITECTURE

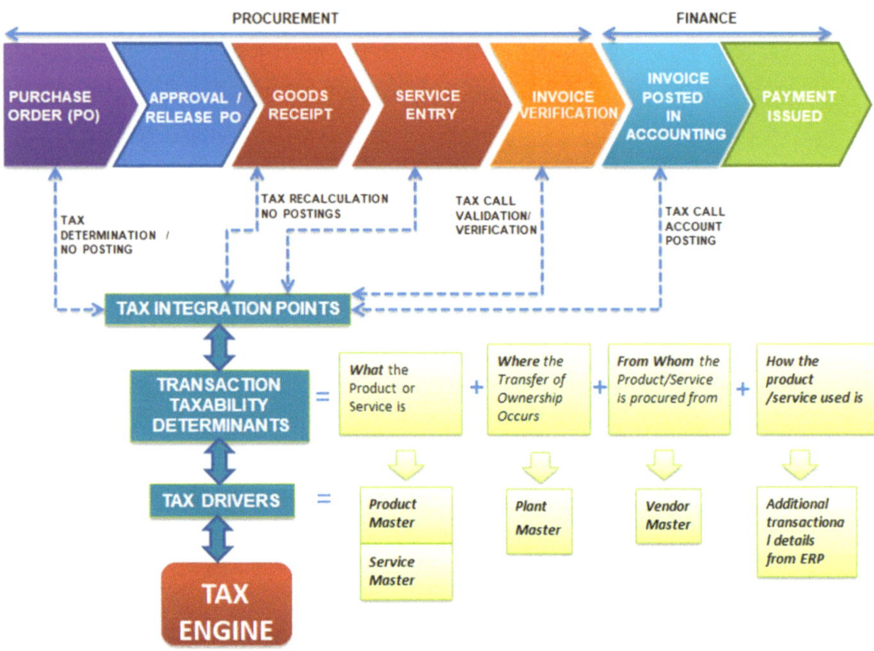

Figure 5.6

ERP's procurement process incorporates steps associated with requesting, receiving, and procuring goods and services required for an organization to operate. In this section, we will try to understand the procurement process, sub-processes, tax integration points, transaction taxability factors, and detailed key tax drivers.

5.5.4 ERP Procurement Process

Figure 5.6.1

A standard Procure-to-Pay process includes the following areas

- Purchase Order (PO) Creation
- Approval /Release PO
- Goods Receipt /Service Entry
- Invoice Verification
- Invoice Posted in Accounting
- Payment issued

The Procurement and Financials modules in ERP are where all the steps associated with a purchase are recorded.

5.6.2 Tax Integration Points

In this section, we will examine the procurement sub-process that calls the tax engine, i.e., the Tax integration points.

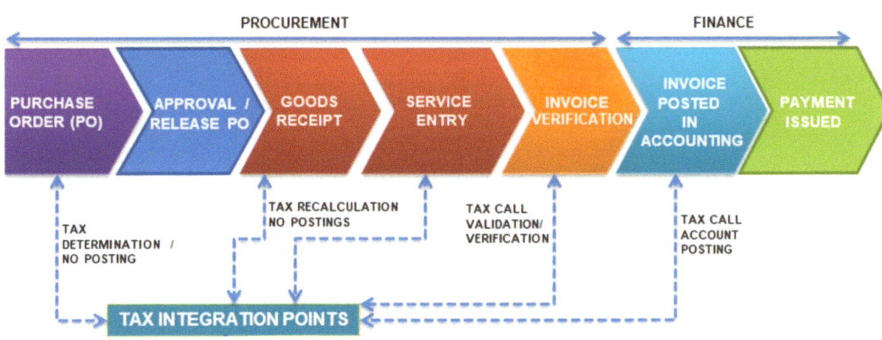

Figure 5.6.2

As shown in Fig. 5.6.2, not all procurement sub processes require tax determination.

- **Purchase Order (PO):** During PO creation, a call is made to the tax engine solely for tax determination. The tax engine returns the tax rate and tax amount for the PO amount; however, it's not posted to the accounting.

- **Approval /Release PO:** In this step, the procurement team analyses the PO and checks finance, material, quantity etc. parameters in reference to purchase requisition and approve/disapproves the PO. Once approved, its flows to the Goods receipt step. No call is made to the tax engine in this sub process.

- **Goods Receipt/Service Entry**: Depending on the system and the type of transaction, a call to the tax engine for recalculation can be made on the Goods Receipt, but no posting is created. Similarly, service PO's in ERP may generate a call to the tax engine for recalculation. In both scenarios, the tax rate and amount are returned but not posted to the accounting system.

- **Invoice Verification:** A final call is made to the tax engine to recalculate taxes and validate against the vendor invoice. Depending on the client's setup, the liability can be posted immediately, or the invoice can be parked for further review if the tax returned by the engine falls outside a certain tolerance.

- **Invoice Posted in Accounting:** Call is made to the tax engine to enable tax posting in the GL and creation of an accounting document in the ERP finance module for the purchase (vendors) invoice.

- **Payment issue:** Once payment is issued to the vendor for the vendor invoice, the entry is updated in the ERP. No tax call is made.

5.6.3 Transaction Taxability Determinants & Tax Drivers

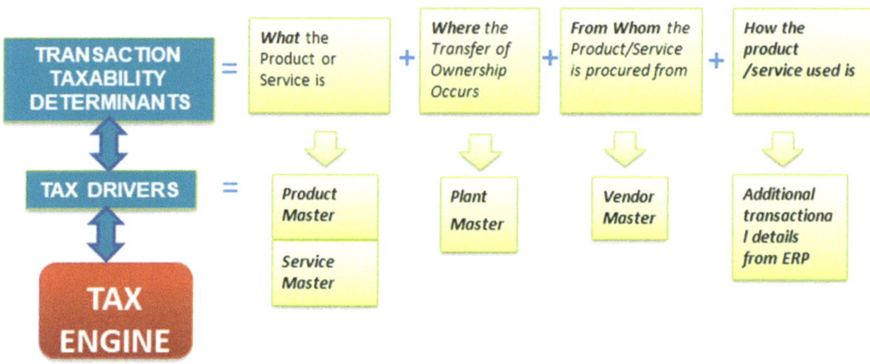

Figure 5.6.3

In this section (Figure 5.6.3), we will understand the taxability factors that determine a tax engine's behavior, as well as the key tax drivers in ERP that impact its tax determination functionality. It's important to note that, for a given project, not all tax drivers are required to be leveraged. The type and quantum of tax drivers leveraged for integration and implementation are directly dependent on the firm's unique business tax flows requirements and its solution design. Though a few tax drivers are mandatory, a few may be optional for some projects.

- **What the Product or Service is:** The product master (Material or material group) or commodity code generated from the ERP or within the Tax engine (via product mappings) is a key taxability factor for tax determination. In a tax authority regime, tax laws have specific tax rates for products and services.

Goods Product Master: From the goods material product master, the following four tax drivers can be leveraged.

- Material Tax Classification
- Commodity code

- Excise duty group
- Material Type

Service Product Master: If it's a service, the following two are applicable.

  - Material Group
  - Service Tax Classification

- **Where the Transfer of Ownership Occurs:** This is identified by the Plant master. For a tax engine, it's essential to know the applicable tax jurisdiction where the goods or services are supplied.

Plant Master: The plant is the location where goods are delivered. The following tax drivers are leveraged for the tax engine.

- Addresses
- Plant Code
- Plant Tax Classification

- **Who the Product/Service Procured is from:** To establish sellers jurisdiction, a tax engine properly requires the Vendor's address data, which is obtained from the Vendor Master.

Vendor/Customer (Buying entity) Master: The vendor master holds the keys to several key tax drivers, listed below.

- Address Information from relevant partner functions
- Corporate registrations, Tax registrations (e.g., VAT ID)

- **How the Product or Service Used is determined**: Either from the product master or from additional transactional details in the ERP. This assists the tax engine in identifying the usage of a product or service. For example, in many jurisdictions, goods or services procured for research, scientific, or academic purposes are exempt or zero-rated; if they are for resale, they may be subject to full tax.

- **Additional Transaction Detail from ERP:** In addition to the above-listed tax driver, the following tax drivers may also be leveraged in the tax engine tax determination process.
  - GL Account
  - Handling Type
  - Valuation Type
  - Item Category
  - Shipping Condition or Inco Term
  - Order type

5.7 ERP NATIVE TAX VS. TAX ENGINE VS. TAX ADD-ON (PLUG-IN'S)

As of now, there are three practical solutions available in the market for automating and digitalizing tax determination.

- ERP Native Tax
- 3rd-party Add-on /Plug-in tax software
- 3rd-party external tax engine

In this section, we will compare the use of ERP Native Tax, a 3rd-party tax engine, and 3rd-party add-on software's functionalities for the automation and digitalization of the indirect tax determination process. A firm may handle 100% of its indirect tax transactions with an external tax engine, or use a native ERP Tax solution alongside a 3rd-party tax engine. In the case of hybrid tax solutions deployment, especially with Native ERP Tax + Tax engine, it's generally observed that, for the US, Canada, and Puerto Rico jurisdictions, tax engine is used, as the US alone has 14,000+ tax jurisdictions (unique tax treatment combinations). It's practically not feasible to manage such a volume of rate changes, rule updates, and the deployment of hundreds of tax codes.

There are still cases where the native ERP Tax solution is used globally. And nowadays, we also see 3rd-party add-on tax software being deployed in firms' ERP tax landscapes to automate tax determination. In short, one may encounter any one of the three or a combination of tax determination software deployed in a firm, so don't be surprised. Let's see the functionalities offered by all three solution approaches and corresponding pros & cons.

5.7.1 ERP Native, Tax Engine, Tax Add-on System Architecture

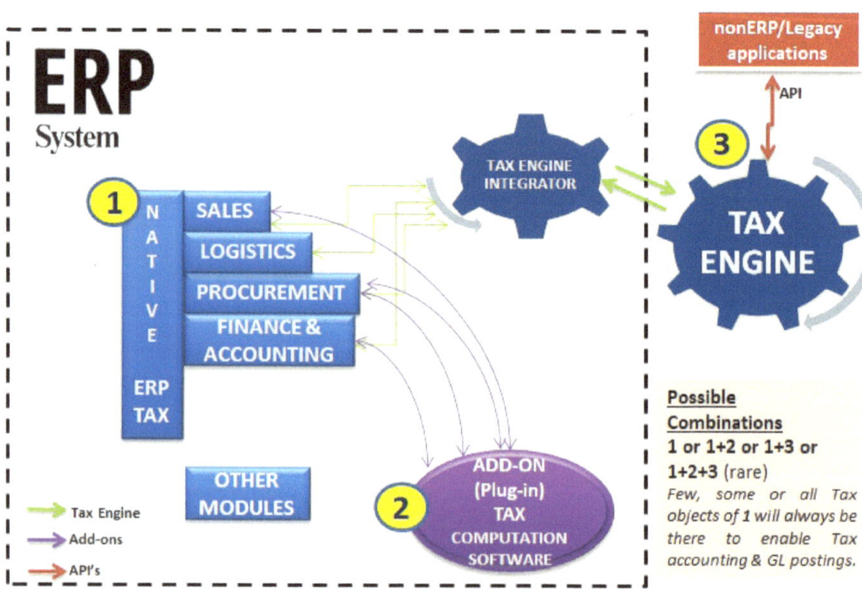

Figure 5.7.1

However, first, we will check out the Tax IT landscape for the three solutions involved to gain better insight, as shown in Fig. 5.7.1, we can see:

- **[1] ERP Native Tax functionality:** A native ERP Tax functionality, i.e., the solution is offered as part of the standard product (e.g., Finance, accounting, sales, and procurement modules), and no separate integration or license is required. For example, SAP Tax has Tax procedures, condition types/records, tax codes, etc., Oracle E-Business Tax has Regime, Tax jurisdiction, tax status, tax rate, etc. These native ERP tax solutions are pre-integrated with the sales, procurement, logistics, and financial accounting modules, and with a few company-specific configurations, tax determination is activated.

- **[2] Add-on (Plug-in) Solutions:** Such Tax determination solutions sits (are installed) within the ERP system as resident aliens, using predefined programs imported into the ERP system. These add-on solutions get integrated with the sales, purchasing, logistics, finance, and accounting processes of the ERP and support tax determination. There is no external interface (API) separating the ERP from these add-ons and tax-related parameter computation is performed internally within the ERP. These Add-ons create a functional, technical menu within the ERP for configuration and operation, allowing users to access them without navigating to or logging into an external application.

- **[3] External Tax Engine**, which is 3rd party tax software, requires integration with the ERP—standard or custom API. Also, nowadays, these 3rd party tax engines have developed standard products (e.g. Vertex Accelerator+, ONESOURCE Global Next) which integrate with the ERP application seamlessly and such set up can be imported into the ERP using standard way (e.g. Transports in SAP, Oracle configuration package import), these 3rd party tax engine integration package also creates a user and configuration menu within the ERP to enable set up, extract transactional tax logs and run reports. Thus, in cases involving 3rd-party tax engines, we may observe either standard integrations or direct API connections.

- **Hybrid Approach:** For example, in a case where a firm uses Oracle ERP for business and Coupa for procurement, we may observe that the standard integration product for third-party tax engines sits in Oracle for tax determination in sales and finance/accounting transactions. Coupa is directly calling the tax engine via an API for Purchase order /Vendor Invoicing tax determination; later in the ERP, the invoices arriving from Coupa are reposted and associated financial postings are again run through the tax engine's standard integration product. So within the tax engine landscape, one may observe one-on-one or hybrid integration strategy involving the integration type (API –standard, custom, hybrid integration) between ERP, non-ERPs, legacy ERPs, and the tax engine. However, the tax computing machine, i.e., the tax engine, remains the same across all such scenarios for the entire enterprise.

Now we will compare the three tax computation software on the four aspects below.

5.7.2 Automation of Legal & Technical Tax Content

Automation of Tax Rules driving Tax Rates (%), Tax Amount, Rate Classification of commodities & Tax determination accuracy. Tax rate rules, encompassing 14500+ tax jurisdictions globally (14,000+ in the US alone) for tens of commodities in a firm's business model, are dynamic. In short, there may be tens of tax authorities, hundreds of associated tax rules, and thousands of tax rates impacting a multi-national business. Moreover, these are dynamic and ever-changing.

- **Native ERP Tax**: ERP lacks automated tax set up that reads tax authority laws and legislative changes for commodities.

Tens of conditions in the table will require hundreds of Tax codes. Diligent fail-proof maintenance is impossible.

- **Tax add-ons/Plug-ins** have no tax content of their own; they're solutions that ease tax setup in ERP based on client business tax flow models. That is, the firm's business tax models are automated, and tax rates are established; such software doesn't codify the tax laws in its applications. It's all maintained on a case-by-case basis. If there is a rate change for a specific commodity in a particular jurisdiction, it's not automated. Either it needs to be done by the 3rd-party add-on/plug-in software firm or maintained by the tax department, with IT support.

- **External Tax engines** have a tax research team across the World. They ensure Tax software systems are up to date, i.e., changes in tax laws are absorbed digitally (monthly tax content update releases), leading to accurate tax determination, i.e., minimal or no revenue loss. Worldwide tax authorities and their tax laws are codified in the tax engine, making it an Artificial Intelligence tax solution encompassing countries; their tax authorities, corresponding tax laws, rules, and tax rates.

5.7.3 Automation of Business Tax Scenarios

Automation (configuration) of Transactional Tax business scenarios (Finance Tax supply chain), both as per Country tax administration laws and enterprise Tax Policy (Business Tax Flows). For example, in the EU, there are multiple tax scenarios: Intra-EU, Reverse Charge, Triangulation, TriTrade, and Import/Export Tax. This Tax treatment (Tax type) may be based on Buyer/Seller location, Tax registrations, Ship To/from, Invoice To/from, Plant location, etc., tens of scenarios may exist. To appropriately identify these scenarios, the taxing jurisdiction and ERP tax code (to book the transaction to the correct Tax Boxes of Tax return) are mission-critical, and a robust, agile, and dynamic tax setup is desired.

- **Native ERP Tax**: In the native ERP, one has to maintain a large dataset (tables containing record) and custom program configuration (e.g. Condition types, condition records, access sequences in SAP) involving Entity + Ship To/From + Invoice To/from +Goods /Service +Plant +VAT Registration and many other key tax driver combinations to navigate and capture the correct scenario. Later, defining and maintaining hundreds of Tax codes and dynamically updating them is a very arduous and error-prone task, leading to delayed solutioning, high IT costs, and compliance risks.

- **Tax Add on's /Plug In**'s: Add ons, i.e. solution built in the ERP, enhancing ERP tax application During the initial implementation (i.e. captured business tax flow), it may work fine based on UAT testing scope, however, that's not a reality in general, company business models and associated tax policy is dynamic and changes do happen in financial supply (mergers, acquisitions, new entities, spin off, new supply chain routes), for such cases Add-ons will fail as they have no artificial intelligence of their own to accommodate this change. Every time a new business tax model is introduced or an existing one is updated, a custom configuration is required that aligns with the ERP business development cycle.

- **External Tax engines**: A modern tax engine, using its calculation engine, tags the transactions with a unique 4-5 digit alphanumeric identifier containing transaction 'DNA' (scenario datasets), the latter at their interfaces or within the tax engine, the corresponding Tax code is populated (e.g., Tax code qualifiers concept in ONESOURCE Tax engine, Tax decision code in Vertex). Since tax engine applications have entire sets of worldwide tax laws codified, they can easily detect new business scenarios (subject to the passage of applicable tax drivers into the tax engine) and apply the necessary tax treatment. This is tax AI; it works like a virtual chartered tax accountant mindset.

5.7.4 Tax Tools for Tax / Tax IT associates

User-friendly tax area, rate look-up tools for the Tax functions /Business users/IT & enterprise wide Taxonomy document for sales procurements business.

Tax functions also needs insights into existing tax setups, the taxability of commodities, tax jurisdiction rates, Tax area ID (Zone), and retrospective and future tax rates to answer business queries pertinent to sales and purchase processes. Otherwise, one has to browse each tax authority portal, a highly time-consuming, painful process. Also, in cases of doubt, a tool that allows a specific-scenario unit test to be run to identify the tax treatment is highly desirable; otherwise, in many instances, tax departments have to consult a third-party tax advisor, which costs money.

- **Native ERP Tax**: There is no such functionality in native ERP.

- **Tax Add-ons/**Plug-Ins: There is no such functionality in Add-ons. They have no tax content of their own, which represents the global tax authorities' tax laws and legislation automation.

- **External Tax engines**: Provide user-friendly tools to look up specific tax rates for a selected jurisdiction and a commodity on a past, current, or future date. Tools to identify applicable tax jurisdictions and sub-levels (e.g., State-City-County-District –sub levels in the US), and determine the tax laws and rules (Sections, clauses, and descriptions in English). Moreover, internal unit testing can be performed without running a transaction in the ERP. Taxonomy file maintenance is also feasible to maintain by leveraging taxability matrix from such tax engines.

5.7.5 Development and Maintenance (AMS) Aspects

AMS, Maintenance, Enhancements, New Requirements, Miscellaneous change /service requests. Tax is dynamic, with new requirements, enhancements, and ongoing AMS activity that often require swift action to prevent business interruption.

- **Native ERP Tax**: Any change to ERP requires standard Quality Assurance (QA), Change Management (CM), and Release Management (RM) processes. Also, new requirements and enhancements are not as easy to build and deploy as rigorous testing and approvals, and utmost caution is required to avoid cross-functional impact and operational disruption to the production system. Work also involves business, functional, and technical associates.

Reversing a bad move to production in the ERP system takes time, and such faults often trigger senior management escalations and inquiries.

- **Tax Add-ons/Plug-Ins**: Same Quality Assurance (QA), Change Management (CM), and Release Management (RM) process applies, as the solution is an Add-on's which sits within the ERP and follows ERP process; any change in the ERP requires a more process-led workflow, increased admin work, regression cycles, cross-functional team impact, etc.

- **External Tax engines**: Enabling a change in the Tax engine is much swifter, and there are lower IT costs involved. Change can be made fast, aligned with demanding tax IT requirements. Though it also follows the standard SDLC process, since much of the tax-related configuration and rules/rates are maintained in the tax engine, there is minimal dependency on the ERP. After UAT testing/approval, moving the built from test system to production system of tax engine landscape is very swift and since fix is done inside the tax engine, in case of move to production failure, the built fix can be deactivated (end dated) at the click of the mouse.

There are many other comparative analysis parameters applicable. Parameters like license and implementation costs, single- or multi-instance, landscape containing ERP, feasibility of non-ERP, e-commerce, web portals integration, and suitability based on the geographic scale of operations, resource expertise requirements, practical tax control framework, compliance and reporting, e-Invoicing, etc. requirements.

5.8 GREENFIELD ERP TAX TRANSFORMATION FOR EU

The chapter delves into a specific viewpoint on the European ERP Tax transformation scenario, under a Greenfield project approach (start from scratch), comparing the adoption of native ERP tax functionality, a tax engine, and tax add-ons. European transactional tax computation process is complex, involving many models – Triangulation, Plant's abroad, cross-border exports and imports, Intercommunity supply of goods & services, and domestic reverse charge. The chapter will help readers better understand European tax technology expectations and walk them through adopting the right technological solutions for their business model and tax footprint.

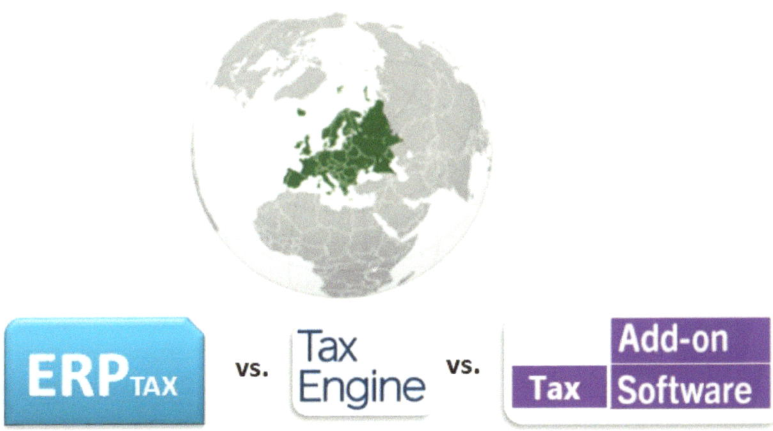

Figure 5.8

- **Reasoning**

In EU jurisdictions, ERP Tax transformation generally involves Tax automation, Tax transformation, and Digitalization of Tax Compliance Reporting. Tax transformation involves two areas: (a) Tax determination and (b) Tax Compliance & Reporting. While accurate tax determination for business transactions (Tax Rate, Tax Amount, Tax jurisdiction, and Tax Code determination (GL postings) is vital, Tax compliance & reporting, the downstream process involves tax logistics and financial data review, validation, checks, and VAT return preparation submissions to tax authorities. However, as there is the saying 'Garbage in Garbage Out', if the Tax determination is not accurate, there will undoubtedly be issues in Tax Compliance & reporting, leading to incorrect VAT submissions, other statutory and supplementary filings like Intrastat and EC sales list, and additional country-specific submissions. In short, the final objective of the entire tax transformation exercise is the submission of accurate, traceable, and auditable legal and statutory returns.

EU Tax regimes have more classification of enterprise tax flow tax treatments. For example, Intra-EU, EU/Domestic Reverse Charge, Triangulation, Tri-Trade, Import/Export VAT, VAT recoverability parameters. If one adds up Input/Output and rate classifications (Standard rate (ST), Zero Rate (ZR), Exempt (EM) Reduce Rate 1. Reduce Rate 2, Reduce Rate 3, Out of scope (OS) etc.) of commodities, hundreds of scenarios may exist, and moreover, each scenario may be unique. That transactional line item tax value needs to be posted in a specific tax Box in the Tax authority return. To facilitate this, the ERP system needs a tax code that defines a specific transactional business scenario, enables posting, and is finally mapped to the tax box in the tax return. Also, accurate VAT determination, alongside the transactional flow to the relevant Tax code GL, is vital for Tax compliance and reporting.

- **Approach:** For ERP involving Tax transformation programs, a good approach is to do reverse engineering of the solution, starting from VAT returns and e-invoicing requirements and identifying the key tax drivers, tax codes, transactional tax, finance, and logistics data required for VAT reports. VAT returns and e-Invoicing requirements should define the ERP - Tax engine / Native / Add-on solution architect, not the other way around. A superior accuracy in tax determination will support VAT compliance, returns, and e-invoicing.

- **Recommendation:** For tax computation accuracy, if the organization size is medium to large, i.e., has a presence in over 20+ EU nations, with global presence, multiple VAT registrations, and a 50+ product service portfolio, and a complex supply chain spanning outside the EU region, then installing an external tax engine is highly recommended.

External Tax engines are conceptualized, designed, and built to automate the Tax determination process, just as ERP systems automate corporate business flows.

However, if the organization has a presence limited to the EU, with few cross-border business flows, a small product/service portfolio, an add-on tax software can serve the purpose, enabling tax financial supply chain rules and associated rates to be automated and maintained.

A native ERP-led Tax determination solution is recommended only when an entity has a minimal business flows and limited jurisdictional presence, a few product portfolios, an overall unique taxability scenario of fewer than hundreds, and VAT filing requirements in few jurisdictions. Native ERP systems may not contain sufficient logic to support and automate tax determination for businesses with complex VAT flows. This exposes a company to tax compliance risks.

5.9 SUMMARY

In this chapter, you've learned about the various methodologies adopted for tax determination – Native ERP Tax, Tax Engine, Tax Add-ons (Plug-Ins). The chapter covered the functional architecture, modules, and processes involved in these tax determination tools. Just as an ERP is the core of business process automation, a Tax determination is the core of tax work, as documents are posted in the ERP only after tax is calculated. Readers also received an overview of the taxonomy, a practice adopted by firms to manage the taxability of products and services for business users. You've learned about the integration between the ERP and the Tax engine, with deep insights into the sales and procurement lifecycle, tax determinants (tax drives) and sub processes tax footprints. A detailed comparative analysis of ERP v/s Tax Engine v/s Add-on's will support you in developing a solution consultant mindset in projects. In the next chapter, we'll travel downstream and dive into Indirect tax compliance and reporting.

CHAPTER 6

TAX COMPLIANCE & REPORTING SOLUTIONS

This chapter introduces readers to the operation, implementation, and overall workflow of modern tax compliance and reporting solutions, supported by both native ERP systems and 3rd-party tax solutions. It's an interesting area of tax functions, as they have been working in this area throughout their professional journey. Readers will learn how tax technology software works for compliance, internal audit, and tax return preparation and submission. Tax compliance, audit, and preparation lead to submissions of tax data to statutory and legal authorities, and that's the final objective of the entire tax work. Readers will understand the functional architecture of modern tax technology software, which will greatly support their work in designing, building, testing, and deploying such solutions, or in supporting, reviewing, and assessing work done by third-party software integrators (SIs). As said earlier, tax software firms brands, product names, modules, and parameters may differ; however, the internal solution architect – the application program workflow remains the same, because the requirements is defined by the tax authority.

6.1 GLOBAL INDIRECT TAX COMPLIANCE

A country's tax administration legislates a set of laws regarding the imposition of indirect taxes on business transactions, involving the collection, filing, and remittance of taxes to the Government. The tax compliance process consists of complying with the applicable tax laws, collecting and paying the correct taxes, filing tax returns, and paying due taxes to the tax authority within the stipulated time period. Alongside the above aspects, the tax compliance process involves monitoring tax laws and assessing the impact of rule and regulatory changes on its business model. Establish, evaluate, and improve pan-organizational tax practice to follow the tax compliance procedure, i.e., adhering to the tax rules regarding business sales, procurement, and financial supply chain transaction taxability, and regular internal audits and documenting, storing, and archiving of business transactions.

Tax compliance is a legal necessity; non-compliance can lead to tax audits and inquiries, and, if discrepancies, inconsistencies, or fraudulent activities are observed, fines, penalties, and jail terms can result, hurt the company's reputation, disrupt business operations, and impede business growth and expansion.

Tax compliance is regulated by the country's tax authority, established by the government; e.g., the UAE has the FTA, India has the GST Council, the US has the IRS, the UK has HMRC, and the Netherlands has the Belastingdienst. These tax authorities collect all tax types, including Direct and Indirect.

Global indirect tax compliance involves adhering to the tax regulations prescribed by multiple countries tax administrations. Since each tax administration has its own tax law and corresponding rules, ensuring tax compliance becomes complex. With frequent regulatory shifts across countries due to economic changes, ensuring compliance and managing tax obligations in a multi-country tax jurisdiction becomes tougher.

Native ERP systems are not capable of managing multi-country tax compliance and reporting requirements because they are designed to automate enterprise business processes, not tax processes. With the upcoming global e-Invoicing mandates, which will eventually lead to near real time or real-time reporting, firms relying on native ERPs will be forced to comply. As a result, in this modern era, various tools have emerged; professional tax compliance reporting software has been born to support the complex, multi-country, multi–jurisdictional, tax compliance, and multi-report-type reporting requirements of organizations. These AI-driven software solutions are revolutionizing tax compliance and reporting by enhancing automation, accuracy, and efficiency.

Vertex, Avalara, Thomson Reuters, Sovos, SAP DRC, Big 4, and other tax technology firms also have their own product range, and nowadays there are tens of vendors and suppliers in the market offering tax compliance and reporting software. However, no matter what the brand is, the product name, or the internal components or function names are, the core fundamental workflow remains the same. Just like we see many diesel cars –Tesla, Toyota, Mahindra, Suzuki, BMW – the brand, outer design color, engine shape may differ, but the core, i.e., the functioning of the diesel engine through a four-stroke cycle: intake, compression, power, and exhaust is common in all. Tax compliance and reporting software core functional architecture is also generic.

Examples of indirect tax reporting include periodic VAT, GST, and sales and use tax filings. Standard Audit File for Tax in Europe (SAF-T), EC Sales. A country may have one or more tax filing requirements;

e.g., Spanish tax authorities require submission of VAT reports, EC Sales, Intrastat, Form 347, and Form SII, each with its own unique format, field data parameters, and submission frequency.

Indirect tax submissions may be legal and statutory. In Austria, legal and statutory reports include the Annual VAT return (U1), the Advance VAT return (U30), EC sales, CBSS, and Intrastat. Ireland has supplementary VAT in addition to VAT report, EC Sales, Intrastat, and Ireland Return Trading Details. Thailand has a text file for PP30, PP 36 VAT Return, VAT Return –Extended, South Korea has VAT return, AP VAT Ledger, AR VAT ledger, Non-Deductible Input VAT declaration, General taxpayer VAT declaration, Italy has LIPE, EC Sales, SDI, etc.

6.2 TAX COMPLIANCE & REPORTING REQUIREMENTS

Compliance &reporting requirements processes	Supported by Tax Compliance Reporting Software	Supported by ERP	Can be managed in-house by tax functions offline or some tools
Tax determination on sales, purchase, finance transactions	No	Yes	No
Extraction of Finance, Logistics, Tax from the ERP for reporting	Yes Automated	N/A	Yes (Manual)
Internal Audit: Checking the data for any anomalies, it's root cause analysis (RCA) and executing corrective	Yes	No	Yes (Labor intensive, error prone)

and preventive measures (CAPA)			
Monitoring of tax laws and assesses the impact on its business model due to changes in rules and regulation	Yes	No	Yes (Labor intensive)
Assess, establish and improve pan organizational practice to follow standard tax compliance procedure	Yes	No	No
Preparation, review, filing of tax returns in the format prescribed by the tax authority	Yes	No	Yes
Submission of supporting transactional tax data to the tax authority in a prescribed format	Yes	No	No
Payment of taxes to the government tax authority within the stipulated time period	Yes	Yes (Payable process)	Yes
Finance& tax document data storage and archiving for per the mandated specification by tax authority	Yes	No	No

Table 6.2

As shown in Table 6.2 above, the major tax compliance and reporting requirements are listed. Moreover, these tasks are organized in a table that shows whether these requirements can be managed within the ERP, in tax compliance reporting software, or offline by tax functions. It's important to note that the table symbolizes the technological aspects of process automation. The tax function is involved in every step of the tax determination, compliance, and reporting journey, whether as a user, guide, facilitator, executor or approver. The objective of Table 6.2 is to identify the tax processes that modern tax compliance software can automate, streamline, and digitize. With the evolution of AI and technological advancements, there may be many additional processes modern tax compliance reporting software can accommodate; its solution consulting teams can provide further insights. Always a point to remember – tax and technology are both dynamic.

6.3 TAX COMPLIANCE AND REPORTING SOFTWARE'S ARCHITECTURE

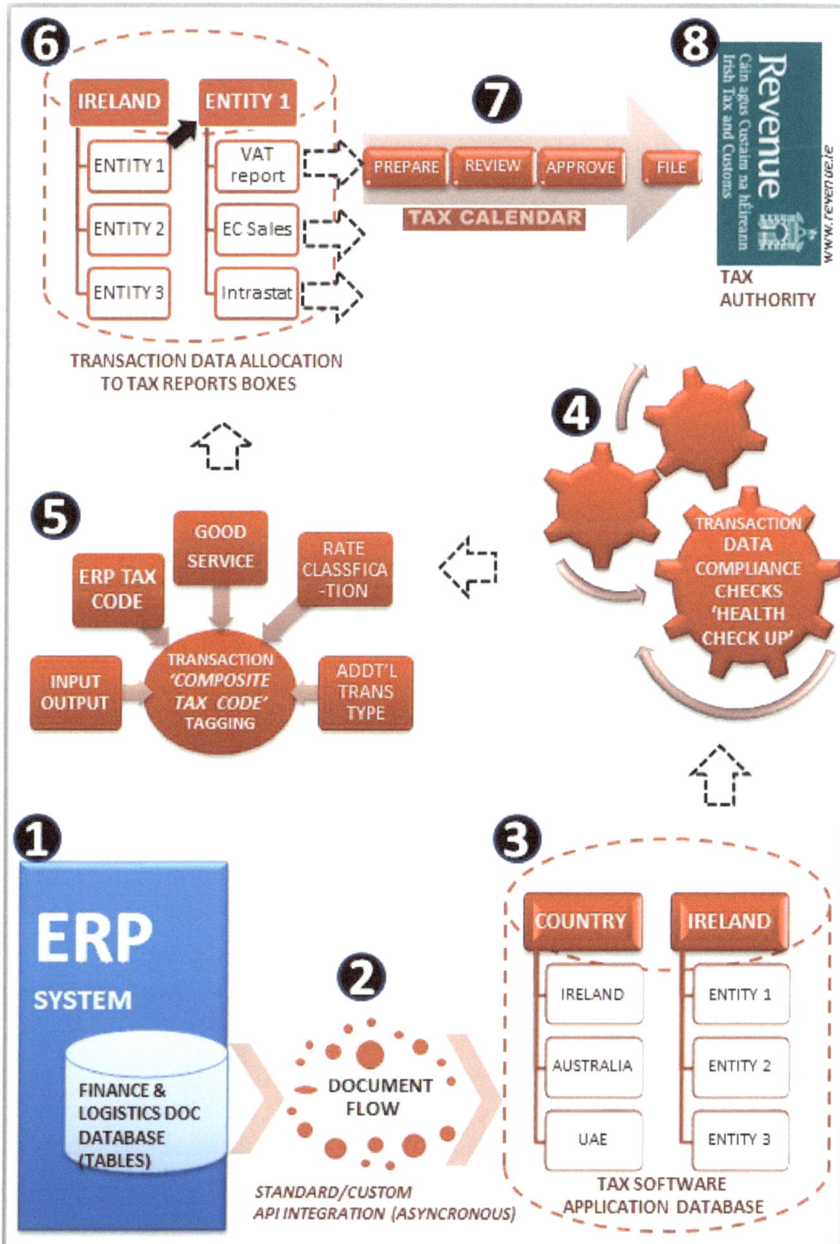

Figure 6.3

Now that we know the requirements, let's see how modern tax compliance and reporting software is developed. As can be seen in Figure 6.3, we can see the entire tax compliance process, with eight workflow components, and their functionalities.

6.4 TAX COMPLIANCE -REPORTING SOFTWARE'S WORKINGS

6.4.1 Workflow Step 1: ERP Transactional Data Generation

Figure 6.4.1

In the first step, the sales, purchase, and finance transactions are executed in the ERP system, the tax rate, amount, and tax GL are determined, and the document is posted. Now, it's important to note that tax returns require data that has legal significance, i.e., the documents on which the tax is actually collected or paid (not in theory but in record). Such documents are also called legal documents, such as sales and purchase invoices and financial accounting documents. Documents such as sales–purchase orders, quotations, and delivery docs are not legal documents for tax compliance and reporting, though they may contain tax data; tax is not realized in practice unless the sales or purchase invoice is posted into accounting and payment is made or received.

6.4.2 Workflow Step 2: Export-Import of Transactional Data

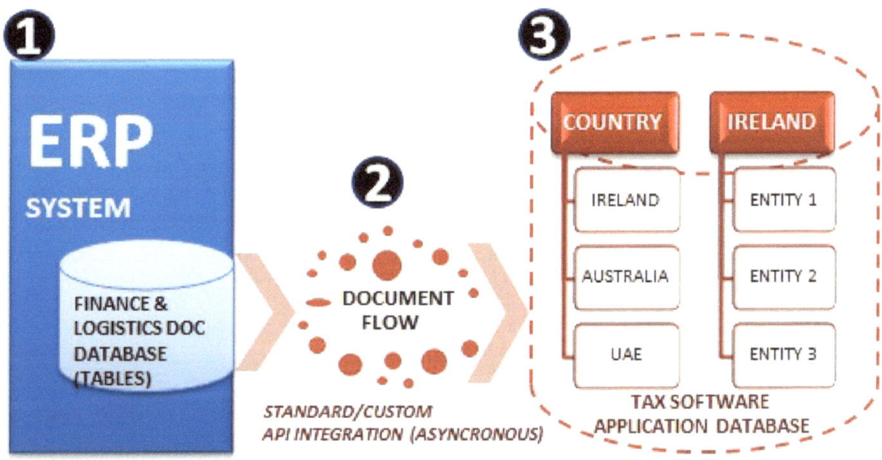

Figure 6.4.2

In this step, the tax compliance and reporting software extracts legal document data from specific ERP database tables. There may be one or more tables subject to the export-import process. Moreover, modern compliance reporting software also extracts logistics data, alongside financial data for corresponding documents for robust compliance checks (Workflow process 4-to be explained later), and additional tables may get involved in the extraction mechanism. The extraction is performed using data mapping (schema mapping), where the source table fields in the ERP system are mapped to the target table fields in the compliance software. At regular intervals, the API (Application programming interface) program runs automatically, extracts data from the ERP system, and stores it in the tax compliance reporting database for further processing.

The quantum of data mapping determined by the scope of multi-county tax reporting requirements, which a firm has operations and is generally designed by reverse engineering the country-Tax reports-Tax boxes level requirements and identifying the data type requirements for individual country tax reports boxes, leading to a data modeling blueprint. Country, entity code (company code), document type, sales/purchase indicator, and tax code may serve as high-level filters for the data extraction process.

This process occurs in the back end and is not visible at the front end. Though technical associates can showcase the data mapping model configuration, which is generally in XML format and the program can be in JAVA, Python, or other ERP-specific code. During the implementation, data integration experts from the vendor team work on this integration aspect alongside the tax functions for their cognizance and validation.

Tax compliance and reporting software firms have dedicated tax advisors, tax law experts at regional and country levels, namely tax research teams, who keeps a track on every tax report type, it's boxes and data requirements published by country tax administrations, later they pass on this information to their product development team (consisting of business analysts and developers), who configure solutions for such requirements and this built is then transmitted to the firms tax software through periodic technical updates, and this is how tax compliance and reporting software's are kept up-to dated automatically e.g. new tax reports, additional tax boxes, structure and format changes etc.

The data is extracted via standard or custom API's (application programming interface) in asynchronous mode (i.e., once the document is posted in the ERP and is captured in the ERP database (audited), at a regular interval, the API extracts the data from the ERP and imports it into the Tax compliance and reporting database. This export-import process can also be synchronous (real-time) for some specific tax authority report types, where the tax authority mandates the submission of invoices and billing documents in real time. As of today, tax return filing is not real-time; with the advent of e-Invoicing models that involve tax authority interfaces, real-time tax reporting will occur globally within the next five to ten years.

6.4.3 Workflow Step 3: Imported Transactional Data Database

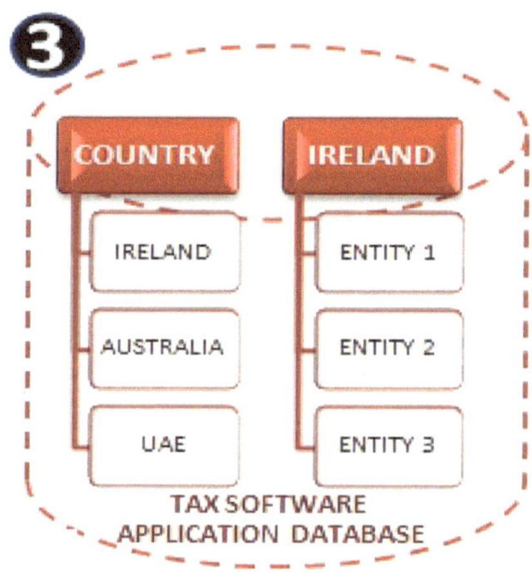

Figure 6.4.3

Once applicable finance and logistics data are in the tax compliance reporting system database, they are reorganized at the country and entity levels. The tax compliance reporting software database is designed to include data containers specific to each country. Within that country, data can be further segregated at the entity level. There may be further segmentation, such as separating the sales, purchase, and finance data sets. All this is available for viewing at the front end for the tax functions. Users can view transactions at the line-item level, segmented by country and company code. The front end provides many filters that the tax function can use to pull up relevant data sets, view it, and perform preliminary checks. The quantum of filters may vary depending upon the initial data export-import filtration drivers deployed, e.g., country, company code, purchase, sales, finance indicators, Tax code, in some cases at tax GL, vendor, supplier, customer levels, and more.

6.4.4 Workflow Step 4: Transactional Data Compliance Checks (Health Check Up)

Figure 6.4.4

This is one of the most critical steps, and tax functions love to execute it. The step involves checking the transactional data for any anomalies. By anomalies, we mean validating and verifying the dataset quality on multiple aspects, before it's considered for tax returns preparation, review, approval, and submission process (Step 7- to be explained later).

Anomalies may occur due to poor quality master data, transactional data entered during the transaction, e.g. checking whether Vendor/Customer has a valid VAT ID listed, and whether that's correct (format, length etc.), analyzing transactional taxability of exempted or zero rated transactions, which otherwise should be taxable or vice versa, whether any listed tax rate and tax amount are exceeded normality, tax collected or remitted figures match up with ERP tax ledgers (manual or using some external or ERP/Tax software tool), right tax codes are correctly punched in (e.g. transaction is intra EU supply, tax code is domestic), currency conversion accuracy, tax amounts matches tax rate, reconciling document no's with ERP etc. and other tens of checks.

This process is also called mini internal audit cycles, which firms run regularly before the tax return preparation process.

The tax compliance and reporting software has built-in standard tax data-checking logic, and further customization is also possible depending on how far a firm's tax functions would like to go. Tax functions can select such compliance components from the menu and conduct compliance checks on the data.

Modern tax compliance and reporting software's are rapidly deploying artificial intelligence (AI) programs within this process to assess data further, identify anomalies, and 'red-tag' and highlight transactions for further checks by tax functions. This is one area where artificial intelligence has a significant scope for improvement.

6.4.5 Workflow Step 5: Transactional data 'Composite Tax Code'

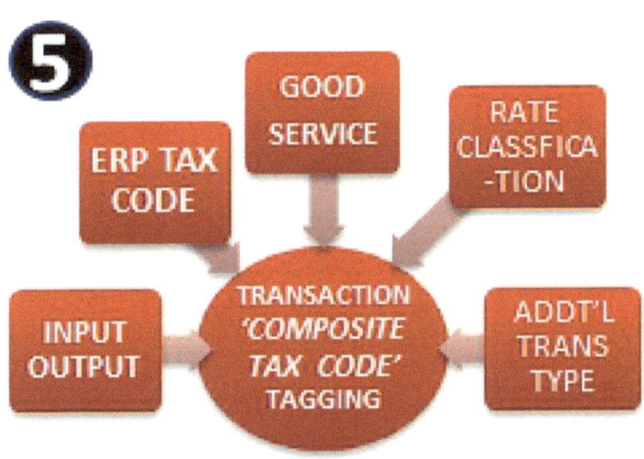

Figure 6.4.5

Once compliance health checks are achieved i.e. the tax functions check process, sanitize and correct the data, and ensure its accuracy; it's ready for the next step. In this process, line-item transactions are tagged with a 'Composite Tax Code'. A composite tax code is like a 'DNA' sequence (the scientific code that uniquely identifies an individual) for the transaction.

It's designed to route the transaction and its data to specific tax reports and their tax report boxes. The software's artificial intelligence understands the business tax scenario at the line-item level. It creates a composite tax code with the following parameters: Country, Entity Code (Input/Output – Goods/Service), ERP Tax Code, Rate classification, etc. Now, the transaction line items are tagged with this composite tax code, which the tax software application uses to identify the transaction and route it to the tax reports.

An illustrative example of such composite tax code is below.

UK A005 I 3X ZR RI M

UK	*A005*	*I*	*3X*	*ZR*	*RI*	*M*
Country	Entity	Input (I) /Output (O)	ERP Tax Code	Rate Classification (Zero rated)	Doc Type (Invoice)	Scenario (Import)

For example, in the above data set, we can see how the software creates a composite tax code, and this composite tax code contains all the attributes of the line-item scenario details and system can use this to route the finance tax values to applicable legal and statutory tax returns boxes. It's important to note again that overall architectural design of the tax compliance reporting software's is designed from country specific tax reports and associated tax boxes data requirement and that is reversed engineered into the entire downstream software application mechanism, not the other way around i.e. ERP system process (company specific business requirements) doesn't define this system engineering, instead country tax administration reporting requirements defines the engineered solution.

6.4.6 Workflow Step 6: Tax Data Allocation to Tax Report Boxes

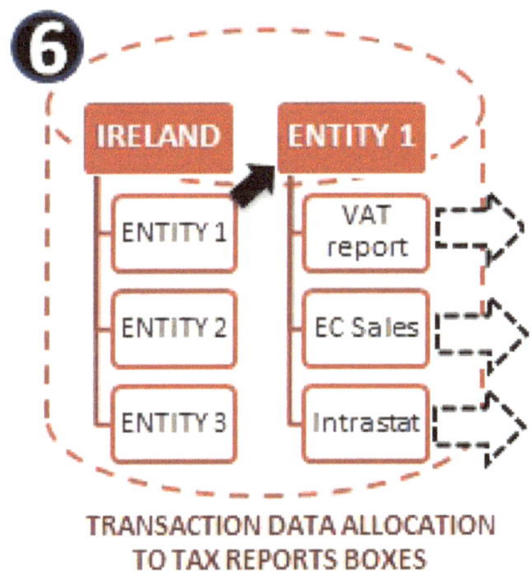

Figure 6.4.6

Post composite tax code tagging, the transactions are absorbed by the application in various country-specific tax reports. Tax compliance and reporting software provides predefined tax reporting templates (forms). It is kept up to date through regular updates (technical feeds inserted into the tax software by tax software vendor firms; e.g., if the tax authority introduces a new tax box in the tax report, the software vendor's research and development team develop this built and release an update to the firms the software, which are automatically absorbed or applied manually.

A document may have many line items and not necessary all line item transaction are targeting a specific tax report box, for example if a document has three line items, one for standard rated goods, another for reduced rated service, and third one for zero rated insurance, their tax value target boxes in a tax report may differ, that's the reason documents in these tax compliance software's are broken into line item transactions. These line-item-level transactions are the actual data sample for tax software working.

These transactions are stored in the tax compliance software's databases as per the data archiving mandates of the tax authority. A firm now has two sets of transactional databases: one in the ERP and another in the tax compliance reporting software. This functionality is convenient during audit defense and reconciliation. These tax compliance and reporting software's have a sophisticated, well-organized, and structured 'tax data lake' for reporting, a functionality that standard ERP lacks.

6.4.7 Workflow Step 7: Prepare > Review > Approve

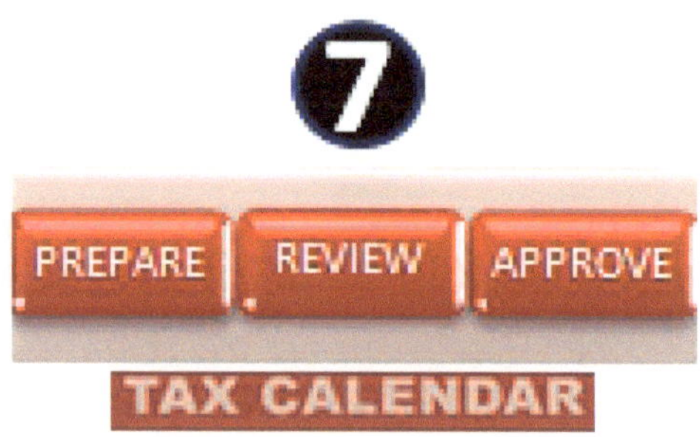

Figure 6.4.7

The above process applies to associates from the tax department; they have dedicated associates in each country and serve as tax return preparers, reviewers, and approvers. Once tax reports are ready in the system, they are pushed to this user-friendly front-end interface, where tax functions can view not only pre-populated tax reports with data in the report boxes, but also the associated transactions at the line-item level relevant to the report and boxes. The software provides two views to the tax functions: Transactions related to the tax report (for a specific country-entity-tax report type) and the tax report output, i.e., the form with boxes and values to be submitted to the tax authority.

Further to this, tax functions can check the report box values and the associated line-item transactions that contributed to each box. That level of fine granularity and reverse traceability is provided by tax compliance and reporting software. The software also provides a view of tax functions on the due dates approaching for various tax authorities and tax reports, and the status (Filled, Due, Overdue), a sort of tax reporting management calendar, which further supports compliance and empowers the tax functions to avoid missing any tax return deadlines.

As seen in the Figure 6.4.7, as a first step, the tax functions prepare the tax report; in this step, they can see a pre-populated report with data in the boxes. The reviewer conducts some additional final high level health checks are done at report box levels to ensure tax reporting accuracy further e.g., if output tax box value is abnormally more than tax input in sync with previous returns with linear business operational, if tax box services has a value when a firm is only selling goods or whether the non-recoverable taxes (non-deductible), exempt, export amounts seems suspicious etc.

The software provides the reviewer a functionality to look-up the associated transactions that are hitting that specific tax box and further validate and verify them and identify any final anomalies for its (document line item) rectification in the ERP system or do manual edits in the tax boxes, citing comments (in cases when tax filing date is near and rectification in the ERP or document cancellation or reversal will take time). Finally, the report is ready for the tax approver to view in the tax software. It's like an official formality: the tax manager or tax director conducts a final check, places their digital signature on the tax report, and approves it for filing with the tax authority. If the approver is not comfortable, they may also send it back to the reviewer with their comments for reassessment of the tax report. Access levels are strictly maintained, monitored, and audited, and only designated preparers, reviewers, and approvers can access this module within an organization.

6.4.8 Workflow Step 8: Tax Report Filing

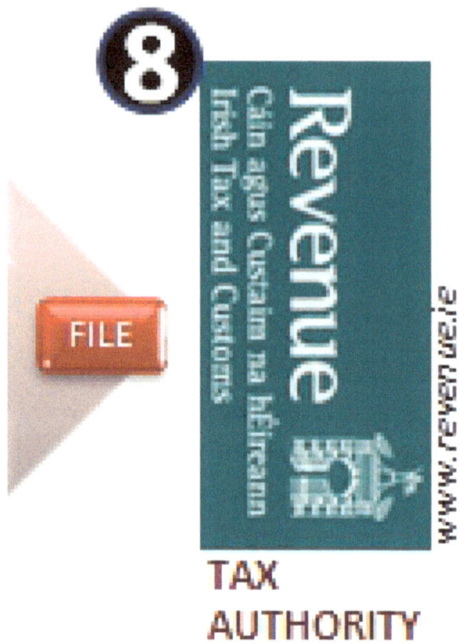

Figure 6.4.8

In this final step, the approved tax reports are filed at the tax authority portal. There are three ways to file. (a) Either paper based and posted to the tax authority – this paper based process is hardly adopted nowadays by tax authorities (2) manual filing, i.e. logging into the tax authority portal using credentials, viewing the standard report template and entering box values in it and submit (3) e-filing, via which the tax software files the approved tax report to the tax authority directly via an API which tax software firm has certified for. The majority of the world's tax authorities offer e-filing functionality, and tax software vendors obtain certifications, a process in which the tax vendor registers with the tax authority and demonstrates that the output file matches the tax authority's report format and parameters.

In addition, many tax authorities require corresponding transactional data submissions having a specific structure, format and field data relevant to the tax report for that specific period. The tax compliance and reporting software also facilitates this functionality. Once filing is complete, the tax authority issues a payment notice detailing the tax due, and the accounts payable team makes the payment to the tax authority using the standard ERP payable process. This completes the entire tax compliance and reporting lifecycle.

6.5 SUMMARY

In this chapter, we've shown you the tax technology aspects of Indirect Tax Compliance and Reporting. You have learnt the basics of tax compliance and reporting, generic requirements, the functional architecture of tax compliance reporting software, and its workings in relation to the tax process and sub-processes. You know how tax compliance and reporting software collects, processes, and transforms business tax data, enabling tax reporting and submissions to the tax authority. Countries' tax administrations are often changing their tax filing expectations –report types, format, structure, data parameters, and e-filing /submission technology- and you are now better equipped to support the IT and tax vendor in getting such legal and technical changes incorporated into your Tax IT landscape, ensuring compliance, accuracy, and legality. For tax functions, compliance and reporting are the most critical work areas, and they must be completed within a fixed deadline; otherwise, penalties, fines, and the risk of an external audit loom. In the next chapter, we'll discuss E-Invoicing, its impact on tax, and technology.

CHAPTER 7

E-INVOICING AND TAX TECHNOLOGY

The chapter introduces e-Invoicing to the readers. E-Invoicing is not tax technology; however, since an e-Invoice - an invoice transmitted from supplier to buyer (in a specific document structure, format and field value parameters) now interfaces with the tax authorities directly or indirectly, it leads to synchronous and asynchronous tax data submissions to the tax authorities database while running sales and purchase invoice transactions. This enables real-time tax data capture by the tax authorities. E-invoice is not giving firms a second chance to audit, rectify, and resubmit tax data to the tax authorities, once it's issued, approved and accepted by the tax authority; thus, having a qualitative, accurate tax determination and invoice billing transmission system set up is a must for e-invoicing-impacted jurisdictions. With ViDA – VAT in the digital age framework, the majority of European nations will go for e-invoicing, and it's already implemented in Latin America, the Middle East, India, and other Asia Pacific regions. The chapter will help readers understand the e-invoicing technological framework, its integration with ERP and Tax technology software, and the overall process workflow. Readers will be better positioned to understand e-invoicing solutions, their workings both functionally and technically, thereby supporting sales and procurement processes while ensuring e–invoicing tax compliance and legal compliance.

7.1 WHAT'S E-INVOICING

An e-Invoice is the transmission of invoices between buyer and seller. It's an electronic format for document transmission, and the buyer and seller can be businesses, customers, or governments, leading to multiple combinations such as B2B (Business to Business), B2C (Business to customer), B2G (Business to Government), and G2B (Government to Business).

A PDF invoice or e-factura (Latin America), e-bill (USA), e-billing, e-receipts, e-way bill (Asian countries), which we see in the current accounting/ ERP system, is also an e-Invoice because it's a digital 'e' electronic document (not paper). The structure, format, and data elements may vary depending on the supplier and country-specific laws. However, in this topic, we are discussing the upcoming global e-invoicing subject, which involves not only a buyer and a seller but also the tax authority, an e-invoice service provider, and e-invoicing routing networks (e.g., Peppol) for cross-border transactions, and a format that is not PDF.

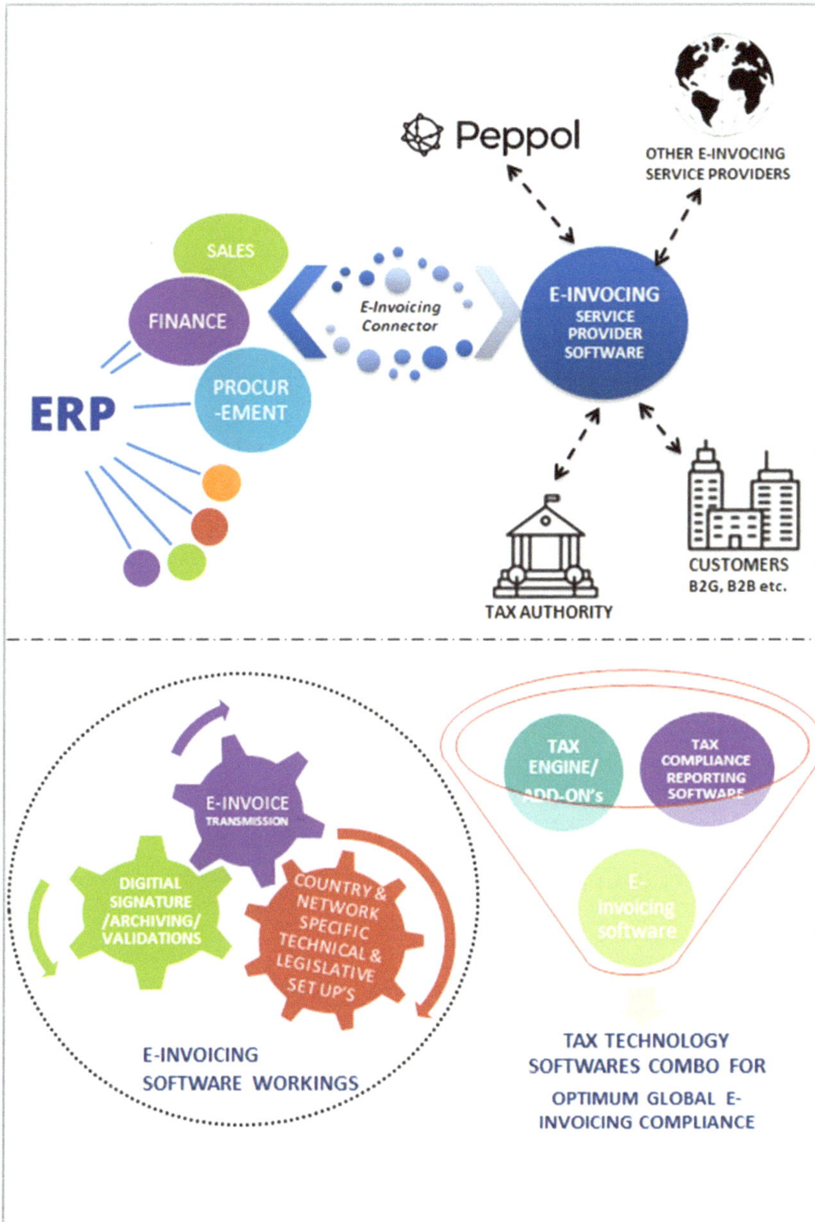
Peppol
OTHER E-INVOCING SERVICE PROVIDERS
SALES
FINANCE
E-Invoicing Connector
E-INVOCING SERVICE PROVIDER SOFTWARE
ERP
PROCUR -EMENT
TAX AUTHORITY
CUSTOMERS B2G, B2B etc.
E-INVOICE TRANSMISSION
DIGITIAL SIGNATURE /ARCHIVING/ VALIDATIONS
COUNTRY & NETWORK SPECIFIC TECHNICAL & LEGISLATIVE SET UP'S
E-INVOICING SOFTWARE WORKINGS
TAX ENGINE/ ADD-ON's
TAX COMPLIANCE REPORTING SOFTWARE
E-invoicing software
TAX TECHNOLOGY SOFTWARES COMBO FOR OPTIMUM GLOBAL E-INVOICING COMPLIANCE

Figure 7.1

With the 'VAT in the Digital Age' (ViDA) program and different legal and regulatory mandates across countries, regions. An e-invoicing will become a global phenomenon, driven by technological advancements. Few countries in Europe (e.g., Austria, Greece), Latin America (e.g., Argentina, Brazil, Chile, Mexico, Columbia) and Asia (e.g. India) have already adopted early e-invoicing models which include submission of e-invoices to the tax authority either in real time or near –real time (immediately after post audit phase (after transaction has concluded and posted in the ERP)).

Under the upcoming setup, the e-invoice structure, which as of now is custom (buyer& sellers invoice format, structure, and data elements), is now being standardized (universal) regarding structure, transmission format, and data elements under the global e-Invoicing program adopted by multiple-country tax administrations.

Now, it's important to note that if any real-time e-invoice transmission model involves a tax authority, it triggers an immediate audit of that business transaction by the tax authority. Tax compliance comes into play because the tax authority database now has a record of that e-invoice, along with the tax collected or the payment details, alongside standard financial and logistics data. The supplier or buyer doesn't have a second chance to edit or rectify the e-invoice (although the credit/debit notes process will continue), the vast majority of approved invoices will get audited in the tax authority database.

Some examples of products and firms that offer e-invoicing solutions include Pagero, Vertex, Avalara, Sovos, Fonoa, Zoho, Payhawk, Xero, Coupa, SAP DRC, and other Big 4 and Top Tax tech firms also have their own products.

7.2 E-INVOICING SOFTWARE WORKING

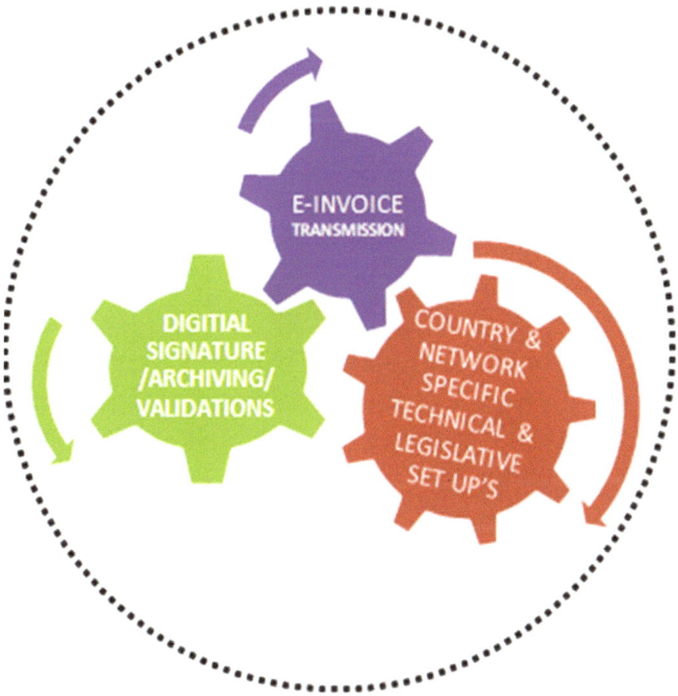

Figure 7.2

An e-Invoicing software (application, database, and APIs) is designed to allow the product to interface with the buyer and seller ERP systems, Tax authority platforms, and global networks, e.g., Peppol. The API's/Connectors - communication protocols, file formats, and structured data elements sets are updated as per the legislative and technical changes prescribed by tax jurisdictions and networks. Also, within the software, there is a set of data validation programs, backed by custom rules and AI, which perform data validation. It includes a database for digital archiving of e-invoices, digital signature, functional dashboards, and other features required for end-to-end E-invoicing.

An e-Invoicing software doesn't do tax computation or conventional periodic reporting. However, since it involves touchpoints with the tax authority, performs transactional tax data validation, and facilitates real-time reporting, it's has tax technology impact, not merely an API or document router and transformer role.

7.3 GEOGRAPHICAL & TRANSACTIONAL TYPE SCOPE

Mandatory regulations across regions are driving global E-Invoicing adoption; many nations have already adopted it, and by 2030-2035, the majority of nations will adopt it.

E-invoicing can have Business-to-Business (B2B), Business-to-Government (B2G), Business-to-Customer (B2C), or Government-to-Business (G2B) transaction type scope. Countries are going forward in a phased manner on this.

More information can be researched at below e-invoicing trackers.

- https://peppol.org
- https://www.ey.com/en_gl/technical/tax-guides/e-invoicing-developments-tracker
- https://www.avalara.com/eu/en/learn/guides/digitisation-of-tax-reporting/e-invoicing-global-tracker.html
- https://www.vatcalc.com/global/live-vat-gst-transaction-e-invoicing-global-tracker/
- https://cleartax.in/s/e-invoicing-mandates-by-country

7.4 WHY E-INVOICING

Tax authorities targets minimum tax evasions (VAT/GST/Sales Tax gaps), promote pro-environmental business practices (e-invoice is digital, not paper based), improve revenue collection, fiscal transparency (expected revenue from tax) and importantly monitor the transactional tax data (real time or near real time e-audit) using Big data or AI for any fraudulent, illegal, sanctioned business flows, enabling accurate VAT refunds -that's why they are moving forward to such models. There are many other factors, including financial supply chains, transfer pricing, market developments, payment solutions, and the digitalization of trade, that are driving global e-invoicing adoption.

7.5 E-INVOICING WITHOUT TAX AUTHORITY

E-Invoicing without a tax authority leads to periodic tax reporting.

In this section, we will examine the various e-invoicing models without tax authority involvement (direct or indirect), as well as the reporting-type obligations.

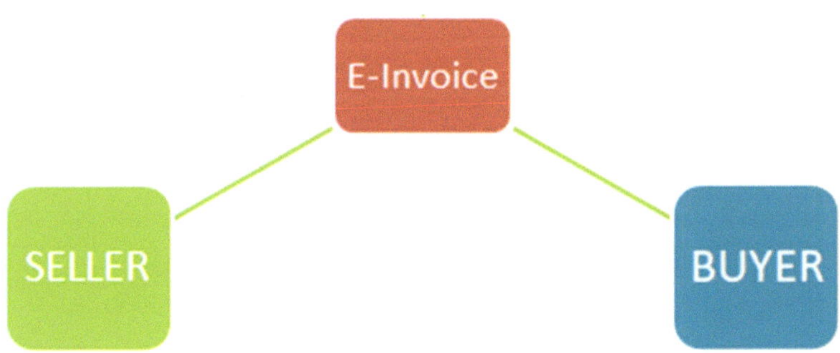

Figure 7.5

One can see in the Figure 7.5 above that the e-invoice is shared between the buyer and the seller, with no 3rd party involved. This model leads to periodic reporting, an example in this case prevalent in EU nations is the SAF-T Standard Audit File –Tax), VAT return, EC sales list, Spain SII. These tax reports contain post-audit data (after the transaction has concluded and is posted in the Accounting/ ERP system). It's not real-time reporting to the tax authority.

It's important to understand that an e-invoicing model that excludes the tax authority will result in periodic tax returns/reports rather than real-time or near-real-time reporting. In the current state of e-invoicing, there are two or three parties involved: the buyer, the seller, and the network.

7.5.1 Direct /EDI (2 Corner Model)

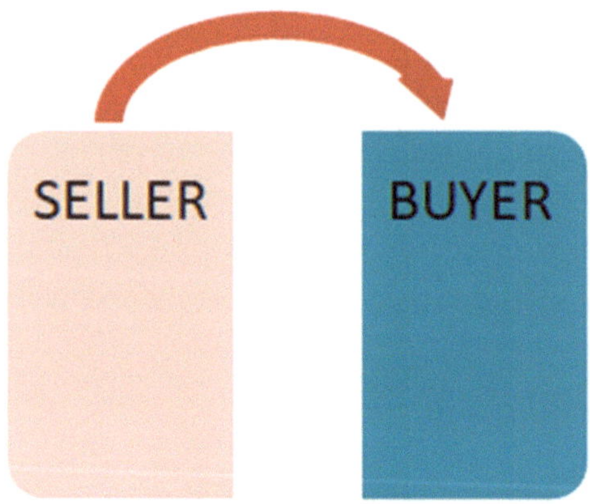

Figure 7.5.1

As shown in Figure 7.5.1, e-invoices can be sent directly from seller to buyer via email, paper, customer portal login, ERP Intercompany billings, or another EDI tool. Firms may use data scanning and optical data recognition software to automate this process.

7.5.2 Network (3 Corner Model)

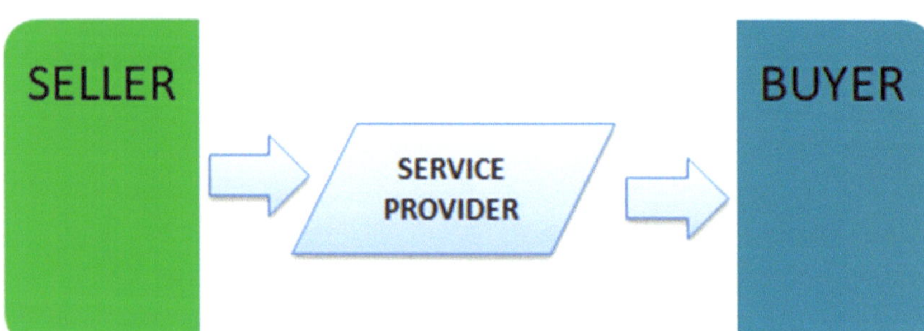

Figure 7.5.2

As shown in Figure 7.5.2, in this model, the seller sends the invoice through a network (service provider). It works on a defined format, structure, and communication protocol. The buyer's ERP procurement process absorbs the invoice, and further processing (validation, approvals, and payments) takes place. Under this, both buyer and seller leverage a network (a mode of transmission) to send and receive invoices. The supplier may send the invoice in any format (PDF or XML), and the network ensures the output invoice data format is compatible with the buyer's ERP procurement process. Basically, the network performs invoice format transformation to ensure compatibility with the buyer's ERP system.

e.g., SAP, an ERP firm, introduced the Ariba network (SAP Integration Suite/Gateway) for data exchange, where suppliers can register, create, and send invoices to buyers running their business on SAP through this network. However, in this model, the supplier, even though their accounting/ERP system is not likes the buyer's (e.g., SAP in the Ariba network case), they can register on it and generate an invoice through it.

7.5.3 Interoperability (4 Corner model)

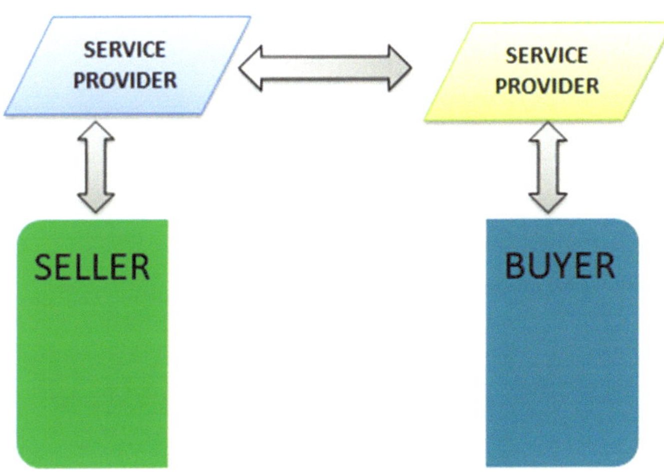

Figure 7.5.3

As shown in Fig. 7.5.3, in this model, the supplier and buyer exchange invoices via preferred service providers. In this model, both the buyer and the supplier can choose their own service providers, who can communicate with each other. These service providers have legal agreements, data formats, and communication protocols, and international standards that are established by associations (organizations) like OpenPeppol, established by the European Commission, and GENA (Global Exchange Network Association). Now, these organizations, e.g., OpenPeppol, offer the Peppol network, which these e-invoicing service providers may use for domestic and global e-invoicing and e-procurement data transmission (cross-border). E-invoicing service providers need to register and get certified with such global networks; these service providers are also called Peppol access points, which taxpayers can use (take services).

In all of the above e-invoice models, the tax authority remains a non-party. First, the invoices' financial and payment data are posted in the buyer's and supplier's ERP systems, and later, based on the tax report and the country's tax administration's mandated periodicity, tax returns are filed with the tax authority. That means the tax authority gets access to data only after the transaction is processed, posted, and stored in the ERP.

7.6 E-INVOICING WITH TAX AUTHORITY

E-Invoicing with the tax authority leads to real-time/near real-time reporting. In this section, we will examine the various e-invoicing models **with** tax authority involvement (direct or indirect) and the reporting-type obligations. It's important to note that though in many jurisdictions having E-invoicing model implemented, periodic reporting of tax returns data to tax authorities will not get phased out completely, for example, in LATAM nations, E-invoicing has been prevalent since years, still periodic tax filings are required.

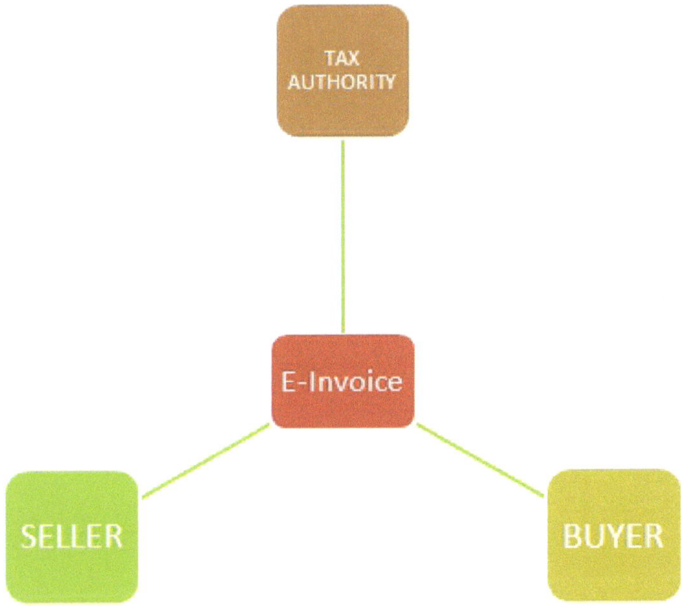

Figure 7.6

One may see in Figure 7.6 above that the e-Invoice process now involves a 3rd party, i.e., the tax authority. Its involvement triggers the need for real-time tax compliance for transactions (sales, purchase invoicing, and financial payments).

The subject of upcoming e-Invoicing mandates (legal & statutory requirements), tax authority-driven requirements, and network-organizational requirements is extensive in its global, regional, and country scope (communication protocols, access points, platform formats, models, document types, data elements). Our goal is to be specific regarding the tax compliance and reporting aspect.

After e-invoicing implementation, e-invoices will be submitted to tax authorities in real time or near real time via vivid e-invoicing models (explained in the latter sections), enabling real-time reporting. This will lead to faster availability of data on finance, tax, logistics, and other data elements (depending on country tax authority regulations, data field requirements may vary from 10 to 50 or more) to the tax authorities. It's real-time: as soon as the transaction leaves the Accounting/ERP system and the exchange occurs between seller and buyer, it's captured by the tax authority and audited (stored in the tax authority's IT database).

E-Invoicing models include tax authority, e-invoicing service providers, and global networks (e.g., Peppol) as parties. That direct or indirect involvement triggers a real-time or near-real-time tax compliance requirement.

There are four models under this setup for the upcoming e-Invoicing.

7.6.1 Real Time Reporting

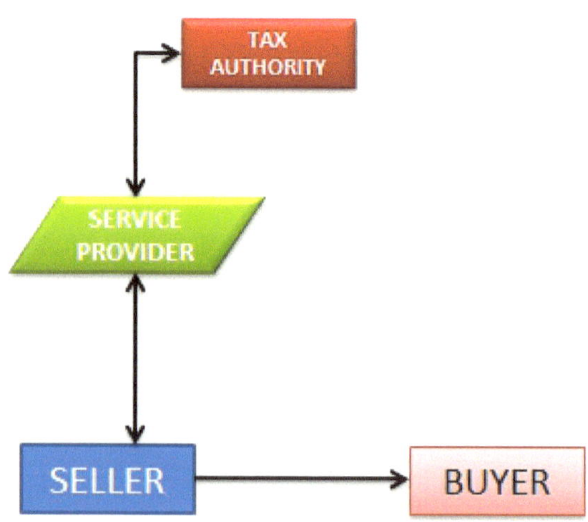

Figure 7.6.1

In the real-time reporting model (Figure 7.6.1), the seller sends an e-invoice to the buyer and to the service provider, which has integration with the seller's ERP and tax authority platform; the service provider then shares the e-invoice with the tax authority in a separate process. In this model, the tax authority provides an e-invoice processing platform, and to access that platform, the supplier requires an accredited (certified) software solution (e-invoicing software) to transmit the data to the tax authority in a specific time period (one to three days) post issuance of invoice, i.e., near real-time submission.

In short, in this model, a taxpayer has to issue two invoices, one invoice to the buyer in an existing format (e.g. PDF etc.) and one to the tax authority 'e-invoice', which has a specific format (e.g. XML, UBL), a structure (header, line item, footer) and data fields via a certified service provider (e-invoicing software).

7.6.2 Clearance Model

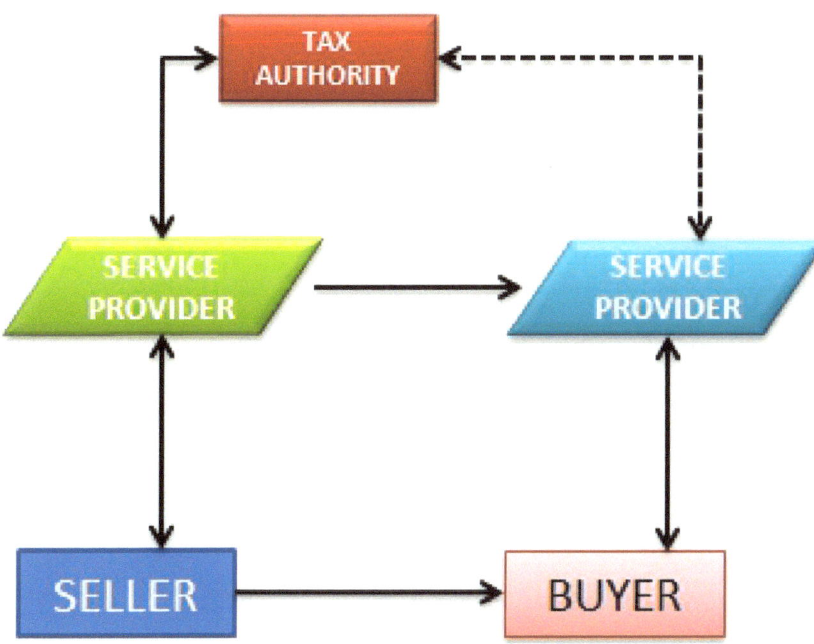

Figure 7.6.2

A clearance model (Figure 7.6.2) involves a tax authority in real time and requires the seller and buyer to report the invoice through the tax authority portal. The tax authority portal validates the invoice for compliance, and then issues it to the recipient; i.e., the tax authority plays an approver 'clearance' role here.

The recipient receives the invoice from the seller and, upon payment; the invoice is further validated in the same tax authority portal, which already has it in its database.

A clearance model may include further sub models and processes.

- *Pre-clearance*: The seller sends the invoice to the buyer via email. The e-invoicing service provider simultaneously sends it to the tax authority. In this case, the tax authority is not directly in the supplier–buyer line of sight, playing a 3rd party role.
- *Post-clearance*: The seller first sends the invoice to the tax authority, and after the tax authority approves it, the seller sends it to the buyer. In this case, the tax authority is directly within the supplier–buyer business line of sight, serving as an intermediary for approval.
- *Simplex and Duplex model:* In Simplex, only the seller reports the invoice to the tax authority for clearance; in Duplex, the seller submits the invoice to the tax authority for clearance, and the buyer also reports (validates) the invoice at the tax portal before making payment.

The tax authority in this case has a database where taxpayer invoices are stored (audited) and retained.

7.6.3 Centralized Exchange Model

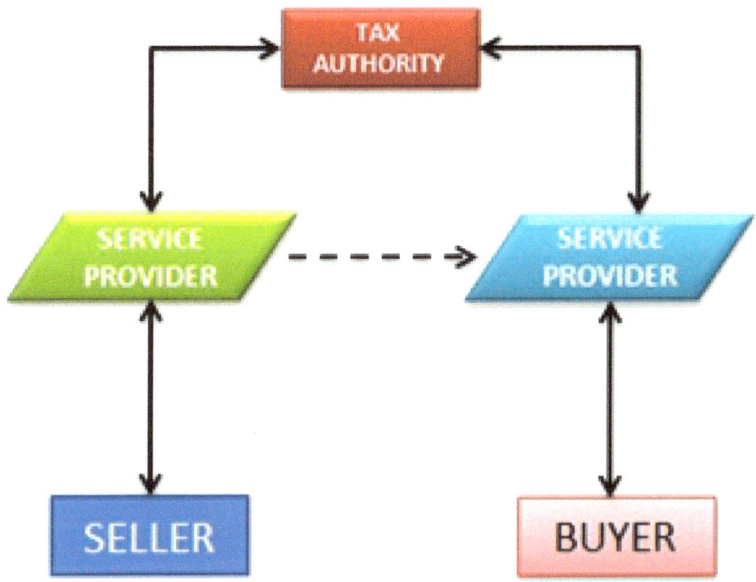

Figure 7.6.3

A Centralized exchange model (Figure 7.6.3) involves the transmission of the seller's invoice to the tax authority portal via a designated e-invoicing service provider. The tax authority validates the invoice (format, registrations, other rules), then sends it to the buyer. In this case, the seller and buyer exchange invoices via designated service providers or through the tax authority platform.

In either case, the tax authority first validates the invoice, and there is no direct transmission of the invoice from the supplier to the buyer, unlike the clearance model.

7.6.4 Decentralized Exchange Model (5 corner)

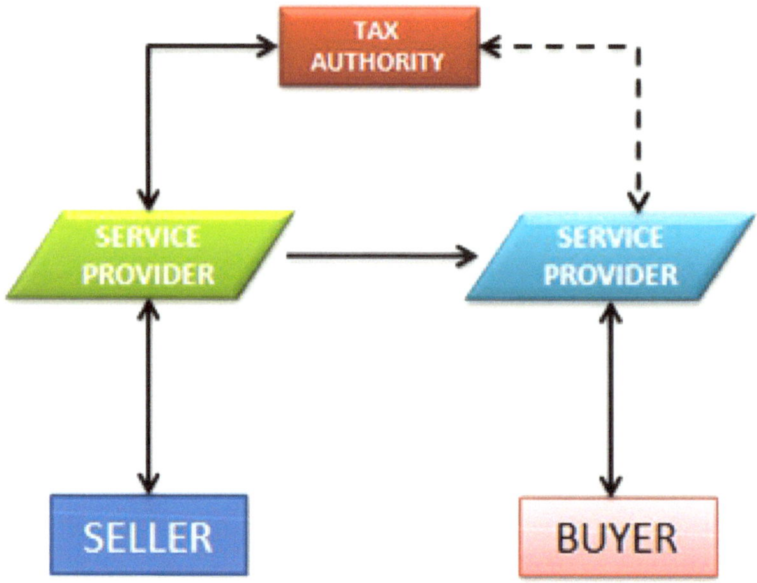

Figure 7.6.4

The decentralized exchange five-corner model resembles the Centralized Exchange Model; it has five fixed parties, as shown in the Figure 7.6.4. Decentralized means that the tax authority is not controlling the entire e-invoice lifecycle process; it's playing the role it's supposed to have – have insights into the transactional tax.

The unique aspect of this model is that instead of the tax authority doing compliance checks, validations, the designated (certified) e-invoicing service providers will validate the invoice.

The e-invoicing service providers in this case, not only supports the e-invoicing format, structure and data fields and extraction from the ERP, but also does a part of tax authority in validating the invoice (data quality and compliance e.g. Tax ID (VAT ID), Product Code etc.) and alongside facilitating the transmission and receipt of the e-invoice between seller and buyer, it also sends the e-invoice to the tax authority with specific data fields as mandated and required by the tax authority. Both buyers and seller may have their own unique service providers – i.e., a 3rd party e-Invoicing software firm; however, both service providers have a common communication interface standard (Interoperability - the ability of computer systems or software to exchange and make use of information) for a successful e-invoice handshake.

To properly understand the real-time/near-real-time tax footprints of e-invoicing, it's essential to have a clear view of the various e-invoicing operational models and their jurisdictional and cross-border positioning.

Note – Both seller and buyer may have same or different e-invoicing service providers.

7.7 DATA FORMATS

As mentioned above, we read about various e-invoicing models; within a model, we may use different data formats for each country. By format, we mean the type of data file with a specific technical structure, e.g., PDF, Word, UBL, XML, etc., and it may vary from one country to another. Example -

- India: GST INV-1
- Spain: Facturae
- Turkey: UBL-TR
- Denmark: OIOXML
- USA: ANSI

The core ERP system, deployed by a multinational with e-invoicing obligations across various tax jurisdictions, is not capable of generating so many different file formats. The e-Invoicing service provider (e-Invoicing software firm) handles this requirement, performing format-related transformations and passing document & data to another service provider, either directly or via networks like Peppol.

7.8 LEGAL, STATUTORY COMPLIANCE INVOLVING E-INVOICING ERP LIMITS AND TAX TECHNOLOGY SOLUTIONS

Now that we have read the various operational models of e-invoicing, including the tax authority, the service provider, and global networks like Peppol, it's time to understand the legal, legislative, and regulatory compliance requirements for e-invoicing implementation. These regulations are prescribed by both country-specific tax authorities and global network organizations, such as Open Peppol, which operates the Peppol network.

This will help us understand the role of ERP, its limitations, and the potential of tax technology to accommodate this requirement. Currently, there are three tax technology products, mainly tax engines, tax compliance reporting software, and e-Invoicing software. To address all e-Invoicing requirements, a firm may deploy a combination of these products.

In the E-invoicing requirement vs. ERP limits vs. Tax Technology solution matrix below, we will analyze prospective solutions and combinations.

Table 7.8: Legal and Statutory Requirements

Requirement	ERP Scope & Limitation	Tax Technology Solutions ▪ Tax Engine /VAT Add-ons ▪ Tax Compliance Reporting Software's ▪ E-Invoicing Software's
Audit trail & Archiving of e-invoicing to enable data retention compliance with jurisdictional requirements	An ERP system can't store the e-invoices in the format and structure in which they are transmitted to tax authorities. Each ERP system has its own unique invoice storage format and structure.	**Tax compliance reporting software + E-Invoicing software** E-Invoicing software, in combination with tax compliance and reporting software, has a database to store e-invoices in the format in which they were transmitted. These e-invoices can be retrieved at any time for audit defense and periodic tax reporting.
Invoice format, structure, and data sets as per European e-invoicing standard and decommissioning non-structured format docs like PDF e.g.,	The ERP system is not capable of accommodating these multi-country format requirements (XML, UBL, and	**E-Invoicing software** e-Invoicing software will support the transformation of an ERP invoice into an e-

EN16931(Ireland and EU standard)	CII). The ERP system has limited formatting capabilities e.g., PDF	invoice format in the format and structure accepted by the tax authority
Taxpayer to send data to the tax authority under applicable e-invoicing mandates and periodic process	The ERP system cannot accommodate this. It's a business accounting system with minimal tax reporting capabilities. In upcoming e-invoicing models, tax authorities will require data in specific formats, structures, and datasets, which ERP is not capable of providing as part of its standard functionality.	**Tax compliance reporting software + E-Invoicing software** E-Invoicing software for real-time/near real-time reporting & Tax compliance reporting software for periodic reporting.
Access point to the Peppol network, tax authority platforms. Submissions of e-invoices, receive e-invoices, and approve/reject e-invoices with a digital signature.	A standard ERP system isn't capable of getting certified. This work requires interface (API) development, with communication protocol, data set requirements, and many other aspects. Moreover, since formats vary from country, including	**E-Invoicing software** E-Invoicing software firms (service providers) have access to such networks; they have developed the product in accordance with the communication standards, transmission protocols, and data set modeling

	structure and data sets, it will be impossible to maintain and sustain.	defined by Peppol and other networks.
Access to Suppliers/Buyer e-Invoice service providers	To enable such communication, the ERP system needs to adopt a specific communication protocol and standard, along with an agreed format and structure, which will require customization of the ERP's standard functionality and frequent development updates.	**E-Invoicing Software** E-Invoicing software service providers have designed their software to send and receive e-invoices compatible with other e-invoicing software service providers, and they keep this software up to date with respect to communication protocols, data sets, formats, and structures.
Mandatory tax fields expected by the tax authority	The standard ERP invoicing process involves defined finance, tax, and logistics fields. For additional fields, customization in the process and format is required.	**E-Invoicing Software** E-Invoicing software integrates with the finance, accounting, sales, and procurement modules and, in addition to extracting standard fields, can extract more fields from the ERP database table and populate them on the e-invoice

		as mandated by the tax authority.
Tax authority access for data security, encryption	The standard ERP will require API /Integration development works for each tax authority applicable. Alongside this, the e-invoice format, structure and field-data requirement developments are also required.	**E-Invoicing Software** E-Invoicing software products come with an out of box integration API/Connectors with tax authorities, because they serve hundreds of clients and also have functionality to populate e-invoices as per the specification.
Compliance with country and network-specific e-invoicing, Legal, statutory, and technical changes e.g., format, structure, data fields, submission methods, and timelines	Standard ERP has no capability for this. It's not e-invoicing automation software, and its product team has no components or legal framework to support this. In the ERP, we will have to code for each country as per the changes.	**E-Invoicing software** E-Invoicing software vendors have dedicated research teams that monitor and analyze legislative and technical updates, and scan for and create new requirements for the product Dev. team. Ops. Team for its incorporation in the software. Vendors can build once and deploy globally, and maintain.
Tax data validation – As seen in the decentralized model (5 corners), the tax authority expects validation of specific tax	ERP cannot validate tax rate, tax amount, and other aspects (e.g., Tax ID/VAT ID) of e-	**E-Invoicing Software** E-Invoicing software includes pre-check

data parameters (e.g., tax rate, tax ID, product code, master data) of the invoice before tax authority submission/reporting.	invoicing; it's a finance accounting software	tools and AI to identify anomalies in e-invoices and can resend the invoice to the taxpayer for further rectification. This software, in combination with tax reporting and compliance software, can perform checks on tax parameters such as tax rates and tax IDs (VAT Reg.)

7.9 NON-LEGAL FUNCTIONAL REQUIREMENTS ERP LIMITS AND TAX TECHNOLOGY SOLUTIONS

These requirements are non–legal, i.e., may or may not be mandated by the tax authority or global networking organizations such as Open Peppol; however, they are vital for operational functionality.

Table 7.9: Non-legal functional requirements

Requirements	**ERP**	**Tax Technology Solutions** ▪ **Tax Engine** ▪ **Tax Compliance Reporting Software's** ▪ **E-Invoicing Software's**
Real-time tax computation, as the e-invoice is to be transmitted post creation, and the	Yes, ERP systems can compute tax in real time, either standalone or via a 3rd-party tool such as a tax engine or a tax plug-in (tax	**Tax Engine** E-Invoicing software service providers don't do the computation of tax,

tax should be accurate.	add-on) for greater efficiency.	nor do the tax compliance and reporting software providers. However, a taxpayer can deploy an external tax engine for tax computation, ensuring compliance with global tax authority rates and rules with ease.
Cloud-based platform to connect with e-invoice service providers	ERP systems can be on-site and cloud-based. However, when a firm operates in multiple countries, it may face various e-invoice service providers, each with its own communication and integration protocols and document format requirements. ERP is not capable of accommodating this.	**E-Invoicing Software's** The tax technology solution involving an e-invoicing service may be able to handle multiple e-invoicing service providers, requiring clear communication protocols, document formats, and structures.
Master data availability & accuracy	Yes, master data resides in the ERP system and should have accurate datasets for the financial accounting system to enter values on the invoice; for this, the work needs to be done in the ERP itself. **1.** Identify the relevant data gaps in master data **2.** If data elements exist, implement additional data table fields integration with the certified integration	**E-Invoicing Software's** Not capable and designed to do this, as it's beyond its scope and control. However, the software provides validation checks, and based on that, the taxpayer can update and rectify the master data. In the current market, there are tools for master data sanitization.

	software target field data sets. In case they aren't available, create and incorporate these data fields into the master data and upstream sales, procurement, and finance processes, later to be mapped to e-invoicing service provider software and transmitted. **3.** Passage of these data alongside the data fields available in the standard invoice.	**Master Data Management Tools**: In the current market, there are master data sanitization tools, through which master data elements can be rectified.
VAT reconciliation on e-Invoices across multiple countries and real-time visibility	ERP has no capability	**Tax compliance reporting software + E-Invoicing software's** E-invoicing software coupled with tax compliance and reporting solution will fulfill this requirement.
Multiple ERP /non-ERP accounting systems landscape	In this case, each ERP accounting system will need a separate integration with the tax authority and networks.	**E-Invoicing software's** Service providers software may integrate with multiple ERP/Accounting systems.
Integration with finance, sales, and procurement processes, data transmission	In ERP, separate connectors will be required to extract finance, sales, and procurement documents and data fields, and later transmit them to	**E-Invoicing software's** E-invoicing software comes with standard APIs/Connectors that map source-to-target data fields from sales, purchase and

	third-party service providers or tax authority platforms, which will require development and ongoing maintenance.	finance processes, though some customization is always required; the expected target format, structure, and data fields are predefined, as they're client-independent.
User-friendly business-as-usual operational functionalities – View, Monitor, track, download e-Invoices (approved or rejected)	An ERP system will contain ERP invoices, but not E-Invoices; thus, it will not support users (tax, finance, sales, and procurement) in their business-as-usual operational work.	**E-Invoicing software's** E-Invoicing software has dashboards with multiple user-friendly functionalities to view, monitor, review, edit/rectify, and download e-invoices.

7.10 IDEAL TAX TECHNOLOGY LANDSCAPE FOR E-INVOCING

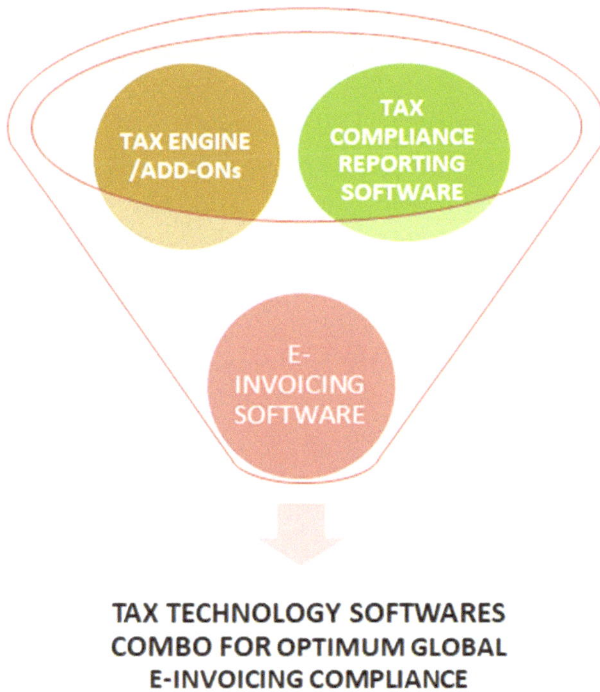

Figure 7.10

From the above-listed legal, statutory, and functional requirements, it's evident that the taxpayer's ERP/Accounting systems are not capable of accommodating these legal and technical e-invoicing requirements, and that enabling e-invoicing from the ERP would not be cost-effective. Deployment of e-invoicing software is a must. A good solution for firms with multi-national presence is to have a good balancing landscape consisting of a Tax Engine /Tax Plug-ins) (for determination), a tax compliance reporting software (for existing periodic tax reports compliance and submissions), and e-invoicing software (for e-invoicing specific jurisdictional communication and real-time reporting requirements).

7.11 SUMMARY

In this chapter, we looked at the big picture of e-Invoicing and its direct and indirect impact on tax reporting. Globally, many countries' tax administrations and regions (EU) are already mandating e-Invoicing, and in the next few years, it will be the standard way to send and receive invoices worldwide. We started by establishing key fundamental concepts of e-Invoicing, especially the various models, with and without tax authority involvement. How e-Invoicing software is functionally architected and how it interacts with the ERP, e-Invoicing partners, buyers, suppliers, and the tax authority, providing a three-dimensional view of its end-to-end workings. We've shown how legal, statutory, and technical requirements and challenges e-Invoicing poses for organizations, and how a good mix of ERP and Tax technology solutions can address them, concluding with an ideal IT landscape. Readers now have insight and foresight into e-Invoicing, its workings, and its impact on tax reporting. In the next chapter, we'll discuss Business & Tax Process with & without tax technology. Such a comparative analysis will foster creativity, hindsight, and foresight, leading to better solutions.

CHAPTER 8

BUSINESS & TAX PROCESS – WITH & WITHOUT TAX TECHNOLOGY

This chapter introduces readers to Indirect tax technology as a whole and provides a bird's-eye view of the end-to-end indirect tax processes and associated tax technologies, automating and digitalizing such processes at applicable stages. It will cover upstream tax processes involving sales, purchase, finance transaction creation to tax determination and downstream processes involving tax data extraction, tax compliance, tax return preparation, and submissions to tax authorities, with e-Invoicing in the picture. This will support readers' understanding of linking individual tax processes with associated tax technologies towards the establishment of the entire tax technology, with and without tax technology solutions, also known as setting up a tax technology control framework.

Indirect tax technology = Indirect Tax + Technology. The use of technology to automate, streamlines, and digitalize the tax processes is called tax technology. Taxes are of two types: Direct Taxes (e.g., Payroll tax, Withholding tax), and Indirect Taxes (VAT, GST, US SUT, etc.). We will be focusing on Indirect Taxes. The first step is to identify the different work areas a tax department does in a firm. It's important to remember here that tax technology is to support tax functions, and tax functions have a specific standard operating procedure for tax work; the technology should support that, otherwise, it's a recipe for failure.

A multinational firm's tax department's primary role is to design, manage, and operate the company's global tax framework. Additionally act as trusted advisor on tax matters, proactively shaping and optimizing tax strategies across countries, support and actively contribute to M&A projects, tax diligence, divestments, finance and corporate restructurings, Support in technical tax advise, from day-to-day questions to project-based initiatives (e.g. e-invoicing), Manage, follow up and coordinate tax audits and other queries from tax authorities; and conducting internal audits (compliance) and returns preparations and submissions to the tax authorities. More detailed information on the tax control framework is explained in section 9.6 of chapter 9.

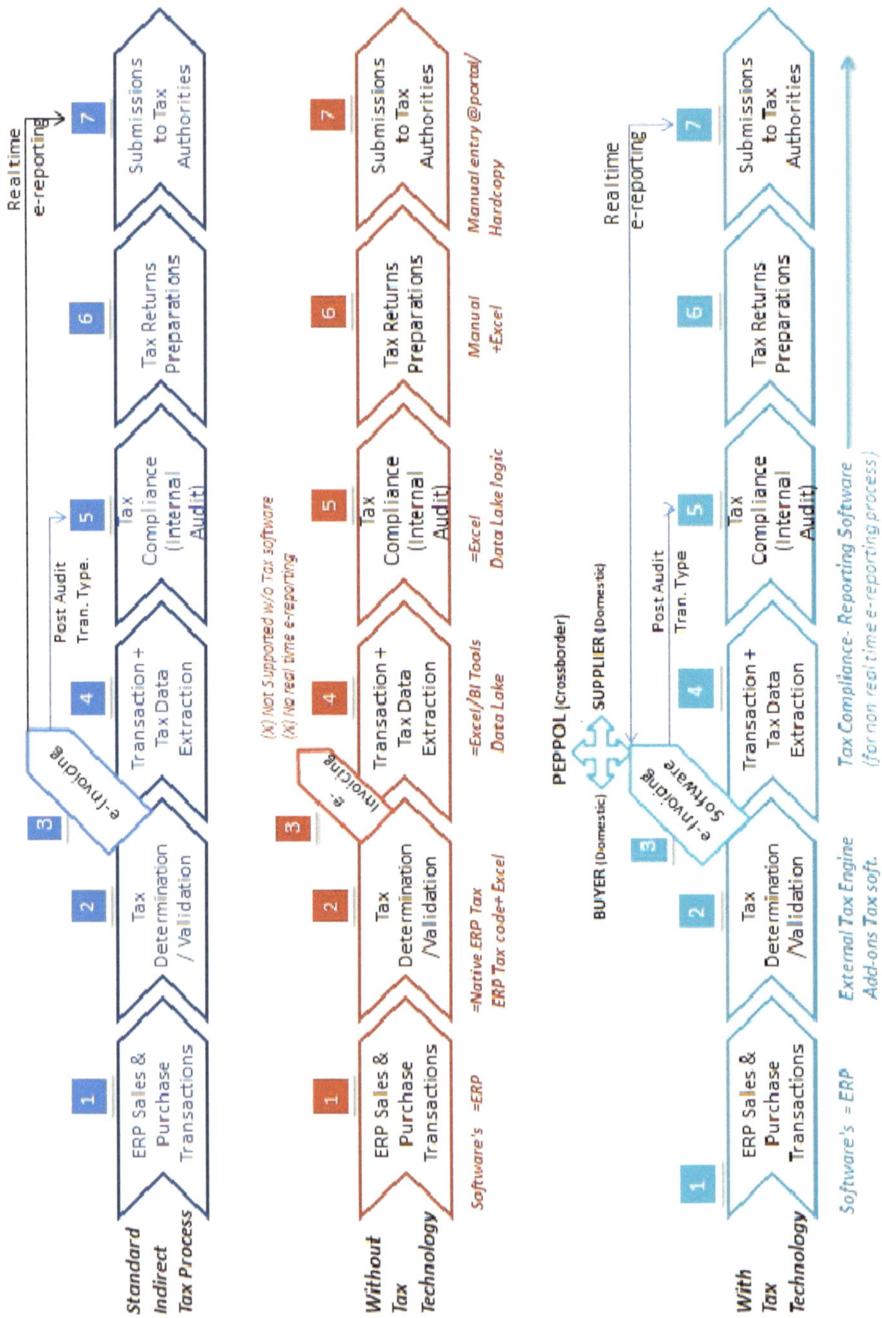
Standard Indirect Tax Process
1 ERP Sales & Purchase Transactions
2 Tax Determination / Validation
3 e-Invoicing
4 Transaction + Tax Data Extraction
5 Tax Compliance (Internal Audit)
6 Tax Returns Preparations
7 Submissions to Tax Authorities
Post Audit Tran. Type.
Realtime e-reporting
Without Tax Technology
Software's =ERP
=Native ERP Tax ERP Tax code+ Excel
(x) Not Supported w/O Tax software (x) No real time e-reporting
=Excel/BI Tools Data Lake
=Excel Data Lake logic
Manual +Excel
Manual entry @portal/ Hardcopy
With Tax Technology
BUYER (Domestic)
PEPPOL (Crossborder)
SUPPLIER (Domestic)
e-Invoicing Software
Software's = ERP
External Tax Engine Add-ons Tax soft.
Tax Compliance- Reporting Software (for non real time e-reporting process)

Figure 8.0

As shown in Figure 8.0 above, there are generally seven processes in a standard indirect tax process.

8.1 BUSINESS TRANSACTION

Business users create sales (quotation, sales order, billing, and accounting) or purchase (purchase order, incoming invoice, and accounting) transactions in the ERP systems such as SAP, Oracle, Sage, Microsoft Dynamics, Workday, or custom/legacy ERP systems. It's standard ERP functionality to enable users to create such transactions. The ERP itself automates the business process; it is the technology for business process automation, digitalization, and streamlining.

8.2 TAX CALCULATION

8.2.1 Without Tax Technology

During this document creation process, a tax amount is needed for final billing or invoice amount creation. Final cost includes product cost (price) + tax amount. In a landscape without tax technology, tax codes are generally created in the system to hold tax rate values, which determine tax amount (tax rate * tax base) and tax codes also drive GL postings.

Under the tax code usage, two approaches are available under the native ERP Tax functionality application.

8.2.1.1 Manual Tax Code Entry

Using an Excel spreadsheet to identify the tax codes to be punched in during transactional creation. In this case, tens of tax codes are created in the system after the tax department issues advice for different business scenarios. Users punch in these tax codes during document creation, which populate the tax rate applied to the overall tax base (net amount), resulting in a gross amount that includes tax.

Under this process of ensuring the correct tax code –tax rate, the tax department has to undergo laborious and research-oriented work (a) understand the financial supply chain, business flows, and taxability (tax rates).

Now knowledge of financial supply chain business flows is an essential learning element with or without tax technology, defining taxability isn't easy, as it requires understanding the tax impact for a business scenarios, quantitatively which may run from few dozen to hundreds depending upon the operating entity geographical scope, vivid product and services and customers, suppliers, plant's, warehouse house location. Also, since tax rates are dynamic, maintaining a spreadsheet becomes an arduous and risky proposition.

8.2.1.2 Automated Tax Code Entry

The process of using native ERP tax determination functionality also involves understanding the financial supply chain, business flows and taxability (tax rates) and then automating them in the ERP using tax driver's tables and associated workflow, in short, when specific tax drivers are populated in a transaction, the corresponding tax code is populated, which has a tax rate embedded. This tax rate is applied to the transaction net amount, and, together with the tax amount, the invoice or billing amount is determined. The only advantage this process has over a solution with manual tax code entry is that users cannot select a tax rate manually for a specific business transaction.

The system will automatically populate the tax code, and the tax rate will be entered. However, this process's success depends entirely on the tax department's definition of tax codes and tax rates, and they must continuously work to incorporate any changes as dictated by the applicable country's tax administration. Here, we are using ERP-native tax technology to automate the tax determination process.

8.2.2 With Tax Technology

However, when tax technology is involved, we bolt an external tax engine into the ERP system. Nowadays we have tax engines, or Tax determination software from firms like Thomson Reuters ONESOURCE range, VERTEX Indirect Tax O Series, Avalara, Sovos (Taxware), and add-ons like Meridian, VATCalc.

8.2.2.1 Tax Engine

A 3rd-party bolt-on tax solution fully automates the sales and purchase tax determination process. The tax determination process involves the identification of accurate tax rates, tax amounts for applicable tax levels (Federal, state/province, (City, county, district, etc. for the US), and nowadays it's able to populate ERP tax codes specific to the business scenario. The tax engine is an artificial intelligence system that incorporates all applicable country tax administration rules and rates into its application. This provides the tax department with significant relief, as they no longer have to worry about identifying taxability across tens of business scenarios. Whenever there is a tax rate change, it's automatically absorbed in the tax engine tax content via periodical updates from its parent entity (tax engine vendor).

All that is needed is to enable the passage of key tax drivers into the tax engine from ERP. Once that's done alongside the standard setup (taxpayers, customers, vendors), the transaction, when created in the ERP, hits the tax engine for tax determination and tax rate, tax amounts for tax levels, and the ERP tax code is populated and pushed back to the ERP for the document to be posted.

Here, we are using a 3rd-party tax engine to automate the tax determination process fully. These tax engines are integrated with the ERP systems using standard and custom API's which can capture and populate a XML file (or other format structures) containing header and line item data (request call) of sales purchase documents and push it into the tax engine, which applies its tax logic and populate the tax rate, amount, code and sends back the XML back to the integrator (response call), later this tax data gets absorbed in the ERP line item. All this happens in real time while the user is creating a document in the ERP system.

The tax engine vendors have standard certified API's for major ERP's or custom API's can also be developed, as most ERPs nowadays have API's for external system integration for both real-time and offline communications.

8.3 E-INVOICING

Conventionally, the business used to send and receive invoices to customers and sellers in paper or PDF format through its ERP system. With the UK's VAT in the digital age (ViDA) consultations, programs, and multiple country-specific statutes, including European Union plans, e-Invoicing is gaining momentum. E-Invoice is not a PDF invoice which is transmitted electronically; it's an electronic invoice with a format with specific data points as mandated by the country-specific tax authority for domestic B2B, B2G, B2C transactions, and a format specified by the EU for cross-border transactions, and a global format to support the PEPPOL framework. E-Invoicing will change the way businesses send and receive invoices. By 2030-35, all EU member states, and other countries, plan to implement mandatory e-invoicing.

Moreover, it may have one or more functional aspects with vivid format and data-point requirements.

- Sending/receiving e-invoices to domestic customers and suppliers - B2C, B2G, B2B
- Sending /receiving e-invoices to/from PEPPOL (Pan European Public Procurement Online), which is an e-delivery network that simplifies cross-border e-procurement
- Sending e-invoices to the tax authority - Statutory (post audit), authority clearance, authority issuer model. Thus, for a firm with a multinational presence, e-invoicing has relevance in solution scenarios.

8.3.1 Without Tax Technology

E-Invoicing without tax technology will not work. A standard ERP solution has no functionality to create an e-Invoice, integrate with PEPPOL, suppliers' e-invoicing solution, and have a real-time interface with the tax authority, i.e., a document with a specified format required by country-specific tax administration or generic e-Invoicing frameworks like PEPPOL or matching up with the supplier e-Invoicing recipient system. In short, without leveraging a 3rd-party e-invoicing software, e-Invoicing will not be supported.

8.3.2 With Tax Technology

Nowadays, there are multiple 3rd-party tax solutions for e-Invoicing; e.g., Thomson Reuters offers PAGERO, and the Big 4 and other key tax tech firms have their own products; e.g., EY offers GIES, and Vertex, Avalara, and many other firms have come up with e-Invoicing solutions. ERP vendors have also developed add-on software, e.g., SAP's DRC (Document Reporting Compliance), which supports e-Invoicing but requires a separate license. These software can fetch sales, procurement, and financial legal documents and associated datasets from the ERP system, and transform them into formats that support e-Invoicing for customers and suppliers e-Invoicing software, universal networks like PEPPOL, and country-specific tax authority mandates. Later can communicate, send, and receive information from customers and suppliers e-Invoicing software, a universal network like PEPPOL, and country-specific tax authorities via integration APIs. As the world moves quickly towards real-time reporting, these e-invoicing software solutions will gradually gain the capability to support e-invoicing, tax compliance, and reporting in a single package.

8.4 TRANSACTION TAX DATA EXTRACTION

Once sales, purchase invoices/billing, and accounting documents are posted in the ERP, the real work starts for downstream compliance – reporting to the tax authorities. The third aspect of tax technology involves the extraction of transactional tax data for tax compliance. The tax department requires this tax report to identify any anomalies and conduct specific validations and verifications before the data set is approved for tax returns preparation. Each country has its own tax administration/tax authority, which specifies a tax return format with tax boxes.

8.4.1 Without Tax Technology

Without tax technology, this process will require extracting data from multiple ERP tables, as neither modern nor old-school ERPs are designed with tax tables for specific countries. The transactional tax data reside in country, entity, customer, vendor, material, and other tables. The ERP system can populate the list of legal documents, e.g., invoicing/billing, accounting, credit/debit notes, etc., data that are applicable for tax returns; however, in a landscape with no tax technology solution, such extraction requires custom program development or reports or queries that can fetch additional data specific to the legal documents for each country. This involves development efforts, and nowadays, since tax authority submission requirements are becoming dynamic across fields, it's a nightmare to run tax operations smoothly under such a custom reporting setup. These custom-developed reports can populate data in desired file formats, such as Excel, CSV, or Text. Later, the tax department also has to slice and dice data from multiple output files to produce a final file, which serves as the source for their tax compliance activities.

In short, in a landscape without tax technology, this Transaction Tax data extraction process not only requires custom development of multiple programs within the ERP system, but also manual data processing of multiple tax output files by the tax department, followed by further refinement. It's a highly error-prone way and often leads to inaccuracies. This process provides no reverse traceability function to the tax department.

8.4.2 With Tax Technology

Under this scenario, the firm has deployed a Compliance and Reporting solution, i.e., 3rd party software. This software integrates with the ERP and can extract sales, purchase, and finance documents from it. Generally, documents are picked via Entity-Tax Code-Document Type (+ additional criteria, as deemed suitable) combinational mappings. Additional compliance fields are extracted using front-end configuration mechanisms on the API/integration side (Source field (ERP) <> Target field (Compliance software) of these software's). At regular intervals, the compliance software application extracts transactional tax data from the ERP, forming the transactional tax data Lake (tax report) in the tax compliance software database. This compliance software has its own database to store client data. Data is organized in a way that allows extraction for a specific country, entity, period, and document type.

8.5 TAX COMPLIANCE

Tax compliance works (internal audit/data health checks) involve checking for anomalies in transactional data before returns are prepared for final submission to the tax authority. For example, ensuring the supplier and buyer's VAT registrations are valid, that the correct tax rate is applied to the transaction, that the scenario is captured in the correct tax code, etc. There may be dozens of such checks to ensure that the upstream determination process is functioning correctly and that the tax data is compliant, i.e., accurate and legal.

8.5.1 Without Tax Technology

In a scenario where no tax technology software is used, the tax department's only visibility is the myriad of spreadsheets using macros, access sequence formulas to populate the final tax data set. This does allow identifying anomalies; however, the checks and validations are done using Excel-based logic, which is prone to error. This was the standard way until the arrival of modern tax compliance software. The tax department has transactional tax data; however, they have no way to reconcile the data back to the ERP system, which is a major fault, as in the case of an external audit by the tax man, they will look up the data from the source ERP system and not from tens of spreadsheets with hundreds of formulas and logic. In such circumstances, it's a nightmare for the tax department to justify its case in front of the tax authority.

Since line item level transactions data quantity may be in thousands or perhaps millions in global firms, ensuring compliance accuracy via spreadsheets becomes overwhelming and laborious. Later, leading to fines, penalties, and more audits, eventually resulting in a negative impact on working capital, reputation, and market goodwill, as such matters become public news. Nowadays, alongside the tax return, many tax authorities also request transactional data at the line-item level in a specified format for that submission. Without tax software, the tax department is ill-equipped.

8.5.2 With Tax Technology

Nowadays, 3rd-party tax technology solutions can store transactional tax data and enable user-friendly tax compliance for tax departments. E.g. Thomson Reuters ONESOURCE Indirect Tax compliance, Vertex Tax Compliance, Avalara compliance, SAP DRC (Formerly ACR), Big 4's, e.g. EY's GVRT, etc. These tax compliance reporting solutions enable tax departments to conduct tax compliance activities with greater accuracy. Tax departments no longer have to maintain spreadsheets or data lakes; instead, these software have many pre-defined rules to identify anomalies in the transactional data extract. The data can be extracted for a specific country, operating unit, period, and by sales or purchase (data filters), and checks can be performed via front-end portals. This also allows the tax department to perform reverse traceability of documents in the ERP system and, since the records are stored in the tax compliance software database, it supports the tax department with audit defense.

In case of an external audit, the tax department can look up the required document dataset and justify their inputs for tax submissions.

8.6 TAX RETURNS PREPARATIONS

Once compliance checks are done and data quality is confirmed. Tax returns preparation involves three processes: draft review, approval, and authorization. The tax department develops the corresponding Tax return draft; i.e., the draft tax return boxes are populated with values, and final checks are conducted before it's sent to the tax director for approval. Once it's approved, the person who has the login/account credentials for the tax authority portal files the tax returns either manually on the portal or mails the tax return package (a hard copy) to the tax authority.

8.6.1 Without Tax Technology

Without tax technology software, this process is again manual. The tax department has to work out the final numbers using Excel formulas or calculators for the relevant tax boxes in the targeted returns and produce a draft.

8.6.2 With Tax Technology

With tax software, this process of tax preparation and submission is automated. First, the assess, review, and approve process has a workflow, which prevents tampering or unauthorized entries or approvals. Each workflow step has designated users authorized for it. Data integrity is intact, and there is no indication of corruption. Moreover, the software automatically sums the numbers for each tax return box and populates the draft tax return. This automation leaves no room for manual intervention while maintaining data quality and process integrity.

8.7 TAX RETURNS SUBMISSIONS

8.7.1 Without Tax Technology

Once the draft tax return is developed, tax functions manually enter the figures at the tax authority portal using their login credentials, or print the tax return and mail it to the tax authority. Nowadays, alongside the tax return, many tax authorities (e.g., the UAE Federal Tax Authority (FTA)) also request transactional data at the line-item level in a specified format for that submission. Without tax software, the tax department is ill-equipped.

8.7.2 With Tax Technology

Post-draft tax returns are assessed, reviewed, and approved. The tax software supports e-filing to tax authority portals; i.e., it has APIs that can communicate with the tax authority portals and post portal login/credentials, allowing the software to submit the tax return or prepopulate the tax boxes with values. Later, the submitted tax returns are stored in the tax software for future reference. Nowadays, alongside the tax return, many tax authorities also request transactional data at the line-item level in a specified format for that submission. In such cases, this tax compliance reporting software is useful, as it can produce output to meet the needs of worldwide tax authorities.

Thus, you have seen how vivid tax processes can be automated and streamlined using advanced tax technology software.

8.8 SUMMARY

After learning about Tax, ERP, and tax technology software, it's time to look at the big picture involving tax technology. You are now equipped with the knowledge covering entire transactional tax lifecycle. From business transaction creation and tax determination to e-Invoicing, Business transaction posting, and the associated Tax compliance reporting process, with and without tax technology. This all-inclusive bird's-eye view will support you in discovering, designing, and building contemporary solutions with and without tax technology and offer world-class advice towards the development of world-class finance tax technology architecture. Now you are in a position to analyze, assess, and contribute to the digitalization and automation of any tax lifecycle process using tax technology. In the next chapter, we will move on to AI (Artificial Intelligence). AI involvement in IT and business tax functions is gaining rapid momentum, and readers will learn about its scope within the overall tax governance framework.

CHAPTER 9

ARTIFICIAL INTELLIGENCE & TAX TECHNOLOGY

This chapter introduces the influence of Artificial Intelligence (AI) in Indirect tax technology. The chapter will guide the users on tax governance with AI footprints, covering each process in the tax lifecycle. Presents a view on how AI will impact tax functions, tax process experts, and tax technologist's work. It compares the delivery capabilities of AI with those of the Tax engine and Tax compliance & reporting software, listing pros and cons for each. AI is fast empowering many IT processes across organizations, and its impact on Business Tax and IT professionals is discussed in this chapter.

In this chapter, we will understand the concepts of AI, GenAI, and their application in the Indirect tax processes of a tax function, as markets globally are buzzing with technologies such as Artificial Intelligence (AI) & it's subsets - Machine Learning (ML), Deep Learning, and Generative AI. It becomes imperative for tax & tax tech professionals to understand their definition, architecture, and high-level functional workings to gauge the role they will play in vibrant tax work supported by tax technologies. For example, modern indirect tax technology software's like Tax engines, Tax compliance reporting software, e-invoicing software, and a few master data validation tools are already using traditional and modern AI in part or whole within their modules for tax works. And are getting further optimized by their firms product, research and engineering teams in getting AI incorporated in sub processes. It's also a fact that AI can augment these tax technology software delivery powers, but can't replace them. Neither can AI replace modern ERP systems (integrated modules workflow automation systems).

In short, the objective of this chapter is to understand AI & its sub-sets (Machine Learning (ML), Deep Learning, Generative AI (GenAI) at a high level, the tax governance framework, its processes and sub-processes, and the associated involvement of AI. This will empower tax function associates to apply AI to their respective work processes. Current market requirements expect tax functions associates transformation into Taxologists –someone who is an SME in tax, which they are already by academic credentials, training, and experience, in addition to having skills towards leveraging AI, i.e., indirect tax technology tools, which come up with AI functions embedded into their applications.

9.1 WHAT IS AI

AI stands for Artificial Intelligence; it's a branch of computer science engineering that involves the study of computer systems that attempt to model and apply the intelligence of the human mind. It refers to the simulation of human intelligence in machines (software + hardware) that are programmed to think, learn, and act like humans. It's the science and engineering that go into making intelligent machines.

The objective of AI is to create systems capable of automating tasks that require human intelligence, such as deriving insights, reasoning, decision-making, problem-solving, and understanding natural languages. AI can enable the desired functioning of both hardware systems, e.g., an automated car manufacturing unit's production process, programmed by software, or processing large datasets and producing desired outputs, e.g., scanning finance tax data from ERP accounting systems to find anomalies.

The sudden emergence of AI is due to the following factors: advances in computing hardware (supercomputing microprocessors), software (algorithms), and the availability of large amounts of data (the Internet, the cloud, sensors, etc.) – a combination of hardware, software, and data. Software is installed on hardware, and data runs on software.

AI cannot replace workflow systems (e.g., ERP systems streamlining the workflow of multiple business functions), UI applications (websites, mobile apps, and desktop applications), and Transaction systems (e.g., e-commerce payment processors, airline reservation systems, and tax engines). AI is also distinct from tax automation. Automation involves arranging a set of clearly defined, repeatable steps that can be applied consistently to time-intensive or error-prone tasks that would otherwise be done manually. However, AI technology can expand automation capabilities by leveraging machine learning, Deep learning, and Generative AI mechanisms to enable more efficient operations.

In the context of indirect taxation, understanding the scope of AI is essential, given that most firms leverage ERP/Accounting systems, which are transactional workflow integration and automation systems. AI can't replace them; modern tax engines and tax compliance reporting systems embed traditional or modern AI logic into their workflow modules and, in effect, are AI or partial AI themselves.

9.2 AI DEVELOPMENT OBJECTS (POPULAR)

- AI programming languages: Java, C++, Python, Go, Julia, Scala, etc.
- AI Framework: Caffe, Deep learning for Java (DL4J), H2O, Theano, Azure machine learning, Torch, etc.
- AI Databases: MNIST, Fashion, IMDB, COCO, etc.
- Freely available databases for AI (a few examples)

  https://www.data.gov

  https://allenai.org/data.html

- AI community (e.g.): https://www.kaggle.com

From a tax perspective, tax professionals or tax tech associates are not required to learn these AI languages, AI frameworks, etc., technical development aspects. AI is a branch of computer science that requires programming skills, but instead should understand prospective AI applications (AI tools) in tax processes, furthering automation and digitalization.

There are already 3rd party firm tools (software) in the market based on AI that support tax work. Tax associates need to understand these tools properly from a user perspective to optimize their use and enhance their efficiency. Also, tax professionals can have their engineering/DevOps teams develop in-house AI tools to meet their tax work needs, for which they need to provide data and requirements to the development team. In short, tax professionals can incorporate AI into their overall tax governance framework, either in-house or by outsourcing it.

Examples of AI: Language translation tools, speech recognition software's, human emotion detection tools, medical diagnosis, personalized advertising (today you are reading about health tip, tomorrow you see advertisements of health products on your mobile phones), pattern recognition and cyber security, Gmail -Spam, Netflix –personalized recommendations, Self-driving cars –computer vision, Google map best route and ETA prediction.

9.3 HOW TO IMPLEMENT AI

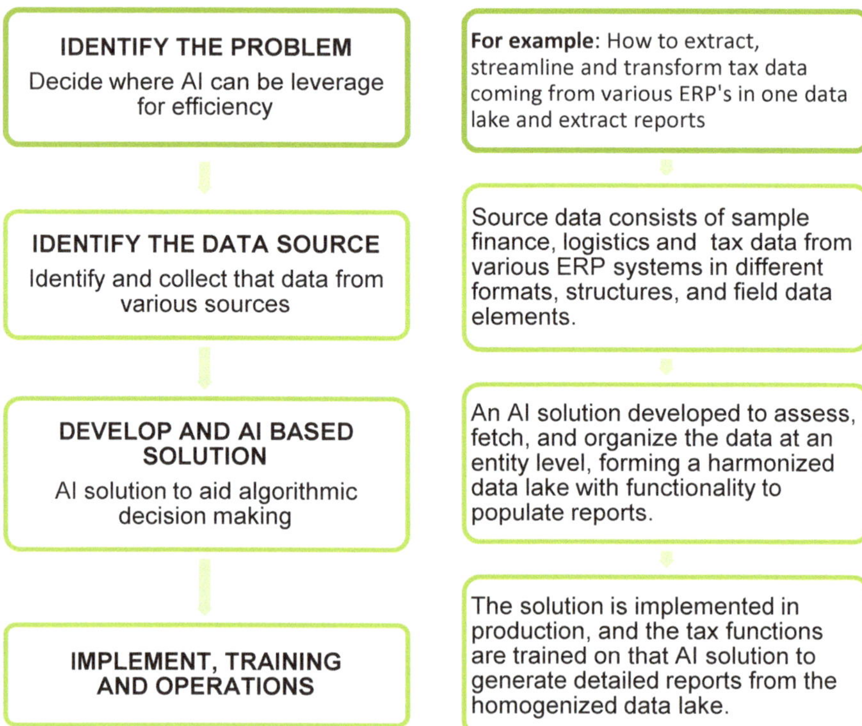

Figure 9.3

In the figure above, one can see the steps involved in developing an AI solution in-house or for the industry. Examples are also provided for easy reference.

9.4 AI SUBSETS

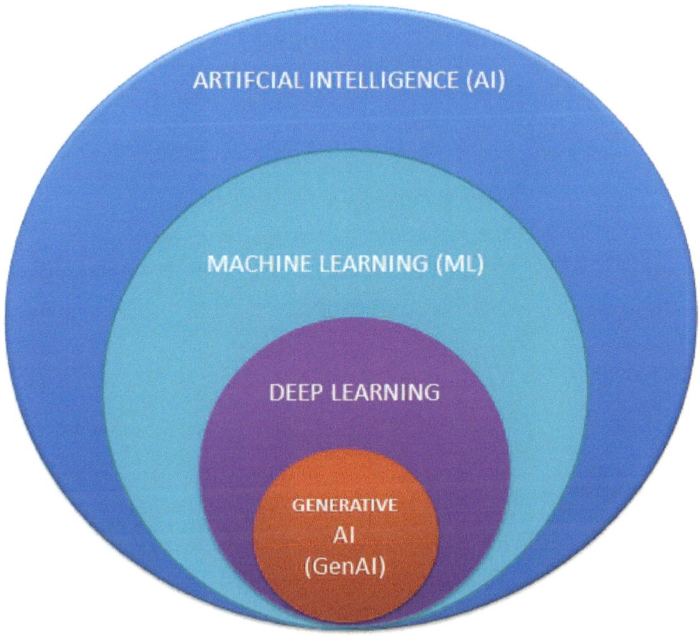

Figure 9.4

9.4.1 Machine Learning (ML)

As the name suggests, it involves educating the machine to learn and then perform specific tasks using software programs and statistical models without repetitive instructions. Machine learning (ML) uses data to make predictions and decisions, and with time (as more data cycles are processed), the accuracy of the machine learning model increases. Netflix's personalized recommendations are a good example of how ML is deployed in the entertainment industry. In this case, Netflix observes the genres of the movies and web series one watches over time (data), identifies their interests, and offers recommendations (decision).

- **How Machine Learning Works**

It's interesting to note that the way Machine Learning is designed, built, and deployed is similar to the software development lifecycle (SDLC); the methodology is the same, and a specialized algorithmic approach is used to develop intuitive analysis.

Software applications are designed using a build–test–deployment methodology using learning data (available in development systems), validation data (available in Test systems), test data (available in UAT systems), and finally releasing the application software (algorithms in ML) to production and later enhancing the software with more features (parameters).

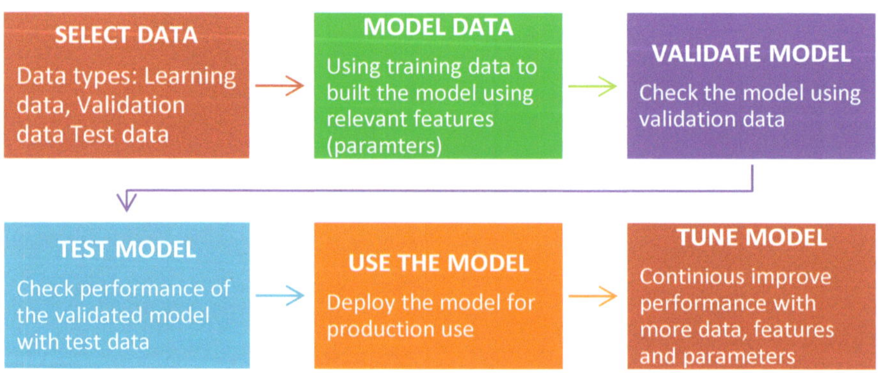

Figure 9.4.1

- **Tax Example**

Firms using ERP systems for finance and tax operations have a specific Tax module within ERP for business transaction tax treatment - tax rate, tax amount, tax code & tax GL determination. In the ERP Tax module, the final tax code for a business transaction is generated through a sequence of steps involving programs and routines that follow a specific flow pattern (an algorithm in ML terms) to scan tax driver tables containing data (Data in ML terms). This is a typical example of how traditional machine learning is embedded into the ERP Tax calculation flow. Also, in this model (ERP Tax), performance continues to improve as new data (tax driver parameters) are added that sync with the dynamic tax requirements, further automating the process.

9.4.2 Deep Learning

Deep learning is a subset of Machine Learning. It utilizes Neural networks (named after the functioning of human brain neurons, also called ANN – Artificial neural networks) at multiple layers (in a hierarchical way) to analyze data and perform tasks such as natural language (speech) and image recognition and processing. It processes data and creates patterns like a human brain for decision-making.

For example, if we see a flying object, we identify it as a drone, plane, or helicopter by recognizing its patterns and features, which are already in our minds from previous observations and learning. Similarly, the ANN learns patterns and feature relationships using data (as it has no natural eyes). Deep learning further augments the power and performance of machine learning. Now the machine has a brain. For example without deep learning, Machine learning can't provide a solution where one can't formulate an algorithmic solution (e.g. identify an image e.g. tax exemption certificate), where much variety of data is there (e.g. populating tax return box value from multiple ERP/Accounting systems data), where a structure needs to be populated from an existing data (populating a country specific tax return form for e-filing from existing data).

- **Examples of Deep Learning:** Image recognition software is a classic example of deep learning. The software captures the image and, later, using the available photo database, it uses features (eyes, mouth, ears) and patterns (color, edges, shape) to identify that human face. Deep learning also involves natural language processing (NLP), which enables interaction between human languages (English, Chinese, Hindi, Spanish, Arabic, etc.) and computers. The objective of NLP is to understand the human language instructions, codify those instructions, and run the software application to perform specific tasks using those codified prompts (instructions). Google language translation, Chatbots, and iPhone Siri are some examples.

9.4.3 Generative AI

Generative AI is a subset of deep learning (Figure 9.4), a type of artificial intelligence that can create new content, such as text, images, audio, and video. As the name suggests, AI that generates new content –it can be a text, photographs, music, or code. Generative AI (GenAI) uses models and algorithms to produce content similar to human-generated content. ChatGPT is a good example of GenAI: given a text description, it can generate an image. GenAI plays a significant role today in creating artistic images and animated movies. GenAI marks a major shift in AI usage, from automation (Machine learning) to analysis, interpretation (Deep learning), towards the generation of new data (Generative AI).

- **Examples of Generative AI:** Gmail -Spam, Netflix – personalized recommendations, Self-driving cars –computer vision; Google Maps- best route and ETA prediction.

ARTIFICIAL INTELLIGENCE
= MACHINE LEARNING (+DEEP LEARNING (+GENERATIVE AI)

In the above depicted robotic cartoon (illustrative). Artificial learning = Machine learning (a programmed machine with software and hardware (here a robot performing repetitive tasks) + Deep learning (Robot with a brain) and Generative AI (Robot with a mouth to speak out 'new content' (not standard outputs) after hearing the instruction from its ears or seeing from its eyes).

9.5 WAYS TO LEVERAGE AI IN TAX WORKS

- **Develop AI tools In-house:** Recommended, if it's cost worthiness and involves less maintenance as tax is dynamic, it will require tax research teams, product development teams. Especially for tax processes which resides at periphery of the tax work, where cost of making mistake is low.

- **Use a 3rd party Tax AI software:** Modern tax technology software's are AI tax tools, they combine the benefits of workflow automation, streamlined processes, digitalization, AI, Machine learning and Gen AI, This is because the tax technology vendors are releasing such products to worldwide markets clients and they have proper research, product development and engineering teams to ensure that the workflow, programs, tax content and output is up-to date in regards to compliance and legality. Their engineering teams are constantly evaluating the potential of AI>ML>GenAI insertions into their established, proven workflows. This is an effective way to implement AI using an iterative approach. Such proven & industry-tested AI solutions for tax technology can be deployed across core business processes, where the cost of making a mistake is severe.

- **A Hybrid Approach:** Use in-house AI tools and also 3rd party tools. For example, using a tax engine (an artificial AI tax computation machine) for tax calculation and an in-house AI tool for tax compliance checks on transactional data.

9.6 TAX GOVERNANCE FRAMEWORK & AI FOOTPRINTS

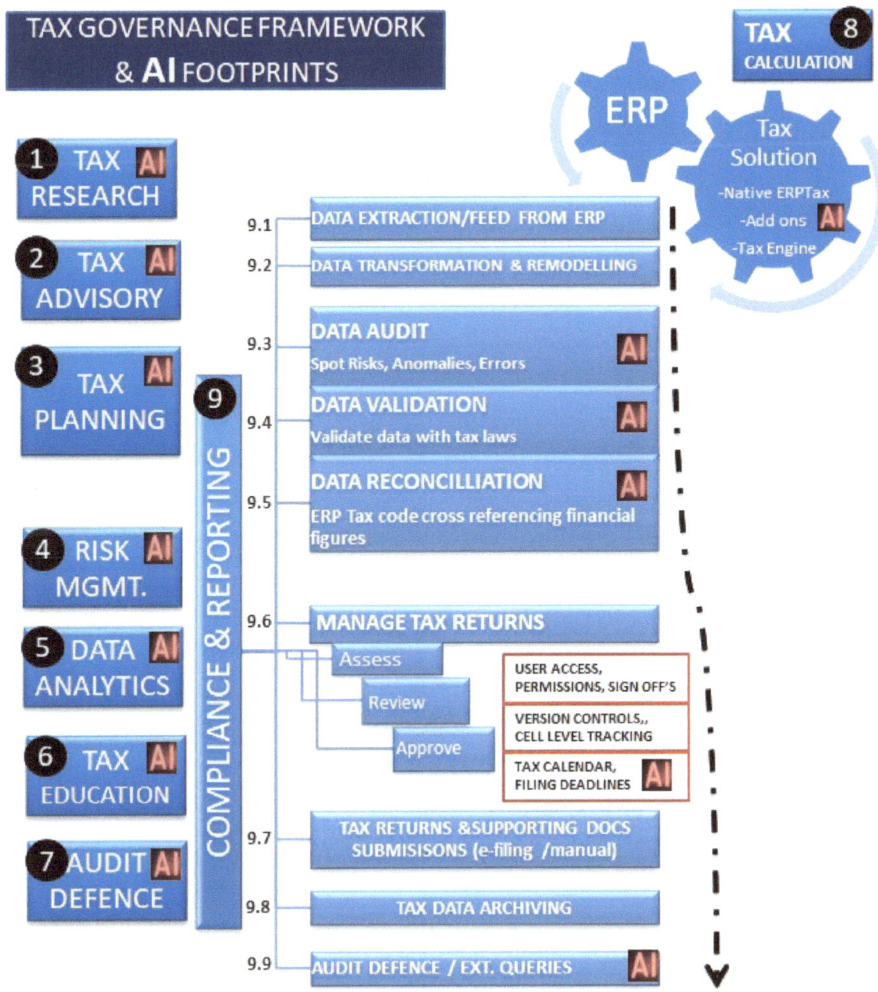

Figure 9.6

As shown in Figure 9.6, a taxpayer's tax function develops a tax governance framework, also known as a tax control framework. The framework may include more components, and different organizations may use their own nomenclature and organize their components differently. Our objective here is not to define an exact tax governance framework, but to know how AI will support each of it's components listed above. The objective of using AI-led solutions is to enable the tax functions to focus on providing tailored advice, creating tax strategies, and tackling complex tax matters, rather than getting stuck in laborious repetitive tasks.

9.6.1 Tax Research

Tax research (Figure 9.6 -1) involves creating detailed tax impact analysis reports and executive summaries to provide actionable intelligence and guide evidence-based decisions for the business. Tax research also consists in developing a business tax flow blueprint—a mandatory document for legal and compliance purposes. A tax function alongside sales, procurement and finance functions needs to develop a comprehensive business flow document that outlines the entire business operational blueprint (manufacturing sites, plants, warehouses, entities, customer bases, supply chain routes, goods/services, etc.) with associated tax footprints. This tax blueprint (business flow diagrams with tax footprints) is often referenced by the business in various situations, e.g., mergers, demergers, spin-offs, new acquisitions, new entities, new supply chain routes or plants, warehouses, logistics, etc., and compliance and regulatory impacts due to tax legislative changes.

- **Non AI Solution**

In a non-AI scenario, the tax function will conduct this research itself, scanning multiple tax authority websites, searching for relevant content, analyzing and interpreting nuanced laws, regulations, codes, guidance, and more, and drawing conclusions. This is an arduous research-based activity requiring multiple resources having their own educational, training, and expertise, since tax legislative changes are always dynamic; what stands today isn't valid tomorrow. In short, the tax functions will require continuous manual monitoring of the World Wide Web of applicable tax authorities, authoritative data, and accredited content to support legal and compliant decision-making in line with business requirements. In a multi-country setup, the work becomes more arduous and research-intensive. Additionally, many firms where tax practices aren't well established or have limited expertise often outsource this work to a 3rd-party tax advisor and pay millions in consulting fees.

- **AI Solution**

Modern AI tax software can scan vast amounts of tax content to find suitable answers that comply with tax laws, supporting informed decision-making and referencing accredited authorities and expert sources. Citation and links to supporting authorities –tax law, rules, and statute, and source documents are provided by the AI in its result. This *'tax law research'* AI tax software continuously monitor and scan thousands of tax department websites worldwide to collect, normalize, and analyze tax developments for informed decision making. The tax research Gen AI tool supports a tax function to look up answers to their tax questions for any specific business scenario. Legal data backs these GenAI tools to ensure compliance accuracy, and they can analyze complex tax structures to support tax planning.

9.6.2 Tax Advisory

Tax advisory (Figure 9.6 -2), whether ongoing or related to a particular transaction, primarily focuses on opportunities and risk management of existing operations. Tax advice from tax functions can range from a simple question like 'Is this material zero-rated in France under resale? To a complex question like 'Should we leverage Spain-based suppliers for raw material intake to UAE plants shipping manufactured goods to India? Business involves multiple cross-functional areas, such as sales, procurement, supply chain, finance, logistics, and manufacturing, and each function may consult the tax function. Business functions need such advice to ensure tax impact is minimal, whether it's direct tax, withholding tax, indirect tax, customs/tariffs, or transfer pricing. Tax not only impacts business working capital (in many cases, it is an expense and non-recoverable), but also increases the commodity's overall selling price, leading to a competitive disadvantage.

- **Non-AI Solution:** For the tax function to answer such questions, it needs to know the entire financial and logistics supply chain and the associated tax jurisdictions. Later, understand the country tax administrations, tax laws, rules, and statutes in those in-scope jurisdictions, and their interpretations, to summarize the overall tax implications of that business supply chain model.
- **AI Solution:** Using AI tax advisory tools, tax functions can get answers from AI for tax research. Tax functions can access supply chain parameters spanning multiple jurisdictions to get quick, reliable answers with source data citations. This ability also makes the tax function self-reliant and internally competent.

9.6.3 Tax Planning (Statements and Reporting)

Alongside contributing to working capital aspects -revenue and expenses, tax also plays a vital role in ensuring Tax statements are accurate, as it impacts working capital, which involves tax as an expense (cost), actual and expected refunds, recoverability aspects, tax credits, etc. Tax functions are also required to provide inputs for the financial reporting, statements, and reports. This helps the business to develop proactive strategies, which is also called Tax planning (Figure 9.6 [3]).

- **Non-AI Solution:** In a non-AI solution, tax functions require custom programs to extract data from the ERP and generate tax data for planning, tax statements, and reporting. This approach fails to leverage tax laws in designing such solutions, and validation is not feasible.
- **AI Solution:** AI tools can scan and read vast amounts of tax data stored in ERP/Accounting system databases and use

machine learning to generate specific outputs as commanded. This allows businesses to have real-time insights into the overall tax status of an entity, business unit, market, etc., leading to accurate financial figures reporting (supplemented by tax figures).

9.6.4 Risk Management

Tax functions have to adhere to local, regional, and international tax laws. Noncompliance will lead to penalties, fines, and imprisonment. Some example of risk management include identifying supplier using an invalid tax registrations on invoices or overcharging tax from customers, preventing fraudulent transactions, stopping transactions involving sanctioned partied, checks on fake invoices leading to tax refunds, or ensuring tax filing deadlines aren't missed, or working on the best supply chain routes to mitigate heavy tax, tariffs and being compliant.

- **Non-AI Solution:** In a non-AI solution, tax functions will not be able to capture such anomalies as data is big and manual or semi-automated checks are not productive and compliant.

- **AI Solution:** AI Tax software can power predictive financial and tax analytics and potential areas of fraud to support the risk management process. Businesses can leverage applicable AI tools to shield themselves from such financial risks, even those hidden in subtle patterns. AI involves machine learning algorithms, such as decision trees and neural networks that use historical and current data to identify and prevent non-compliant, illegal transactions. It enhances risk management through instant access to valuable knowledge and insights.

9.6.5 Tax Strategy by Data Analytics

A tax function strives to develop the best tailored tax strategy. Here, they can use data analytics (Figure 9.6 -5) to identify patterns and trends in a dataset, leading to a more effective tax strategy and decision-making that improves tax data insights and tax-saving opportunities, for example, by minimizing tax rates and augmenting tax credits.

- **Non-AI:** Tax functions will have to develop and design custom data analytical tools using spreadsheets and tools such as Power BI.
- **AI Solution**: AI tax tools are prebuilt with data analytics functionality and work on datasets imported or stored in an existing data lake, allowing the tax function to generate user-friendly graphs, diagrams, figures, and charts with output parameters for tax strategy development with other cross-functional business teams.

9.6.6 Tax Education& Awareness

In this regard, the tax functions need to educate (Figure 9.6 [6]) internal and external associates on tax topics, e.g., what is a tax code, tax type, or tax jurisdiction, commodity codes, taxing jurisdiction, tax type, tax reports, tax engine etc. As tax jargon differs from plain English, business and technical parties involved need a further breakdown of the meanings that have to be provided to various business functions in layperson's terms, repetitively, and to new joiners with less tax tech skills.

- **Non AI solution**: Tax functions have to create content themselves, share and train associates.
- **AI solution**: Generative AI can generate content for tax functions, which they can review and edit to tailor to the needs of the audience, e.g., what a tax code is and how triangulation works in the EU.

9.6.7 Audit Defense

Audit defense (Figure 9.6 [7]) capability is the ability to support the audit imposed by the tax authority and to defend it effectively using validated, verified transactional data. Audit orders by tax authorities occur when there is a tax controversy, i.e., a firm isn't able to provide proper justifications to preliminary queries.

- **Non-AI:** In the non AI solution, the tax function has to perform arduous, time consuming, error prone tasks of reconciling and reverse tracking the tax boxes values to the ERP document line item or search their email inboxes for the advice given by 3rd party tax partners for a specific taxability.

- **AI Solution**: AI tools can support a tax function by identifying relevant legislation, case laws, and rulings for specific transactions' tax treatments. In tax litigation, AI can support document preparation and substantiate tax positions with calculations and explanations as prescribed by the country's tax administration. If there are queries from tax authorities, AI can support the tax function by providing information on the business tax flow data parameters (Entity, ship from, ship to, product, tax treatment etc.) and the tax laws they have leveraged. Just like a in court of law, a lawyer provides evidence and legal arguments with citations to laws, their application in former case judgments to the judge for his cognizance.

9.6.8 Tax Determination

AI can reshape the way they work by automating complex tax calculations (Figure 9.6 [8]).

- **Non AI: Manual tax treatment**: Some firms are still using old-school accounting systems, where a user has to enter a tax code for a business transaction; they check the tax code from spreadsheets and punch that in the document for tax rate calculation and tax GL hit. Although it's advisable to use a proper ERP system with a semi-automated AI mechanism, if a firm wants to continue with such a business practice, they can leverage a 3rd-party AI tool that can support automated tax % treatment upon calling the AI tool.

- **Non AI: ERP Native Tax**

For businesses using ERP-native tax for tax determination, AI tax tools can automate the feeding of tax rates into ERP tax codes in line with the latest tax laws.

- **Partial AI: VAT Add'ons/Plug'Ins:** AI can enhance the Tax Add'ons/Plug'Ins tax calculation software towards automatically updating the tax rate in the tax codes for correct tax treatment applied for a business transaction – an aspect they lack in the current design. Unlike modern, established tax engines, VAT Add'ons/Plug'ins don't have their own tax content; i.e., the worldwide tax laws, tax rules, and tax rates are not codified, and they often require technical feeds from the vendor firm to pass tax rate updates based on the client's business scenario. Their tax research team needs to conduct internal research first and provide the design and built feed to the client, and later, the client IT team inputs that into the ERP. Such firms may use Tax AI tools to automate this process further.

- **AI: Tax Engines:** Modern tax engines are artificial intelligence systems for tax computation; they exhibit qualities of both AI and GenAI. Leveraging this tax software for tax calculation is the optimal use of AI, as these tax software vendors are already at advanced stages of AI in their product development. Tax professionals need to understand the high-level functional workings of the tax engine to understand the AI involved and further optimize it.

9.6.9 Tax Compliance Reporting

Tax compliance and reporting (Figure 9.6 -9) have legal obligations and is the main objective of any tax department. It involves the collection, monitoring, verifying, preparing, and filing tax and supplementary returns across multiple legal entities and jurisdictions. It involves cumbersome manual review tasks and processes. Non-compliance leads to costly penalties. Integrated tax compliance and reporting AI tools are the way forward for firms to minimize compliance risks.

- **Non AI: Manual Excel-based Approach**

Firms without tax compliance and reporting tools: For firms that rely on spreadsheets for these tasks, this is a risk. As a result, tax departments deal with inconsistent data sources and formats. Many tax teams will then turn to Excel, but these work papers often use error-prone tools such as pivot tables and VLOOKUP to populate source data into the spreadsheet. All this cannot be achieved in Excel. With e-invoicing and real-time reporting in place, a manual spreadsheet-based approach for tax calculation, compliance, and reporting is not recommended.

- **AI-enabled Modern Tax Compliance Reporting Solutions**

Deploying modern indirect tax compliance and reporting software (Integrated AI tools) is best recommended to offer end-to-end workflow automation, data streamlining, and leveraging the optimum use of AI. For example, in Figure 9.6, Section 9, one can see all standard compliance steps (9.1-9.9), each following a flow.

Firms can use independent AI tools for specific steps; however, this may not yield the same efficiency as integrated tax compliance and reporting AI tools do. Firms like Thomson Reuters, Vertex, Avalara, Sovos, Meridian, and others in the tax tech space offer integrated solutions (i.e., integrating step 9.1...9.9).

Modern tax technology software has incorporated AI tools into its established, proven workflows. They have workflow automation and AI embedded into their processes.

- **Data Extraction from the ERP**: The step involves financial tax data extraction from the ERP and is often achieved via an API/connectors. There may be multiple sources, e.g., many ERPs, non-ERP accounting systems, spreadsheets, etc.
- **Data Transformation, Remodeling, and Harmonization**: As firms may have multiple ERPs, or the same ERP with many versions (SAP S/4, ECC, R/3), they need

to deal with inconsistent data sources and formats. An AI tool can enable data transformation, modeling, and harmonization at the country and legal-entity levels.

- **Data Audit:** The first step towards data compliance is a tax audit; in this step, the tax function spots risks, anomalies, and errors. For example, AI can assist tax functions in defining a formula or filter in plain English to identify a shortlist, segregate data, or fetch data. Going further, there will be no requirement to write simple or complex formulas.
- **Data Validation:** Post data audit and anomalies identification, as part of corrective and preventive actions, suspicious data (transactions) needs to be validated against tax laws for accuracy in tax treatment. If rectification is required in the ERP tax solution, IT is asked to fix the matter. AI tools can support this process by checking tax laws and enabling cross-checks.

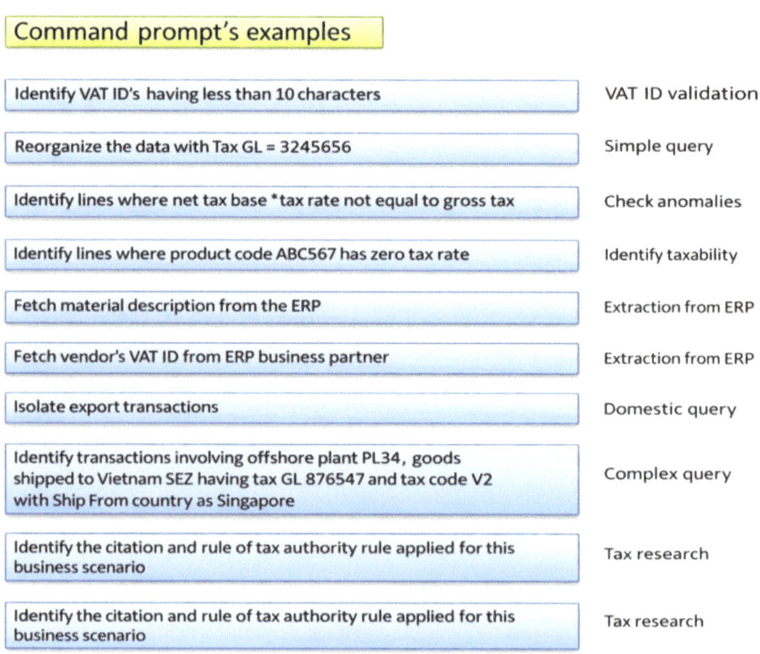

Figure 9.6.8

In the Figure 9.6.8, one can see how AI can be leveraged for data health checks.

- **Data Reconciliation:** Once data health checks are completed, the next step is to move towards reporting. It's time to ensure the figures in the tax boxes match the applicable tax GL accounts in the ERP. This is called tax reporting data reconciliation, ensuring that all applicable documents are accounted for in that period. In a non-AI scenario, it involves extracting data from both systems in Excel and using macros/pivot tables,/Vlookup to do recon. With an AI solution, such cross-checks can be automated.

- **Manage Tax Returns & Filings**

Tax return preparation (Tax work papers process) involves preparing legal and statutory tax returns& supporting documents for submission to the tax authority. The work should provide a clear audit trail and help ensure accuracy, consistency, and traceability.

It involves three steps.

1. Prepare: Preliminary draft tax returns are prepared.
2. Review: Draft tax returns are reviewed
3. Approve: Draft tax returns are approved for submission

Alongside this, in the above process, three additional mechanisms also run in parallel.

- **User Access**, Permissions, and Sign-offs for compliance and to prevent unauthorized access.

- **Version controls**, cell-level tracking (tax return tax boxes, transactional tax line item data feeding those boxes) of changes made during the prepare and review process.

9.6.10 Tax Calendar and Filing Deadlines

This functionality allows the tax function to know the types of tax reports (per legal entity), their due dates, track deadlines, and the applicable jurisdictions and filing status for each report. AI tax calendar and dashboard tools can ensure that tax function has 24*7 visibilities into such areas. Also, AI is valuable for understanding complex tax forms and disclosures; it can translate various languages and interpret data. For example, AI tax tools can help a Dutch-speaking tax associate understand specific tax box expectations in the Arabic-language VAT return.

- **Tax Data Archiving**

Tax data archiving involves storing tax returns, supplementary documents, and associated documents line item transactional data.

9.7 RISKS OF AI IN TAX WORKS

An AI tool is risky if it isn't tailored to the specific tax work. For example, a tax professional can't just upload financial data to OpenAI, ChatGPT and ask it to prepare a VAT return. For that, tax professionals first need to understand the workings of the tax technology product, which embeds AI into its modules and submodules to evaluate quality and build confidence in the results.

AI works on data; if the source data is of poor quality, the AI solution will suffer, and AI solutions, such as tax research, that are not grounded in authoritative data will pose more risk than benefit. For example, while looking for a 3rd party tax engine or Tax Research tool, it's essential to know whether that AI tool can provide tax authority law, chapter, and paragraph, clause level information to substantiate the summary. i.e., how far and good AI has federal, state, and other authorities codified statutes and regulations. AI lacks the human judgmental, strategy development, and personification qualities to address ad-hoc and unique tax situations fully. For example, during a production outage due to a tax error, AI will not be valuable, as it can't provide production support, identify the issue, perform root cause analysis, or take corrective and preventive actions on its own.

Data security and privacy: AI tools used must be scoped to private environments, so that while the AI functionality may be available to its users, the queries or outputs from it do not leave the secure environment. Data privacy and security are primary concerns while using AI due to the sensitive nature of financial information. E.g., GDPR compliance in Europe, CCPA in the U.S., and AI solutions deployed outside private networks must include robust data protection measures, such as access controls and encryption, to prevent breaches and ensure confidentiality.

9.8 BENEFITS OF AI IN TAX WORKS

As outlined in the tax governance framework, Tax AI solutions can provide answers faster from large datasets, enabling tax functions to do more in less time. In tax research, AI is enhancing the accuracy and efficiency of tax functions by codifying legislative and statutory tax laws. This enhances tax functions hindsight, insight, and foresight, enabling them to focus on higher-value activities such as strategic decision-making and cross-border compliance.

AI empowers the tax function to focus on higher-value activities. It's worth noting that AI is not only adopted by the taxpayer tax functions, but many tax authorities are adopting AI into their taxpayer management systems to capture maximum tax revenue, identify fraud, and enforce compliance. AI compliments workflows (streamlining processes), automation software, and integrated systems like ERP by adding artificial intelligence to workflow steps, providing an end-to-end comprehensive solution, mitigating risks from process and data gaps, and reducing overall costs.

9.9 AI VS. TAX ASSOCIATES

Given AI's evolution, tax professionals will remain integral to corporate tax functions. They will likely focus on creating, testing, controlling, and monitoring AI tools (In-house or 3rd party). Human oversight remains essential for complex and strategic decision-making, as well as in high-risk areas. AI is designed to support tax functions, making the job easier, but it does not replace tax professionals. Outputs produced by AI still need human review to ensure accuracy and reliability.

Tax professional's aspects like consulting skills, knowledge, bringing insights, tailored advice, interpretations, ethical considerations, personalized services, emotional intelligence, creative & critical thinking, staying adaptable, analytical judgment, experience &expertise, client interaction, interpersonal relationships building, communications and active listening will continue to be led by tax associates (humans) and cannot be automated by AI.

9.10 SUMMARY

In this chapter, we provided you with an understanding of AI – Artificial Intelligence, its composition, and sub-sets like Machine learning, Deep Learning, and Generative AI in relation to tax works. You've learnt about the overall tax governance framework, which scopes in entire tax functions building blocks, the various components and associated processes, sub-processes alongside prospective AI application footprints. AI tools are not meant to replace ERP, Tax function, or Tax technology software; they can't replace workflow and integrated systems. Instead, they augment the delivery power of such systems, processes, and sub-processes.

Tax governance framework aspects can be effectively managed with an integrated suite of dependable AI-powered tools that streamline tax processes, automate workflows, automate transactional tasks, enhance tax planning, and simplify tax work. In the world of AI, tax professionals will need to develop learning and skills in the functional operations of AI tax tools, understanding how AI processes data, and the ability to interpret and leverage AI output to enhance their work and explain AI-driven results to clients (internal or external). This will elevate their service levels, their project contribution value, and their adaptation to the evolving tax landscape.

Contemporary tax technology software includes built-in AI in specific modules, and software vendors are maximizing its use. Readers can now effectively assess and analyze the tax process, identify AI solutions to improve it, and gain insights into the limitations of AI applications. Readers are also aware of the risks, benefits, and the scope of opportunities that AI delivers, providing a clear vision of what AI can and can't do and enabling a stronger solution value proposition in tax technology work. In the next chapter, we will learn about modern tax technology landscapes encompassing determination, compliance reporting, and e-Invoicing.

CHAPTER 10

MODERN ERP – INDIRECT TAX TECHNOLOGY SOFTWARE LANDSCAPES

In this chapter, readers will understand the modern Indirect tax technology landscape, including firms ERP systems, Tax Engines, Tax Compliance reporting solutions, and e-invoicing software. Understanding the placement of ERP (Finance/Accounting, Sales, Procurement Functional areas) with Tax technology software is vital to have a bird's-eye view of overall indirect tax systems, integrations, and operations for associates working on tax technology projects. Chapter references the modern ERP Tax technology landscape, which works similarly to our solar system: the Sun (ERP system) occupies a central place, and planets (tax softwares) are placed at specific locations and orbit it in particular ways for optimal joint working.

There are mainly two types of ERP Tax software integration landscapes.

- External bolt-in tax software, which requires an external integration between ERP and Tax software using standard or custom APIs.
- Add-on tax software that sits within the ERP system (resident alien) and performs the required task. These add-ons are predefined programs that are imported into the ERP system and create a user- and functional menu of their own within the ERP.

Here, we will discuss the many possibilities for integrating ERP and tax software, with commentary.

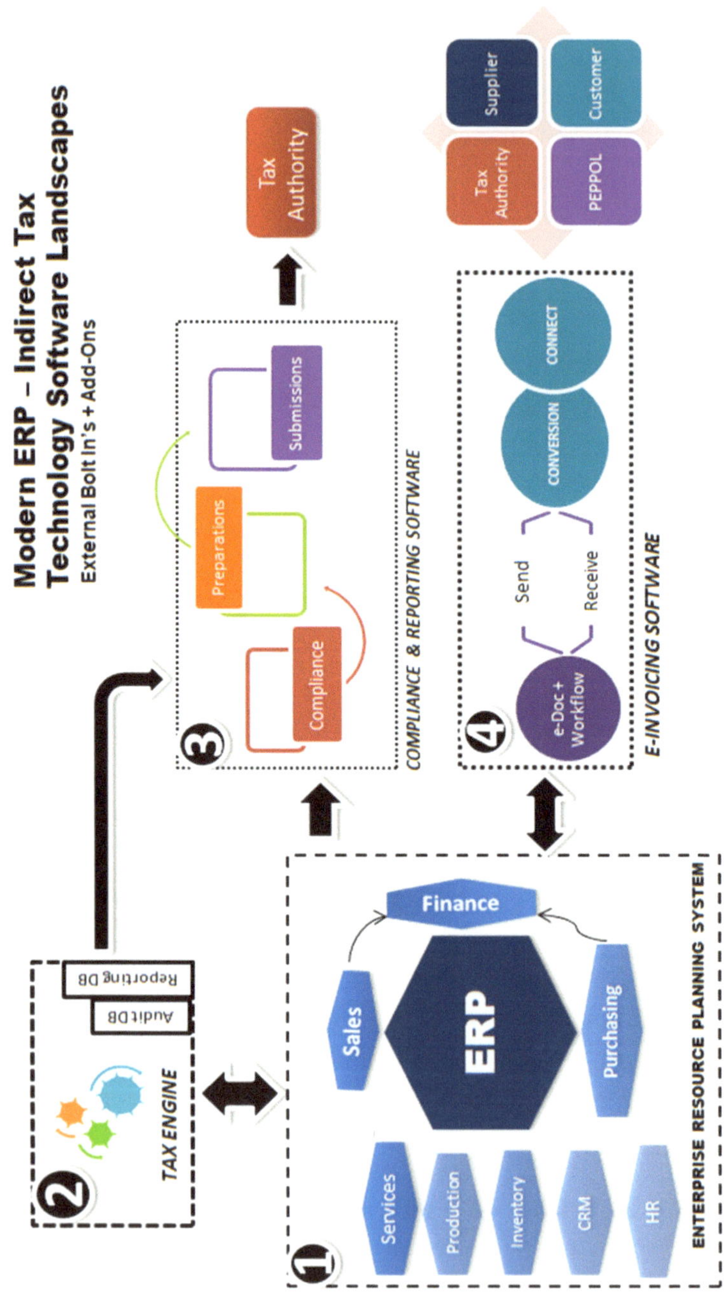

Figure 10.0: Consolidated ERP Tax Technology Landscape

10.1 ERP - 3RD PARTY BOLT-IN TAX ENGINE

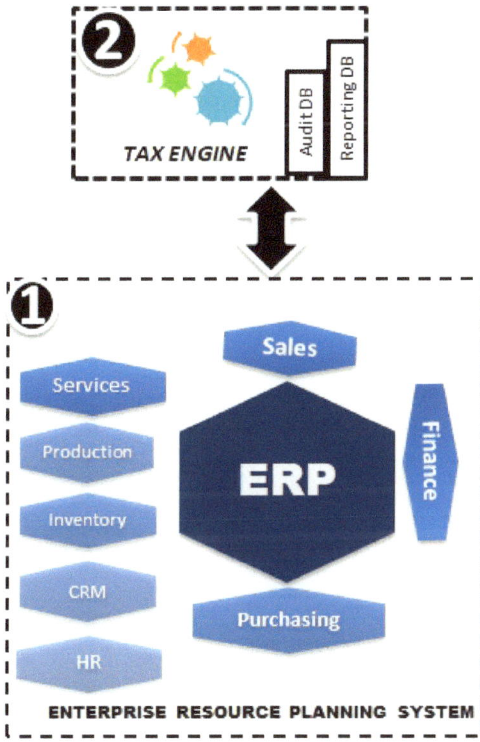

Figure 10.1

An ERP system-to-Tax Engine integration is 1-1. Though there are very few Add-on software products in the market, the majority of firms leverage a 3rd-party external tax engine for tax computation. In Figure 10.1, the ERP is shown integrated with the Tax Engine. It's important to understand that the communication between the ERP and the Tax engine is two-way. When sales, purchase and accounting data is created in the ERP, it makes a tax call (Request call) to the tax engine, which after reviewing the key tax drivers, finance, logistics data produces a tax decision on the tax rate, tax amount for associated tax levels (Federal, provincial/ state, city, country etc.) depending upon the country tax administration requirements. Later, the tax engine returns this data to the ERP via. the integration layer and tax rate, the tax amount is posted to the corresponding document line item.

It's worth noting that nowadays there are standard integrations between popular ERP and Tax Engines and in many instances, such standard integrations, the tax engine can also generate an ERP tax code based upon the transactional scenario parameters. This fully automates the tax computation cycle.

10.2 ERP- ADD-ON (PLUG-INS) TAX CALCULATION TOOLS INTEGRATION

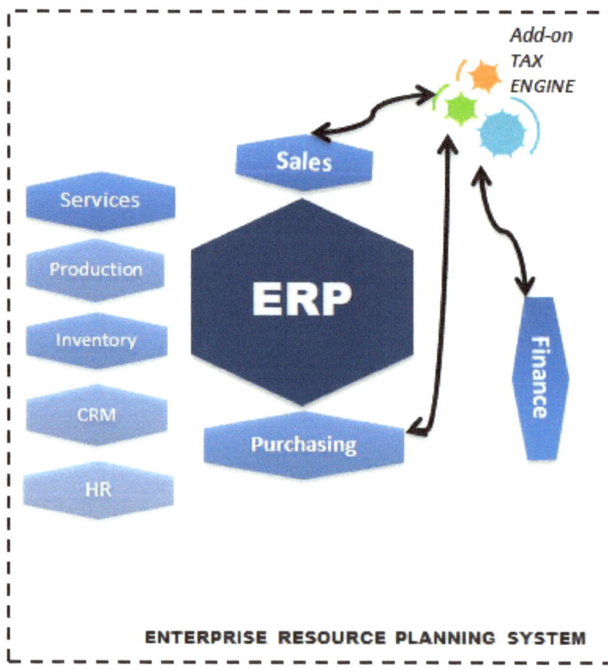

Figure 10.2

In such a scenario, the Add-on (Plug-in) tax calculation tool sits within the ERP system; no external API is involved. These Add-ons are predefined application with programs that are imported into the ERP system and create a user & functional menu of their own within the

ERP. Such an add-on's tax determination software is not capable of delivering the full benefits of a tax engine; instead, it's sort of an advanced version of native ERP tax functionality. Such software needs customization (hard-coded) to reflect the firm's business flows and associated tax footprints to deliver the tax output, much like native ERP tax functionality, which requires configurations.

10.3 ERP – TAX COMPLIANCE REPORTING SOFTWARE

10.3.1 Scenario 1: Direct ERP Integration

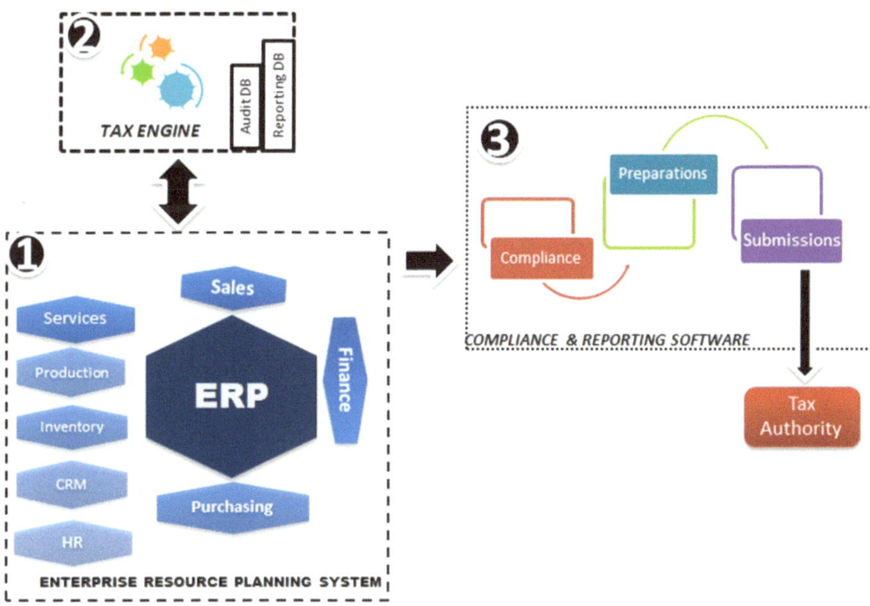

Figure 10.3.1

As can be inferred from Fig 10.3.1 (Flow 1& 3), the ERP system is connected to 3rd-party external tax compliance and reporting software. Once tax is determined in the ERP system (either via native ERP tax functionality or an external tax engine, or an Add-on tax software), the documents are posted in the ERP. This completes the tax determination part.

Next comes the tax compliance and reporting part, where 3rd-party tax software extracts sales and purchase invoices, as well as financial accounting documents, from the ERP, creating a transactional tax data lake for compliance activities, tax return preparation, and tax submissions. Here, you can observe that the flow of data is one-way, i.e., flowing outward from ERP to compliance reporting software. In case of an external tax engine deployed, you can see that the tax engine is connected independently to the ERP. In cases of native ERP tax functionality or add-on tax software (section 10.2), Tax engine is out of scope, as tax is determined within ERP, which is connected to Compliance and reporting software.

10.3.2 Scenario 2: Indirect ERP Integration

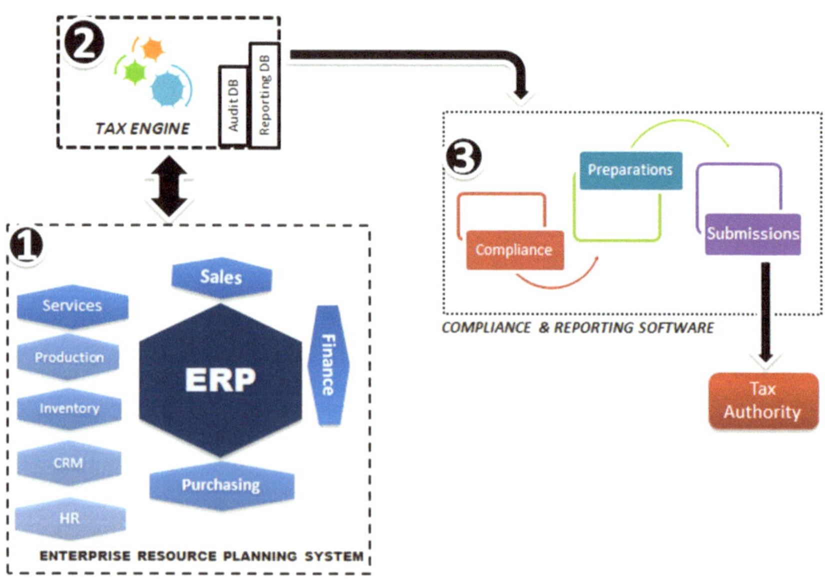

Figure 10.3.2

In the above scenario, you may see that the ERP system is interfaced with a 3rd-party bolt-in tax engine, and the tax engine is interfaced with the compliance and reporting software. Modern tax engines include tax logic that computes tax and support tax reporting and tax audit databases. This reporting database stores the sales, purchase invoices, and financial accounting document information. The tax audit database is hit when posting occurs in the ERP system, i.e., the transactional tax lifecycle is completed.

The tax reporting database is refreshed from the tax audit database at regular periods and is primarily used to extract summarized and detailed tax reports for external purposes.

In some cases, when you have the tax engine and tax compliance reporting software from the same vendor, they try to push for such an arrangement – ERP (1) <> Tax Engine (2) >Tax Compliance Reporting Software (3). From this tax engine reporting database, the Tax compliance and reporting software extracts legal invoice data (sales, purchases, finance) for downstream tax compliance and reporting processes.

In the author's view, this approach (10.3.2 Scenario 2: Indirect ERP Integration) isn't compliant for tax compliance and reporting processes. Because one aspect matter most for Tax compliance and reporting, this is that all relevant invoices should be extracted pertinent to the reporting date period and the associated entity.

In this scenario, there is a potential risk that documents will not be logged in the tax engine database due to vivid technical reasons (e.g. network outrage, connection timed out, missing configuration at integration layer) and, as a result, firm has missing documents which are accounted for tax return preparations and submissions. Also, for credit and debit notes, there may be gaps or duplicate entries, leading to inaccuracies.

There should be some reconciliation of documents parameters like tax amounts, tax GL ledgers between ERP and the tax compliance reporting software before final submissions are made to the tax authority. Getting tax data from the tax engine database is not recommended, and the ERP system should be the single source of truth for both upstream and downstream systems. The tax technology software's should be integrated with ERP directly and not indirectly.

10.4 ERP – E-INVOICING SOFTWARE

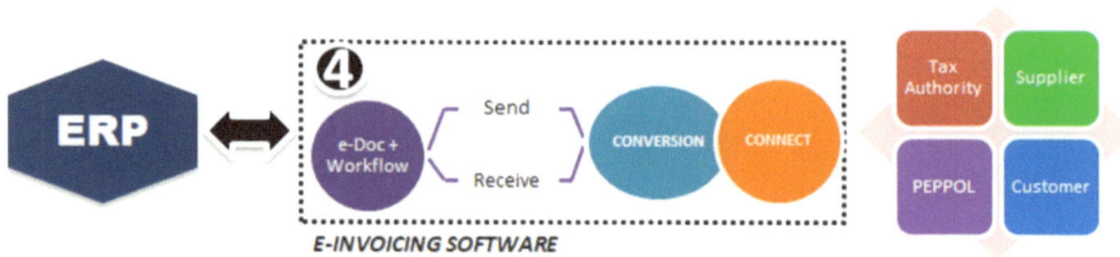

Figure 10.4

As part of new global e-invoicing requirements, firms are looking for software that meets their needs. An e-Invoice is not a PDF; it may use XML or another format. By 2030-2035, businesses in the majority of nations will be required to send e-Invoices to their customers and suppliers, domestically and internationally and use PEPPOL for cross-border. Depending on the country's regulations, businesses may be required to first send the e-Invoice to the tax authority for validation/approval, and, post-approval, either send it to the customer or have the tax authority forward it to the customer. When a tax authority is involved in the business-to-customer e-Invoicing process, it enables real-time tax reporting: tax authorities accumulate financial tax data for the business entity in real time, rather than relying on post-audit periodic submissions.

One may see the flow of data: it's two-way, i.e., e-invoices are generated in the ERP and sent to PEPPOL/Tax Authority/Customer (sales), and the ERP receives e-invoices from PEPPOL/Tax Authority/Supplier (procurement). The majority of ERP systems lack e-Invoicing functionality, as it first requires converting sales, purchase, and finance documents into a particular format mandated by the country administration, PEPPOL, etc. In the case of a firm with multi-country cross-border operations, it becomes a daunting task to custom-build an e-Invoicing solution. As a result, one can see many e-Invoicing solutions in the market, launched by tax technology firms, which now also offer e-Invoicing solutions. One can see that this landscape has no interference from either the tax engine (i.e., the tax engine cannot sit between ERP and the e-Invoicing solution) nor from the tax reporting and compliance software. However, there are products in the market that can deliver both e-invoicing solutions and tax compliance and reporting solutions.

10.5 IDEAL LANDSCAPE

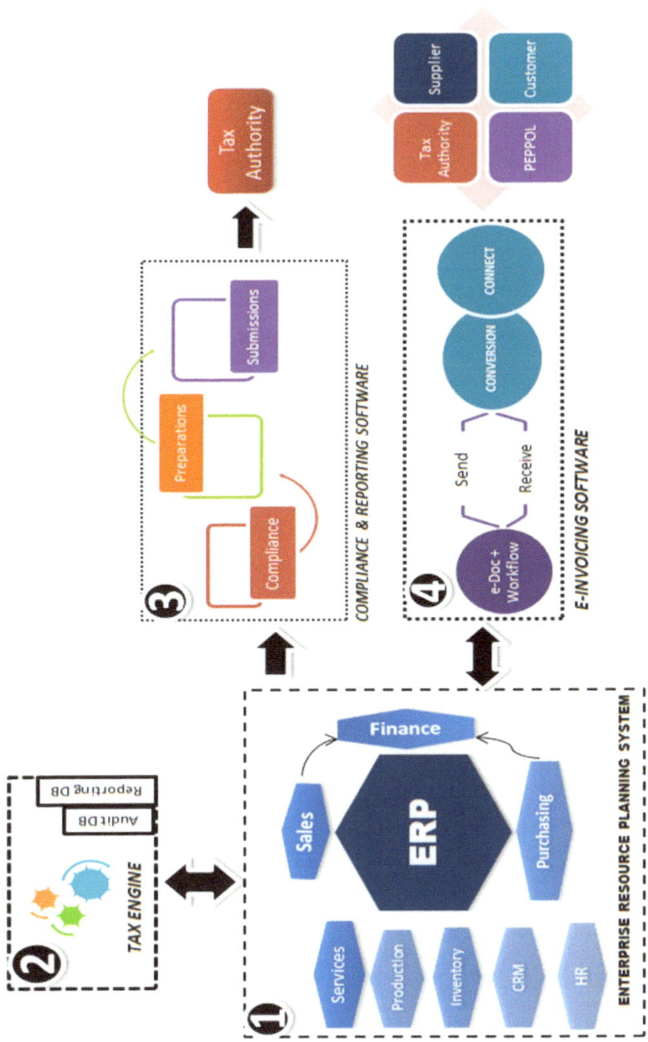

Figure 10.5

As shown in Figure 10.5, an ideal landscape is one in which ERP is centrally positioned, and these tax software's are integrated independently with the ERP system. Just like the planets which revolve around the Sun, and there is no intra-planetary positioning (except the Moon-Earth scenario). Here, Sun – the powerhouse of energy, is our ERP system, and planets are the tax software getting light (Finance tax data) from Sun (ERP). In the authors view, this ERP Tax IT landscape is the ideal landscape which offers flexibility, scalability and less interdependence.

10.6 SUMMARY

In this chapter, you have learnt about modern ERP Tax technology landscapes. To understand tax technology, it's vital to start with the enterprise-level tax architecture, the products deployed, the processes that interface with these products, and the overall integration working in unison to deliver compliance with the law and business policy. Readers working on tax IT projects may correlate these possible scenarios with the client's Finance Tax IT landscape and contribute more efficiently to requirements analysis, as-is-to-be gap assessment, and solution design that is technically and legally compliant. The chapter has educated you on the various ERP Tax integrations, combinational scenarios, direct–indirect interfaces, starting with the ERP –Tax engine, Tax Add-ons, ERP Tax Compliance Reporting, e-Invoicing, and finally leading to an ideal Tax IT landscape encompassing automation, digitalization, and streamlining of end-to-end business tax processes. In the next chapter, we will learn about key considerations towards discovering the right tax software for clients.

CHAPTER 11

KEY CONSIDERATIONS FOR THE RIGHT TAX SOFTWARE

The chapter focuses on the factors a firm and its tax team should consider when selecting the right tax technology software. Today's tax technology market is flooded with hundreds of tax software's, and it's tough to filter out the ones that don't yield the desired results. The chapter revolves around key selection parameters for shortlisting and finalizing tax software: tax authority coverage, ERP-friendliness, Tax content, implementation and maintenance. Readers with solution consulting, pre-sale roles, or teams involved in product screening activities can learn the key considerations and contribute further.

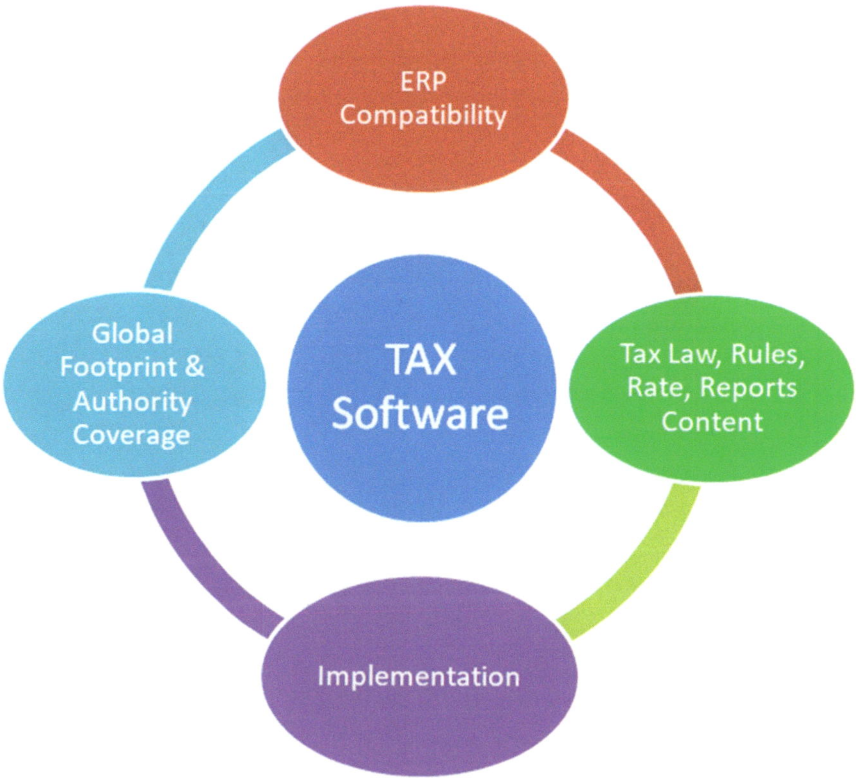

Figure 11.0

Tax engines are modern software (which gained prominence post-2000) that enables a company to automate its tax determination process. As firms expand their global footprints, their finance and tax departments face greater regulatory and compliance challenges in ensuring accurate tax filings. The first step towards being compliant is a precise determination of tax for both sales and purchases. The tax engine's primary role is to determine the accurate tax rate based on the transaction tax scenario, calculate the tax amount, and identify the applicable tax jurisdiction (tax authority). Similarly, tax compliance, reporting, and e-Invoicing software are critical for accuracy, compliance, and communication with external partners and authorities.

Selecting the right tax software is critical to your end-to-end transaction tax process, which impacts your end-to-end value stream supply chain processes –Sales, Procurement, Logistics and Finance. Tax software's & ERP integrate for a long, happy, and financially sound tax business operation.

11.1 GLOBAL FOOTPRINT & TAX AUTHORITIES COVERAGE

Tax engines are practical and cost-effective for firms with many entities (company codes) across more than a dozen countries. i.e., number of tax jurisdictions to report to. E.g., UK has one tax authority; the US has 14,000+ Tax authorities led rate combinations.

The USA is an exception to this. In the USA itself, there are more than 14,000 tax rates (combinations of states, counties, cities, districts, secondary districts, school districts, etc.). Tax jurisdiction is the geographic area, and the tax authority is the Government department that oversees that area for tax purposes. In short, for the US, if your firm has purchase and sales operations in more than 100 jurisdictions, the tax engine case is legitimate. If, along with the USA, your firm has operations in non-USA countries, you should consider the tax engine over your native ERP Tax solution. It's worth to note that the tax engines were designed and developed primarily for the US and later got its geographical scope to worldwide regions in its product roadmap.

Native ERP solutions depend heavily on custom tax code creation; each tax code contains a specific tax rate, and in a scenario of 100+ tax jurisdictions, you may have hundreds of tax codes for both sales and purchase transactions. This is a considerable risk.

If your firm has a significant international presence, more than 25 countries, i.e., you are reporting to more than 25 unique international tax authorities (Country + State/ Province + City Etc.), considering having a Tax engine is a prudent thought.

This is because, in the absence of a tax engine, you will need a standard tax team to manage numerous Tax authorities' tax laws review, changes, and make edits in your ERP. The tax engine will provide greater accuracy and be cost-effective. Similarly, for tax compliance and reporting software, having adequate coverage of tax returns and reports in applicable jurisdictions is vital. E-Invoicing software will support B2B, B2G, and B2C transactions across geographies where the firm has business. In short, firms need to know how far the tax software's geographical coverage scope is enabled.

11.2 COMPATIBILITY WITH ERP

Whether your firm uses SAP, Oracle, Microsoft Dynamics, Sage, or other ERPs for business processes, the tax software's must integrate seamlessly with your ERP. Interfaces are of two types: batch mode (offline, asynchronous) and real-time (synchronous). Since the tax engine's main job is to compute tax in real time, it should have standard connectors to that ERP or be able to connect via API (Application programming interface), which sends and receive data in real time. If your firm doesn't need a real-time tax call, you may also opt for batch mode tax determination. In that case, the integration is primarily via an SFTP folder (Secure File Transfer Protocol folder), which receives files from ERP in CSV, or other format, forwards them to Tax Engine, Tax Engine populates Tax rates and Tax amounts for each line item, and resends the file back to ERP's SFTP folder. During the solution consulting phase, you must obtain in writing that the tax engine is compatible with the ERP and integrates well with it. Preference should be given to tax engines that have standard connectors (customized for specific ERPs), followed by custom API/Web services calls. For tax compliance, reporting, and e-Invoicing solutions, the same compatibility factor holds, as they also involve data extraction, transformation, transmission, and receivables. Nowadays, the integration component of few tax engines sits within the ERP and enables communication.

11.3 IMPLEMENTATION

While buying tax software's is one big deal, getting it implemented is another game altogether. Tax software's implementations are not tough; all you need is the right combination of integration and implementation specialists. In many cases, the tax software's vendor offers implementation cum license packages - That's a safe bet. Your firm must have a crystal-clear answer from the tax vendor on who will implement (integrate, install & run, and support) the tax engine. Is it your firm, the vendor, or 3rd party like Big4, or a combination of the above. In any scenario, you must have the right tax Technology specialists on your team. Tax Technology specialists are sometimes hard to find and many ERP functional consultants claim tax tech skills but fail miserably in hands-on tax technology experience.

In short, if you are implementing on your own, your firm must do a resource assessment of tax technologists in your region. If 3rd party is implementing it, you must ask them about the former or existing client's references. If the seller is implementing it solely, you should still seek credentials and let the parent firm's professional services implement it. The ideal scenario is when a 3rd party implements it, in cases when a firm has no internal competency. The statement of work (SOW) and the contracts for sale, license, and support should be robust.

11.4 TAX CONTENT

Once you're on board with the tax engine, it's the first step towards effective tax compliance and automation. The real journey begins now. The tax engine is not a standalone system; it contains vital tax content (Tax jurisdictions, Tax authorities, tax rates, tax rules, product tax-ability information, etc.). This content is dynamic, meaning the tax rates for different products and tax jurisdictions keep changing over time, per the circulars of the tax authorities. Hence, the tax engine must keep itself up to date with the content it receives, which is automatically updated from its firm's content management teams in the cloud. Tax engines may or may not support all applicable countries (tax authorities), products, or services. In this scenario, a significant risk arises: your firm will need to customize the tax engine to comply with expected tax rate requirements.

However, when you do customization, your firm becomes liable to maintain and update that logic; in short, you are back to ground zero, the works that tax SME's were doing in Excel, now they are doing in the system. Thus, before finalizing the tax software, a firm's tax function should list down all unique taxability scenarios. The tax engine that supports the maximum number of combinations per your firm's business scenarios wins this point. Also, tax vendors should have a defined support system for content-related production tickets.

For tax compliance, reporting, and e-invoicing software, too, content does matter, a tax reporting software should have the applicable reports in the format and structure to cater to specific country tax administration, and e-Invoicing software also need legal and technical content updates (transmission protocol, Tax authority, Peppol interfaces and acceptable e-Invoicing formats). Though there are a dozen+ factors to consider before shortlisting the right Tax engine for your firm, the above four are the most vital heavyweights.

11.5 SUMMARY

In the chapter, we've covered the solution consulting (pre-sale engineering) aspect of tax technology, which is an advanced skill area. Readers with Tax, ERP, Tax Technology, and Business knowledge are now in a position to provide consultation to clients and internal Tax functions on 3rd-party tax software solutions. Whether they are compatible with the current legal, statutory requirements, compatibility with the existing ERP landscape, ease of implementation and maintenance, and legal/technical updates. As tax is dynamic, so are tax technological solutions. Firms do undergo ERP transformations every few years, and tax transformation goes in parallel. During the initial discovery phases, applicable product selection discussions do occur, and tax functions are consulted by enterprise architects and the steering committee board to send proposals and bids to tax software vendors for demonstrations and prototypes. At this phase, readers will be able to participate, contribute, and provide a detailed pros & cons analysis of their tax functions on applicable aspects for final product selections. In the next chapter, we will learn about the tax technology organization. structure and various cross-functional roles working in cohesion for optimum business tax delivery.

CHAPTER 12

TAX TECHNOLOGY ORGANIZATIONAL STRUCTURE: ROLES & RESPONSIBILITIES

The chapter introduces the readers to the overall enterprise organizational structure involved in tax technology. Alongside the tax technology software solutions know-how, it's vital to understand the organizational structure, it's stakeholders in tax technology work, individual skill work streams (cross-functional business, GPOs, GSS, tax functions teams, process experts, Tax IT associates). Their placement, roles, and responsibilities in overall tax technology work for better alignment, communication, and solution delivery. The chapter delves deeper into each role and describes the associated work in detail, especially the distinct types of indirect tax technology roles and their value propositions within the solutions. Alongside this, readers will be able to better understand the job market, roles, and responsibilities during job applications to recruiters, and can effectively talk with the interview panels. The chapter will educate readers on tax technology organizational architecture, leading to better task ownership and accountability.

We will explore further the different roles and responsibilities that encompass tax technology careers. Generally, in cases of ERP Tax transformation projects (Greenfield, Brownfield), either the entire tax technology piece is implemented in-house or a 3rd party like Big Four or other IT consulting partner or it may be a hybrid structure (In-House +IT firm), there may be external tax advisory partners too. Also, since tax is dynamic –Legislative, statutes, rules, law of tax authority keep changing, alongside the company financial supply chain, business models, mergers, spin-offs, acquisitions, migrations, having tax implications.

Post-implementation or transformation, alongside regular production support / Application maintenance services (AMS), there is always ongoing work such as enhancements, new requirements, mini projects like upgrades, technical maintenance, and new integrations. In short, a firm's tax technology journey is always in motion.

First, it's essential to understand the generic tax & tax technology organizational structure prevalent in the firms with whom these roles will interface.

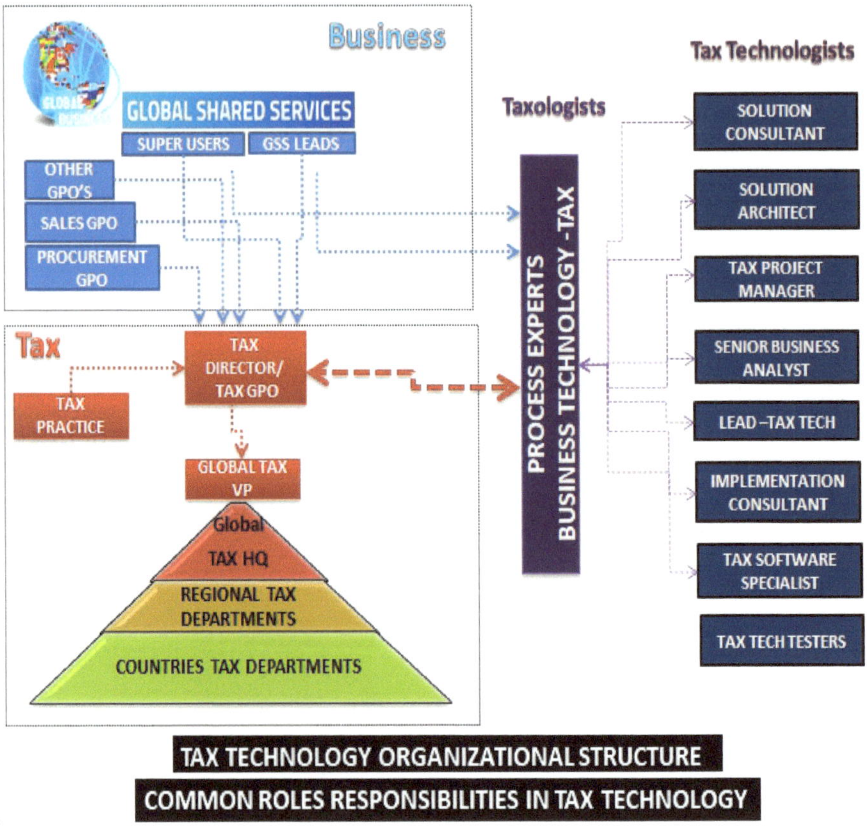

Figure 12.0

12.1 TAX TECHNOLOGY ORGANIZATIONAL STRUCTURE

As shown in Figure 12.0, a firm's tax technology organizational structure comprises four areas.

12.1.1 Tax Department

The Tax departments of multinational firms have Global HQs, regional hubs, and country-specific tax practices, depending on the quantum of business operations. The country-specific tax department or associates or external tax advisors report to the regional tax department (APAC, EMEA, NA, LATAM, INDIA, etc.), and these regional department tax directors or associate directors report to the Global Tax HQ, which is generally the company's parent country base, where it was founded and started. The Global Tax HQ leader is the Tax Vice President, under whom is a tax director, who has his own team of tax associates (the tax director's office) reporting to him. The Tax Director's office is also known as the Tax GPO (Global Process Owner). In huge organizations, the Tax Director's office and the Tax GPO may be located in different places. It's the Tax GPO/Tax director's office that interfaces with the business. However, the tax department organizational structure may differ from firm to firm, and there may be multiple power centers, e.g., NA, EMEA, APAC, LATAM, or centralized power resting with Global Tax HQ. The Tax function interfaces with the Tax authorities, and whenever there is any change in tax laws, rules, rates, legislation, statutes, or any impact on firms' tax-related business models, they reach out to the Process Expert / Business Technology team.

12.1.2 Business

An organization's business is run by global shared service centers (GSSs) organized by region. These GSS centers support the company in enabling and executing the sales, purchase, financial accounting transactions – PO/SO, Invoices/Billing, payments to vendors/ suppliers, and a myriad of other business transactions. GSS centers have leads, and whenever they encounter a tax issue, they are supposed to reach out to the Tax Director's office/Tax GPO, or the Process Expert/Business Technology team.

12.1.3 Process Experts

This team is composed of Taxologists – person who knows tax and technology and can act as a bridge between the Tax department and Tax IT (Tax technologists). This team acts as an interface between the Tax Department and Tax IT associates. Basically, this team assesses, analyzes, and documents the requirements with the tax department and works with tax technologists to get the demand delivered.

12.1.4 Tax Technologists

This team is composed of tax technologists who work towards requirement delivery – Documentation (BRD), design, build, test, and deploy as per the change management, quality assurance delivery framework of the organization. It involves Tax and IT, i.e., tax technology. Tax IT symbolizes the delivery of tax requirements in IT systems (ERP, Tax software).

12.2 TAX TECHNOLOGY ROLES

In this section, we will discuss the standard tax technology roles present in the market. There may be many other titles and job designations; however, they may be a combination of roles and responsibilities from the following roles. It's important to note that not all of the roles below are always present on a firm's tax technology team. It depends on the project scenario.

12.2.1 Business Technology Tax /Process Experts

Although they are taxologists (individuals who know tax and technology), senior tax technologists working in firms' tax technology often migrate to this role as process experts or business technology tax. The role is quite senior and requires subject-matter expertise in the firm's financial supply chain/business models & associated tax footprints, tax software, and tax knowledge. This associate is the key bridge between the Tax Department, GSS leads and Tax IT team. They are responsible for ensuring that tax projects, enhancements, and bug fixes are implemented on time and in compliance with the firm's tax policy and legal/statutory deadlines. There may be one or more process experts for tax determination, tax compliance reporting, or e-Invoicing, depending on the firm's size and global operational scope.

Such associates generally work in-house and are employees of the firm, as this role is critical to the firm. In a few cases, we have such associates from 3rd party consulting firm working as contractors or consultants.

12.2.2 Solution Consultant /Pre-Sale Engineer

A solution consultant is an associate who helps solve complex client tax problems or helps a firm identify the right tax solution in tax software for the ERP operational landscape.

There are two types of tax solution consulting. Pre-Implementation pre-sale engineer - One who gets involved in early project phases to help market, demo, and sell a 3rd party tax software products to a firm. Post implementation solution consultant - one who has profound knowledge of software and ERP tax technology, and helps the firm to solve complex problems leveraging additional software, interfaces, customization, or process change. Solution consultant-level associates have vast knowledge, skills, and years of work experience in tax technology.

12.2.3 Implementation Consultant

This role involves an individual who knows how to configure and implement the tax requirement in tax software solution. An implementation consultant is not heavily involved in the design and requirements discussions; they receive the requirements and, sometimes, the technical design document, and work towards implementing the solution. An implementation consultant knows tax software well and is skilled in optimizing it for tax solutions.

12.2.4 In -House Techie

An In-house tax technologist is an associate who is an employee of the firm and supports process experts or the business technology team in delivering solutions, either directly or through 3rd-party IT firms managing AMS projects. They have a good understanding of the company's business tax models and are proficient with the tax software solution. Nowadays, firms are getting serious about having one or more in-house tax technologists, so the movements of 3rd-party consultants don't disrupt their tax technology work.

12.2.5 Business Analyst

A business analyst role (senior or junior) is to assist the process expert or business technology team in ensuring the requirements are well documented and discussed with the tax technology team. The requirements should be well-written and understandable to the IT team. The tax department uses many jargons and has its own communication style. This is where a business analyst jumps in alongside a process expert or a business technology team to transform the message into a form, including scope, on which a tax technology associate can begin the work and understand the delivery expectations. Sometimes, business analysts are also involved in UAT testing, configuration, and technical documentation.

12.2.6 Tax Solution Architect

A tax technology solution architect role involves designing the overall tax systems, processes, sub-processes, architectural diagrams, and flow diagrams. They work alongside enterprise solution architects to ensure the tax solution architect aligns with the overall enterprise solution design. A solution architect designs the As-is and To-be architectures for transformation projects. This architecture involves tax software solutions, their placement in the overall ERP landscape, the flow of business transactions, 3rd-party tax software, integrations, interfaces, and associated tax touchpoints. The position may or may not be permanent, and often solution consultants or process experts support the enterprise solution architect team in seeding tax solution architecture, or, in the case of 3rd-party IT vendor involvement, it's the Tax PM or a senior business analyst who works on it. Any firm needs to have the architecture in place and well-defined so that Tax & Tax IT associates have a crystal-clear understanding of the overall landscape, processes, sub-processes, interfaces, etc.

12.2.7 Project Manager

A Tax PM is someone who can manage moderate and large tax projects and has project management skills. They are generally deployed during major transformations, upgrades, spin-offs, or ongoing mergers. This person reports to the overall project steering committee and the tax director. They have knowledge of tax technology and project management and can seamlessly integrate the tax project implementation plan with the overall project plan, ensuring compliance and synchronization. Such roles are need-based and are rarely seen in the market. In the majority of cases, 3rd-party IT firms implementing a tax solution deploy such experts to support the tax technology team assigned to the client project. A Tax PM manages resourcing, budget, backfills, hiring/firing, project plan development, monitoring of work, and other aspects related to the overall quality assurance framework. Generally, such individuals know ERP, integrations, and tax software, which helps them identify requirements effectively and deliver a solution delivery plan to senior management or the project steering committee.

12.2.8 Tax Software Specialist /Product Managers

A tax software specialist is a person who is highly skilled in the tax software product, e.g., Tax engine, tax compliance reporting software, or e-Invoicing software. Such individuals are expected to work on specific software and may or may not need end-to-end tax technology knowledge and skills. Sometimes, such individuals are also referred to as product managers, who ensure that the tax software product is up to date with the tax content, technical patches, and other software maintenance updates. Upgrades are regularly and timely seeded/implemented into the tax software throughout its lifecycle.

12.2.9 Tax Testers

A tax technology tester is an individual who supports testing work – test suite, test plan, test case development, and execution – Including Unit testing, System integration testing, and supporting the business (tax function) with user acceptance testing. A tax tester knows the scenario well, ensuring accurate master data is used for document creation and that the expected outputs (tax rate, tax amount, tax return – tax box value, etc.) are provided for a specific business scenario (use case). They know how to execute testing, manual, semi-automated, or automated, and test documentation tools and workflows involved. This is an important role, as firms are now seeing major operational issues post-Go-Live due to improper, inadequate, or gap-filled testing during the user acceptance testing (UAT) phase.

As mentioned in the beginning, not all roles are required for a project delivery. However, the skills, knowledge, and experience listed are indeed part of the solution involved. There may be cases where a business analyst plays a Taxologist or process expert role alongside the PMO for Tax, or an in-house tax technologist plays a process expert, GPO, etc., role in a hybrid role. Program leadership needs to appoint seasoned, experienced leaders to manage the tax technology program, which generally runs in parallel with enterprise transformation programs, ensuring the team's organizational architecture is comprehensive, robust, and self-reliant.

On this, Alexis Aimard, a renowned tax technologist (US), has some words of wisdom.

“One aspect I’d add is how this framework can also be a powerful tool when joining a new team or project. Often, not all of these roles exist within an organization, leading to gaps in ownership or understanding. Mapping against this structure early on is a great way to identify potential gaps and clarify responsibilities—whether that means strengthening certain roles internally, bridging across functions, or ensuring that partners and consultants cover missing areas. In that sense, your framework doesn’t just describe the ideal state; it also serves as a diagnostic lens for understanding where a team stands today and what’s needed to achieve a more complete and resilient setup.”

12.3 SUMMARY

In this chapter, readers learnt about the overall business, tax, and IT organizational structure prevalent in organizations. Understanding this aspect is essential for understanding who does what and how things work in an organization when it comes to tax technology requirements, projects, and incidents. Readers also gained insights about the diverse tax technology roles in the market and the responsibilities associated with them. In Fortune 500 firms, many tax technologies are used to manage tax operations, and readers are now better positioned to understand the work they do, the skills they possess, and the knowledge they bring. Also, during job postings and interview discussions, readers can now effectively understand the work requirements. In the next chapter, we will discuss the expected tax technology skills that should be included in a professional profile.

CHAPTER 13

ESSENTIAL TAX TECHNOLOGY SKILLS

The chapter introduces readers to the basic and advanced skills required for tax functions, tax process experts, and Tax IT associates required in tax technology work. The online tax technology knowledge base is limited, and many associates struggle to identify the skills needed to work in tax technology. The chapter explores various skill facets required in tax technology works for impactful value driven delivery, which includes knowledge areas encompassing Solution consulting, Tax knowledge, Tax processes lifecycle, Business tax flows, Tax software's, ERP Tax software integrations and bit of project management skills to align the delivery in regards to the change management, release management and quality assurance framework of software development and delivery lifecycle. The chapter benefits readers by providing a deeper understanding of this knowledge area and by guiding them through the necessary learning steps to gradually develop their knowledge in theory and later in practice, enabling them to become indispensable, multi-skilled professionals in the current tax technology market.

A tax technology consultant is the key bridge between the Tax Department and IT, can serve roles such as an in-house consultant, a member of a system integrator (SI) implementation team, an AMS, or an independent 3rd-party consultant deployed for a shorter period for greenfield or brownfield projects. They possess some basic knowledge of Tax and have expert knowledge of Tax solutions. They are not a Tax SME; instead, they can effectively elicit tax requirements, design the solution, define technical specifications and deliver solutions.

Figure 13.0

Below are some IT consulting skills and strategies for Tax Technology consultants.

13.1 SOLUTION CONSULTING

Ability to effectively listen, communicate, understand the problem statement and associated pain points, As-is and To-be scenarios (actual vs. expected), fit-gap analysis, solution discovery, technical viability, and proof-of-concept/prototype development in a non-prod environment are key attributes for successful solution consulting. As a Tax technologist, one needs to keep their ears and eyes open to new tax laws and policies proposed by the country tax administrations alongside client tax policy requirements. Maintain an agile, fertile mindset to ensure such demands are documented in the project tools for tracking. The consultant can effectively articulate the tax requirements into technical specifications and provide a solution design. Consultant should have a good understanding of the tax solutions – whether native ERP or 3rd party tax engines or add-ons, etc., and how these tax software can accommodate proposed tax requirements.

13.2 TAX KNOWLEDGE

As a tax technology consultant in a multi-national organization, your business point of contact is local, regional, and global Tax SME's (Tax Manager, Tax CoE, Tax Directors, etc.), who are Tax experts. They know their firm's tax business flows, jurisdictional tax requirements, and Tax determination, compliance, and reporting obligations. For you to effectively communicate with these SME's, basic Tax knowledge is expected. A global tax technologist should know what are the different tax types and how these taxes are levied on a sales or purchase transactions– e.g. basic know how on Value Added Tax (VAT), Goods Service Tax (GST), US Sales Use Tax (US SUT), Canadian HST/QST/PST, Brazil (ICMS, IPI, PIS, and COFINS) and other indirect taxes, jurisdictional specific charges, tariffs. This knowledge and skill are essential for effectively understanding the applicable business scenario, its scope, and the type of tax implications the Tax SME is discussing. One may learn this skill by reading tax articles, listening to publicly available tax webinars, attending roundtable conferences, talking to tax professionals, reading global tax reports published by Big4's or pursuing an academic qualification in Tax.

13.3 TAX LIFECYCLE

A Tax technology consultant should know what the end stage of any Tax IT work is. The transaction tax lifecycle has four phases: (a) Tax Determination, (b) Tax Compliance, (c) Tax reporting, and nowadays, with (d) e-invoicing, an additional phase is added.

The end goal of any Tax activity is to ensure accurate filing of tax returns and other statutory submissions to the tax authority. With e-invoicing gaining momentum, real-time reporting of transactions to the tax authority is now a legal obligation.

The primary focus is on addressing the tax authority's legal and statutory obligations. For that, ensuring accuracy and compliance is of supreme importance to avoid fines, penalties, and other reputational and goodwill losses in the event of an external audit. A Tax technology consultant needs to understand the psyche of the tax department and where they are coming from, rather than a technology-driven approach. That is, rather than focusing on what tax solutions offer, one has to ensure that upstream tax processes appropriately support compliance, reporting, and other statutory submissions. For the tax function, it hardly matters which technical solution is installed; what matters for them is whether that IT solution can get them the required data, data that is sorted, organized, accurate, and compliant. In short, a seasoned tax technologist should view tax requirements through a tax lifecycle perspective: Tax reporting/e-invoicing> Tax compliance > Tax determination.

13.4 BUSINESS TAX FLOW'S

Each firm has its own unique way of doing business for sales and purchases. A company has legal, registered, representative entities, sales organizations spread globally, warehouses, manufacturing plants, and purchase organizations. The operational model differs from company to company. These are called business flows, and each business flow has tax footprints on the reporting country jurisdiction. The company has a well-documented blueprint for these business flows, and it's generally used with super users, sales, procurement, local, and regional business leads. Tax functions also has access to the company's business flow and operating model, and are regularly consulted by businesses for tax matters. Knowing your firms business flows helps a tax technology in two ways

1. Consultant to communicate and understand the problem statement effectively, do a IT fit gap analysis of as-is, to-be solution, design a robust solution and ensure legitimate UAT testing, leading to qualitative solution delivery.

2. Consultant can check whether ERP /Tax IT solution configured and customized by system integrator during the implementation accurately reflects the business flow blueprint and identify potential gaps for corrective and preventive actions i.e. continuous process improvement.

13.5 TAX IT SOLUTION

A consultant should possess profound functional and technical know-how of the tax solution, whether it's a 3rd party tax engine, tax compliance reporting software of an external vendor, or an ERP-native tax solution. They should have hands-on experience in implementing the agreed design and requirements for tax solutions. Knowledge of tax solutions, their architecture, and functionalities will help a Tax technologist determine the right solution design for the requirement and propose approaches that aren't disruptive, are sustainable in the long term, and serve the end purpose of the entire tax work, i.e., efficient tax compliance reporting. A tax technology consultant should not only be able to provide solutions but also implement them. The consultant must also handle product management for the tax solutions, including regular monthly tax content upgrades, technical upgrades as suggested by the vendor, ensuring configuration redundancy is not present, and avoiding unnecessary customization when out-of-the-box functionality serves the purpose. One has to communicate regularly with tax solution vendors and partners on issues, product roadmap, performance, and other tasks.

13.6 ERP TAX IT SOLUTION INTEGRATION

Nowadays, many ERP systems are in the cloud, and cloud-based SaaS tax solutions are working well. A tax technologist should have knowledge and skills on the Tax solution and how it integrates with the ERP's sales, procurement, and other processes where tax has a footprint. The entire tax technology determination process relies on the transmission of Transaction tax data from the ERP to the Tax software and vice versa, the integration (API) plays a vital role in ensuring the movement and transformation of the key tax drivers, and its transformation (ERP-Tax solution data model mapping) at the integration layer is compliant with the design. The majority of tax solutions use the XML/JSON formats to transmit transactional tax data between ERP–Tax Solutions and tax authority. The ability to read associated XML/JSON structures and parameters is an essential skill for root cause analysis and solutioning.

13.7 PROJECT MANAGEMENT

A tax technologist should have basic project management skills, not just functional and technical skills. A tax requirement can be global, regional, or local, and may be of moderate or high complexity, leading to a large project, a mini project, or a minor fix.

The requirement may include solutioning discussions with cross-functional teams like finance, procurement, sales, master data or vendor technicians, as it may involve or impact their systems and processes. Also, the solution needs to be delivered via the standard SDLC process, involving quality assurance, change management, release management workflows, and teams. Approvals from Business

Technology/Process experts and Tax managers, with justifications, are also required for solution approval and UAT, etc. Relevant resource allocation, delivery timelines, and cost assessments are also needed for project management tools. All this work requires a project manager's mindset.

13.8 MENTOR, EDUCATOR & TEAM BUILDING

A tax technology consultant understands the systems and processes involved in the end-to-end tax lifecycle; in fact, he knows the company's complete transactional tax architecture. Often, a tax technology consultant must educate and inform the tax functions, other stakeholders, and the project management office on solution approaches, risks, root causes, and problem statements. Nowadays, tax teams and super users also have strong insights into tax solutions, and one has to make a strong, convincing pitch with facts and figures to gain stakeholders' confidence.

A global tax technology consultant also has to build up a team of fellow tax technologists, who may not know tax solutions or be from finance or procurement teams. He needs to educate, train, supervise, and mentor them from time to time to ensure optimal delivery. Sometimes, one has to build a Tax CoE (Center of Excellence) and a team from scratch for AMS/Production support post-project implementation. A global tax technologist needs to have leadership, team-building, and an educator-mentor mindset.

A good online resource to get insights into contemporary tax technology solutions and community is https://www.taxtech500.com.

13.9 SUMMARY

The chapter has educated the reader about the various skills one needs to learn and develop throughout their tax technology professional journey. These skills are interrelated; a balanced approach to them is required to succeed as a tax technologist. Tax technology is not just about having know-how on tax software, but encompass a broad range of knowledge base and skills like solution consulting, tax knowledge, tax lifecycle, firms business flows and tax footprints, tax software's skills, integration functionalities, a bit of project management and notably the art of mentoring, up skilling and team building towards Tax IT CoE (center of excellence) development within the tax functions. Having awareness and knowledge of such skills has helped readers identify the gap and will motivate them to overcome it via external and internal learning. In the next chapter, we will examine the knowledge areas and skills expected by the interviewing panel during tax technology interviews.

CHAPTER 14

KNOWLEDGE AREA& SKILLS TO ACE TAX TECH INTERVIEWS

The chapter prepares readers for tax technology interviews, in which a panel of tax function comprising of tax process experts, and Tax IT associates assess the interviewee's skills and knowledge. The chapter delves into the psyche of interview panels. Today's tax technology landscape integrates all four processes: ERP, Tax determination, Tax Compliance Reporting, and e-Invoicing. These processes work in unison and are interdependent. The interview panel would like to get an overall picture of the candidate's skills and knowledge base to judge skills, learning's and expertise, so that minimal re-skilling and resource development is required, post hiring. The chapter will support readers in better preparing for interviews and in-person meet-ups, and in gaining hindsight, insight, and foresight on the client's legacy, as-is, and to-be tax technology landscape, processes, and problem areas, leading to a successful, fruitful discussion and hiring.

With digitalization and automation, the tax technology market is growing rapidly. There are three types of tax technology software in the market.

- Tax Engines, which automate the tax computation aspect
- Legal/Statutory Tax compliance software that assists the tax departments to review, draft, and file tax returns to the tax authorities and other statutory bodies
- E-Invoicing software, which interfaces with the ERP and supports the buyer-seller e-Invoicing process
- A candidate may see the corresponding role in the job description and prepare accordingly. Tax technology interviews can range from moderate to high complexity. In this chapter, we will analyze the knowledge areas and skills an interviewer may be seeking in you to hire you. Interviewer may be a seasoned tax technologist, Tax SME (Tax Specialist), Tax GPO (Global Process Owner), Tax process experts, or a Tax super user, or the panel may consist of the above combinations who interview you. Having given tens of interviews during authors 15+ years in tax technology and taken dozens, below are some knowledge areas a tax technologist should be well aware of. The content can be a good interview question checklist for the interviewer and the panel, too.

Image 14.0: Tax Technology Interview Panel

14.1 ERP PROCESS WITH TAX TOUCH POINTS

First, it's essential to know which ERP software the client is using to run its business – SAP, Oracle, Sage, Microsoft, JD Edwards, or procurement software like Coupa, Ariba. A candidate is not expected to know all modules functionally; focus will be on modules with tax touch points, such as sales, purchase and finance. The panel will focus on how well you know each sub-process (step) within the sales and purchase process, along with the associated tax touch points. In short, identify the ERP and stay up to date on its sales, purchase and finance accounting processes, lifecycle, and tax footprint. Without basic ERP sales and purchase process knowledge, a candidate will be deemed unfit for a tax technology role.

14.2 ERP -TAX SOFTWARE INTERFACE (INTEGRATION)

Tax software needs to be integrated with the ERP; nowadays, out-of-the-box predefined interfaces are in vogue, and tax software firms have ready-to-bolt-in interface capability. These integrations have their own names; e.g., the Vertex tax engine has Accelerator+, and ONESOURCE has Global Next, etc. However, many clients are still running legacy ERP versions and have custom interfaces with tax software. Try to identify the interface type and learn more about it. Tax technology work (tax processes digitalization and automation) is nowadays scattered across three spectrums – ERP-native tax, Interfaces, and 3rd-party tax software. Modern interfaces are not just a means to map the schema (data modeling/field mappings) of ERP with that of tax software; they play much bigger roles, such as serving as a tool for reports, data lakes, request-response log files, enabling tax code generation, and enabling business partner-related location data transmission. Tax software that sits within ERP doesn't need a separate interface, e.g., Meridian tax engine; some Tax compliance reporting and e-Invoicing software may or may not require a separate interface (e.g. SAP DRC sits within SAP ERP). Similarly, there may be 3rd-party interfaces involved, e.g., MuleSoft with COUPA (a procurement tool). A candidate should also focus on the type of interface the tax software provides and the functionalities it offers for the tax process.

Client panel will be more comfortable with a candidate who has good know-how functionally (not technically (programming)) of the interface and effectively supports operations, as tax technology work involves three frontiers – ERP, Interface and tax software. Knowledge and skill are desired on each frontier to deliver value.

14.3 TAX SOFTWARE

This is very important. With the advent of tax technology, nonstandard company-specific tax policy or the financial supply chain models are primarily automated in tax software to minimize development work in ERP, which is why tax software is in the market: it's a mini ERP type tool focused on tax. Whether it's a tax engine, a tax compliance reporting tool, or e-Invoicing software, a candidate should have fundamental knowledge and skills in the primary sub–modules that make up the tax software, i.e., the process architecture. The tax technology runs on tax software. While on ERP, business users post transactions, and the interface enables transmission (handshake). The desired outputs (Tax rate, Tax Amount, Tax code, Tax return, e-Invoice) are generated via tax software. A transaction, once entered into tax software, travels through various sub-sections (application programs) to enable the software to make a decision and provide the required output. A candidate should know the entire journey legs and key milestones it hits - from entry until exit. Also, a candidate should be well aware of the functionalities provided by various sub –modules within tax software, this to answer any specific scenario related question during the interview process, and i.e. how solution will be defined in a particular case (problem statement) and most likely the problem statement is real, either it's an open ticket at client end or it's a solved one with some complexity.

14.4 ERP NATIVE TAX

Having a tax software onboard doesn't mean that ERP native tax parameters are totally bypassed; a few components will always be there, irrespective of how far tax technology goes, e.g., tax regimes, tax code, tax GL's, master data tax parameters (e.g. commodity code, tax classification indicator on Material/Service master), and various tax reports. In cases where the client is not using third-party tax software and is running its operations entirely or partially on the Native ERP tax solution, a candidate should be well-versed in the native tax setup within the ERP and how it supports determination, reporting, and related processes. In cases where 3rd-party tax software is in the picture, you may see 75%- 80% of the Native ERP Tax setup not getting leverage; still, 20-25% of the Native tax setup and parameters have a place in the show. In short, this area also needs attention.

14.5 MASTER DATA (TAX DRIVERS)

Tax software is like a black box; it doesn't have any transactional or master data of its own. It is manufactured generically, i.e., any client can use it and customize it as per their business needs. A billing/Invoice/accounting document contains many master data parameters, e.g., customer, supplier, plant, material, cost center, and company code. These master data types are key for any tax determination and subsequent tax reporting compliance and e-invoicing. Master data contains key tax drivers that power the tax software program. For example, VAT registration no., City/Province/State/Country/Zip Code/Tax Jurisdiction Code is present on suppliers, customers, and plant master data. A commodity code is an essential master data parameter that helps tax software identifies goods and services. In short, the entire show runs on what we are buying/selling, to whom/from whom we are buying/selling, from where/to where we are shipping, the jurisdiction in scope, and the value of the transaction.

14.6 GLOBAL INDIRECT TAX

Basic knowledge of tax types and associated jurisdictions is required. For example VAT, GST, US Sales Use Tax, and Canada HST/ PST/QST/GST, and other indirect tax types and applicable jurisdictions. A candidate is not expected to know the legislation and statutes of each country's tax authority. Having basic knowledge of the country tax authority/ tax regime, tax type, tax jurisdiction, tax status, tax rates, and recoverability, etc., is expected in the interview, and a candidate can learn about it online at various portals and Big4's indirect tax reports.

14.7 SOLUTION CONSULTANT SKILLS

Knowledge of the above areas will make a candidate confident in facing any interview question and in becoming a solution consultant. Whether a candidate is being hired for project implementation, enhancements, upgrades, transformation, production support, etc., solution consulting skills are the key to delivering value and being valuable. Nowadays, panelists are well-versed in software, and they will undoubtedly give you a specific problem statement and ask for prospective solutions with pros and cons to test your end-to-end knowledge and skills. The solution may be achieved within tax software, at the tax software–ERP interface, within ERP itself, or as a hybrid.

It's essential for the candidate to understand the problem statement and the expected output, and to propose a solution that fits well. The solution may have one or more solution approaches, however, during the interview, it's advisable to propose two solutions (max three), with justifications e.g. To drive a special tax rate for a specific jurisdiction based customer, making a simple rule in tax engine is always easier than to enhance customer master data in the ERP, which has broader upstream impact. Similarly to drive specific tax rate for a set of materials, it's easier to group them under a specific material group tied to a tax engine commodity code in ERP is much beneficial than to make tens of material level product mappings in the tax engine. Or having a separate tax code for VAT returns boxes scenario in the ERP itself is more complaint and legal than modifying a tax code at the interface or tax compliance reporting software. The solution and its justification should satisfy the client.

Golden words: Client looks for a solution which is universal (generic), pro standard, compliant & legal, doesn't disturb existing upstream, downstream process, and involves fewer development and maintenance tasks.

14.8 SUMMARY

In this chapter, readers learnt about the strategy for successfully passing tax technology interviews. To this end, the chapter provided readers with insights into the psyche of the interviewing panel, composed of finance, tax, IT, and the project management office. The chapter educated readers about the areas and skills the panel is likely to assess to gauge overall capability. The content is based on the author's own experiences and interviews given and received during his fifteen-plus years in tax technology across major world regions. Readers are now better prepared to engage more actively during the interview process, which may last a few weeks to months and involve multiple levels. The ultimate objective of developing knowledge, expertise, and skills is to secure a proper job role in an organization, and this chapter has prepared you to address and manage the selection and recruitment process in depth.

INDEX

ACKNOWLEDGEMENTS

I want to express my gratitude to the individuals listed below, who have empowered, trusted, mentored, and supported me during both normal and challenging times. They will always hold a special place in my life. Without their guidance, I wouldn't have achieved success.

Academic

Prof. R.K. Soni (Physics), Prof. Rajesh Sharma (Maths), Late. Dr. G. K. Sharma (Chemistry), Vaishnav Sir (Maths) (High School, Kota (Rajasthan): 1998-2001)

Late. Mr. Dilip Kadam & Mr. Ashok Patil (BVP College of Eng, Pune: 2002-06)

Prof. Michael Kuhl& Prof. John Kaemmerlen (Dept. of Industrial& Systems Engineering, Rochester Institute of Technology, New York, USA: 2007-09)

Professional

Mr. Shripad Deshpande (ICICI Bank, Mumbai:2006), Mr. Bhushan Paladugu (Trisync Technologies,NewJersey:2010), Mr. Alexis Aimard (Hewlett Packard,Houston:2010-13) – My first tax technology Guru, Mr. Stephan Meteors& Mr. Mark Russo (Deloitte, Houston:2014), Mr.

Mark Hunt (Shell, UK:2018), Mr. Mark Freeman (Thomson Reuters, Dubai:2019), Ms. Jessica Smith (Orica, Singapore:2020), Mr. Babu Srinivasan (Autodesk, US:2022), Mrs. Elaine Lundin (Organon, Netherlands: 2023), Mr. Shony Champakara (Cognizant, Netherlands: 2023), Mr. Vinay Sanil &Mr. Tuhin Chatterjee (Tech Mahindra: Netherlands: 2025)

Personal

My father Late. Dr. Ramesh Chandra Sharma (PhD, Human Phycology), a corporate management consultant, and the founder and director of the Center for Behavioral Science Services, was a lovable, caring and protective father. My mother Mrs. Kamlesh Sharma (MSc, BSc), a retired Govt. college principal who in the aftermath of my father unfortunate and untimely demise in 1999 due to blood cancer did all her best to get me and my young brother access to best in class teachers, books, training institutions and colleges, what I am today is because of my mother, forever grateful to god for sending her in my life. My wife, Neerupama, who understands me well, and her presence in my life brought happiness and good luck, making me a family man and father of two cute kids, Abhyudaya and Rudrakshi. My younger brother, Kunal, who stood by me in times of need, and supported local family requirements during my foreign deployments.

My maternal uncle, Mr. D. C. Garg (Jaipur), a gentleman and our maternal family patriarch. My uncle, Mr. Suresh K. Sharma (Atlanta, US), who supported me in my grad studies in the US during 2008-09 recession period. Mr. Ajay B. Puri & family – who provided strategic advices and guidance during my undergrad educational and early professional journey. Good friends like Praveen, Kumar (Pune), and Ankit Dhar (Boston), who were close helpful buddies in undergrad and Grad College, social mentor Mr. Rajiv Varma (US), and there are many other important individuals and firms with whom I will forever be grateful for their presence in my life.

God bless them all!

www.ingramcontent.com/pod-product-compliance
Ingram Content Group UK Ltd.
Pitfield, Milton Keynes, MK11 3LW, UK
UKHW060022051026
15591UKWH00006B/333
9798904511166